THE BONDING
OF
WILL AND DESIRE

The BONDING
of
WILL and DESIRE

JOANNE H. STROUD

CONTINUUM • NEW YORK

Desire **defines us.**
Will **focuses us.**
Imagination **frees us.**

1994

The Continuum Publishing Company
370 Lexington Avenue
New York, NY 10017

Printed in the United States of America

Library of Congress Cataloging-in-Publication Data

Stroud, Joanne.
    The bonding of will and desire / Joanne H. Stroud.
        p.   cm.
    Includes index.
    ISBN 0-8264-0646-7
    1. Will. 2. Desire. I. Title.
BF611.s77 1994
128' .3—dc20   93-51491
                                                                 CIP

Acknowledgments

In a reverie harking back to my childhood I see an outline of a plump cat that can only become full-bodied by etching along dotted lines, and I relate it in my mind to the crafting of this book. Far-fetched? Perhaps, but in each case the outline first forms in the mind, and then countless separate connectives are needed to bring the finished work into focus.

This feline metaphor occured to me as I was teaching a class at The Dallas Institute of Humanities and Culture, which in little more than a decade of existence has become the foremost cultural vehicle of our community. The Institute evolved from the collective vision of Don and Louise Cowan (whose creative thinking and inspired teaching first motivated me to undertake a doctoral program in Psychology and Literature and, after its completion, to teach at the University of Dallas)—of James Hillman (whose interpretation of Jung, an early mentor, opened up ways of carrying on the work of the soul)—of Gail Thomas (whose earthy wisdom and delicate wit kept the multi-directional functions of The Institute from splintering apart)—and of Robert Sardello (whose psychological guidance provided the lodestar that kept the rest of us from straying too far from essential questions). Sardello was of tremendous help in reviewing and strengthening the first draft of this manuscript.

Apart from these Founding Fellows, I have received staunch support in this book's preparation and in my teaching activities from the Institute's able staff. In particular I think of Ann Patrick, Mickey Bright, Mary Bonifield, Frank Lukner, and Melissa Bodenhamer. I would never have become computer-literate or been able to prepare this book for publication without the skills of Marie Basalone. She has been devoted in every way. Eileen Gregory and I have shared an office as well as ideas. She read and critized most constructively the first draft and the final one. I am also indebted to my efficient secretary, Jane Milburn, capable of running her own business, who worked tirelessly in collating my book's thicket of footnotes.

Teaching is an avocation which, when it functions best, gives both students and teacher an interactive exhilaration. The teacher hopes to be able to articulate the subject in broad sweep, but good students insist that he or she fill in the gaps. I have learned as much from students as from books. My classes in Cultural Psychology at the Institute and my monthly seminar in New York City on Jungian thought have compelled me to seek "words to obey my call" (I'm always borrowing a line from Yeats).

My education is grounded in cultural and spiritual psychology. In furthering it, I have been nurtured both in thought and friendship by Nor Hall, Ginette Paris, Mary Watkins, Pat Berry, David Miller, Ed Casey, Paul Kugler, and Tom Kapacinskas.

Finally my family—my husband Ken Bilby, foremost, for his caring, untiring attention, support, and skillful editing (those early years of journalism at the New York Herald Tribune and later writing two books of his own provided the proficiency to be an invaluable help), but also Ethan, Carol, Eric, and Natasha Stroud, who never gave me any doubts of their steadfast encouragement all through the lengthy process of developing what is called "a life of the mind." All of you deserve my heartfelt thanks.

If you pinpoint a book's gestatory process, mine began at a weekend seminar at the Institute on "Images of Will and Desire." This subject was augmented over the years by conferences on such diverse topics as Gaston Bachelard's work on imagination and the psychic impact of the Twelve Olympians. The random nature of the book that evolved suggests a Menippean literary genre (a word my friend Robert Dupree taught me). One can start anyplace. If you don't like any chapter, move on. The form will still emerge, I hope. The cat will still be there.

Table of Contents

Introduction

Imagination is more important than knowledge.
ALBERT EINSTEIN, *On Science*

The complex relationship between will and desire—those building blocks of the human psyche—has never been fully addressed. I do not intend to suggest, however, that this book will encompass all the intricacies involved in the bonding of will and desire. My far more limited goal is to seek the connective images, the interrelated links about which much more must be unearthed before we fully comprehend how desires can be made known and how will can be engaged. Hence this attempt to explore images which synthesize, which bring together the "intimate discord" (Mary Ann Caws's phrase) of will and desire.

In my teaching career spanning twelve years at the University of Dallas and twelve at The Dallas Institute of Humanities and Culture, I enlisted a broad range of scholarly tools in preparing this exploration—mostly psychology, but also some philosophy, some words of the poets, some cultural criticism, and even some of those self-help suggestions that abound in contemporary literature. I have, in particular, leaned heavily on the analytical psychology of C. G. Jung. In reference to his precepts, I have included a sprinkling of myths, poetry, alchemy, and those healing techniques that resonate at deep levels of our collective awareness. The richness of his comprehension is obvious when one attempts to delineate such complex emotions as anger, fear, shame, depression, love, and ecstasy—those essential human responses to being-in-the-world. Among current scholars, James Hillman, Robert Sardello, and Thomas Moore have especially enriched my understanding with their focus on psyche, or soul, as it moves in our everyday lives.

The French philosopher Gaston Bachelard is my primary source of illustrative imagery. I have borrowed his words throughout to instruct and illumine. His method of engaging material images provides a means of dealing with what might otherwise have become an abstract plea for images in an image-less presentation.

I share Bachelard's belief that images are foundational. A focused image summons will to realize the embodied desire. It is erroneous to think that will is the dominant partner. Will operates primarily as an unconscious instinct through each of the realms of body, soul, and spirit. We can feel its surge; we can use it for limitation or for direction. But without the image of the desirable we can never harness its energy to our purposes.

The title of the book comes indirectly from Bachelard. Although he is not a theorist, his distinctive and provocative work on elemental imagination—of earth, air, fire, and water—stirs up images that bond will and desire in response to being-in-the-world. He demonstrates imagistically how our reaction to the world manifests hidden desires and reveals new aspects of our identity if we pay heed to them.

Jung's psychological lucidity and Bachelard's genius for amplifying the image are both catalysts that enhance comprehension of our motivations. In their approaches to imagination as it affects will and desire, they have helped me generate possible answers to the poet W. B. Yeats's accusation that we live in "the age of the disordered will," with the will trying to do the work of the imagination. To fathom his meaning requires understanding of those misconceptions of the will's function that abound in our century. We have equated will with the will-to-control or the will-to-power. Will thus equates with ego. With a strong ego exalted, a strong will-to-control is also glorified. The will-to-action often blinds access to imagination. Then imagination, a far more effective energizer, is devalued. Then, too, love loses out whenever the urge for power predominates. Ultimately our mistake may be to presume that all life and mystery must yield to control.

Chapter One introduces the enigma: how to bond will and desire so that imagination can move forward, flowing and facing the future, instead of being trapped in either the successes or the pain of the past.

Focusing on Eros, the second chapter encompasses a sequential discussion of the role of will as the force of creation, as provenance of the gods, and considers the debate between philosophers and theologians through centuries of Western thought on the divine and the human arenas of action. I also examine the modern era when only the human will seems to matter. In this chapter I seek to elucidate a definition of will by considering the different nuances of meaning that have been emphasized at different moments in time.

Chapters Three and Five investigate the pagan images of love and desire, those energies illustrated in the classical figures first of Eros and then of Aphrodite. The chapters probe how these energies are still operative today.

Against a backdrop of the medieval alchemists, Chapter Four elaborates Jung's and James Hillman's development of alchemical Sulphur, with their additions relating to the unconsciousness of will and desire.

Chapter Six is an examination of how the concept of love is extended into the Christian principle of Agape.

Chapter Seven investigates the interconnection between will and image; Chapter Nine examines the link between will and intentionality, in an attempt to generate some understanding about the genesis of action. (By now you will know that I believe images are the organizers of experience, shaping and focusing our desires.)

In the eighth chapter I have addressed twentieth-century psychological thinking, especially that of the followers of Freud, Jung, and Adler, insofar as it relates to the three central motivating forces: imagination, will, and desire.

Chapters Ten and Eleven discuss the involvement of complexes—both personal and cultural—in limiting or expressing will and desire.

Willful Prometheus, both boundless and desperate, is the subject of the twelfth chapter.

Chapters Thirteen and Fourteen explore the three emotions—fear, anger, depression—that stultify the realization of will and desire. "I can't" is often more powerful than "I can"; "I won't" as important as "I will." These chapters observe the perverse human tendency to define ourselves as much through what we won't do as by what we want to do.

The last chapter is an extended examination of Bachelard's compelling thoughts on the ways of the will and imagination (his favorite subject after science), expanding our awareness of the will's multiple powers to move through imaginative response to the physical world, thereby bonding with our most intimate desires.

Finally, the book is Menippean in genre, like a carousel designed to be jumped on or a vessel to be dipped into serendipitously wherever you please. Each chapter is intended to stand on its own.

Like the poet-philosopher or the alchemist, we need to ask ourselves how we can discover soul—our soul—in matter: the *anima mundi*, a move that simultaneously awakens matter into life. Images of will and desire open up awareness of the interconnectedness of soul in all things. In its essence, this is an exploration of those images that provide metaphoric or symbolic bonds between will and desire and converge in often unconscious fashion to give our lives direction.

The Enigma

The Possible's slow fuse is lit
By the Imagination.
EMILY DICKINSON

Imagination separates us from the past
as well as reality; it faces the future.... If we
cannot imagine, we cannot foresee.
GASTON BACHELARD, *Poetics of Space*

The role of human will in governing personal conduct has long been a focus of scholarly inquiry. Philosophers, theologians, and poets have been fascinated endlessly by the will as a motivating force in human behavior. With the emergence of the discipline of psychology, another voice has entered the arena. Even so, a precise configuration of this most essential urge continues to elude definition.

We know that when we consciously apply will to achieve a goal we experience its energy as determination; from the tension of the set jaw or the clenched fist, we feel it surge through our bodies. But will also may be unconsciously activated by desires we hardly recognize as our own. It is this interplay between will and desire that we shall probe, seeking to solve such enigmas as how each becomes manifest on the field of consciousness. The fact is, both a subtle similarity and a dichotomy continue to exist between these two seminal thrusts.

Textbook references to will are numerous and contradictory. The authoritative *Oxford English Dictionary* offers two definitions, the first: "desire, wish, longing; inclination, disposition (*to do* something)." It is followed by: "the action of willing or choosing to do something: the movement or attitude of the mind which is directed with conscious intention to (and normally, issues immediately in) some action, physical or mental." The first suggests subjective motivations and traits of personality not easily grasped and often misunderstood. The second emphasizes outward action involved in doing something, a conscious choice. In addition to these definitions, the O.E.D. lists a broad range of other synonyms: "volition, resolution, intent, wish, mind, inclination, determination, decision, choice, preference, purpose," and again "desire." In these standard definitions will and desire are frequently used interchangeably. Like personality, will has imprecise parameters. Everyone has a good generalized grasp of its meaning, but who can define its essence?

Can we say that will is simply psychic energy, as many definitions imply? Is this energy physical? Or one of spirit, an *élan*? In what way is will a force, a function, a response to a need, a reaction, or a defense? What role does gender play in the incitement of will? How do anger and fear aid or thwart the will? How does love tilt the equation? Can we conclusively bond will and desire, recognizing that the two belong together but are not identical?

At its most fundamental level, will is the instinct to live, the outward thrusting of our inner vitality. Without it, there is simply no life. C. G. Jung touches on this point: "In the long run no conscious will can ever replace the life instinct. This instinct comes to us from within, as a compulsion or will or command."[1] We are most consciously aware of the power of will when its momentum translates into the energy of action. But even then we are largely unaware of the multiple sources from which it springs and from which it derives its energy. Desire certainly rules and circumscribes choice. Experiencing the pulse of will we can become simultaneously aware of the focus of desire, when we sense it only fleetingly or when we feel it in committed goals. Then we sense a bonding.

Desire itself is unbounded, limitless. Either we are consumed by it or unaffected. Desire sears us, opens up a cavernous space deep inside us. That may be the whole point: desire alerts us. We become aware of our incompleteness through our yearnings that desire translates into demands. We have difficulty quieting desire. The mere effort of attempting to fulfill a desire is actually, in itself, pleasurable. Desire is a passion for the infinite, larger than needs or wants, omnivorous. Susan Sontag says in *The Volcano Lover*, "desire wills its perpetuation *ad infinitum*." In James Hillman's words: "Desire yearns for 'more' and calls this more, Paradise. The gaze above and beyond seems an archetypal requisite of the soul to live a life on earth with passionate purpose."[2] All of the language associated with desire—longing, yearning, wishing, coveting, craving, obsessing—suggests a magnet drawing us toward the future, thus insinuating the eventual possibility of realization of what is merely imagined in the present. Even if only an infinitesimal portion of our cravings translate into reality, the focus must be on the future. When will is harnessed to desire, a sense of moving in a forward direction is generated. Yet, by definition, longing has a transcendental urgency that can be only partially fulfilled, before desire takes up residency anew in untried possibilities and future options. While it is not possible to be immune to these persistent yearnings, we would hardly feel alive without them. Only in despair or ill health, conditions that we pity, are we immune to desire.

In seeking to distinguish between acts of willing and desiring, the inevitable question arises—does will follow or precede desire? As this inquiry is psychological in method, we shall examine the subjective, individual ways that we live will and desire, exploring pathways through which they enter into and determine our lives. If they are happily fused rather than in continual discord, we shall discover the ties that unite body, soul, and spirit. But is it will or desire that ignites the fusion? Again, the enigma!

Today desire is too often relegated to mere sensual appetite, thus limiting its true scope. The Greek idea of desire as the impetus to creation, the quintessence, the prime mover of the cosmos is far more accurate. Will, when not in active opposition, gives form to desire, *follows* desire. The fact that human beings have a will at all—hitherto considered the province of the gods—is an announcement that the divine spark animates the human being. Neither will nor desire is the exclusive domain of the gods or of humans. Can they form a bridge of understanding between the two realms?

By any yardstick the twentieth century is a time of turbulence, of present as well as future shock. Raphael López-Pedraza claims that "cultural anxiety is more apparent, more acute, in times of historical extremes."[3] Some scholars liken ours to the seventeenth century in terms of rapidly transmuted values. The energies of the late medieval age and of the emerging Renaissance clashed with the modern era and its scientific emphasis. It has been said no one living at the century's end could have understood anyone living at the beginning: Shakespearean and Elizabethan mores at the start, Newton at the end. Similarly, our century has gone from kerosene lamps to lasers, television, and interplanetary travels and, as fast as technology has changed, so have our value systems. Love and will, human aspirations and desires, are caught in the whirlwinds of change. New definitions are demanded, and old ones are subject to scrutiny.

Early in this century the poet W. B. Yeats summarized the problem, claiming that this is "the age of the disordered will" with the will trying to do the work of the imagination. If, as in Yeats's aphorism, the primary problem is that we live in a distorted environment, where did we lose the image and imagination? Over the last three centuries, myths, or stories rich in images that previously guided behavior, have been exchanged for reliance on impersonal, scientific data, exacerbating the sense of loss of meaning in our lives. By running faster, we strive to compensate for having lost our way.

How do we reanimate image and restore imagination as a motive force in our lives? How do we reconnect our deepest and most consequential desires with will? Jung's monumental twentieth-century contribution—the theory of the archetypes of the Collective Unconscious—may provide part of the answer. He links desire's immanence within the image together with will as the pervasive necessity that accompanies any archetype—a profound insight. Hillman emphasizes this same point: "Images are primordial, archetypal, in themselves ultimate reals, the only direct reality the psyche experiences. As such they are shaped presences of necessity."[4]

Desire, held in the image, and will, as the inevitable and repetitive manifestation, occur together in these basic psychic structures. Our ability to perceive is circumscribed by archetypes. Jung likens their hold to the possessiveness of a *daimon*:

> Naturally, it is not merely archetypes that govern the particular nature of perceptions. They account only for the collective component of a perception. As an attribute of instinct they partake of its dynamic nature, and consequently possess a specific energy which causes or compels definite modes of behavior or impulses; that is, they may under certain circumstances have a possessive or obsessive force (numinosity!). The conception of them as daimonia is therefore quite in accord with their nature.[5]

While Jung did not emphasize the unconscious modes of will, he was concerned with internal rather than external necessities. But the key point is that he elevated and delineated the image, and thus imagination, as an organic function as important as instinct in the process of becoming:

> The archetype as an image of an instinct is a spiritual goal towards which the whole nature of man strives; it is the sea to which all rivers wend their way, the prize which the hero wrests from the fight with the dragon.[6]

The archetype uniquely holds image, instinct, and spirit in a nuclear whole. Thus Jung began to reweave the essential parts of human nature together. Further contributing to the return of image to its rightful place, Jung promoted the potency of dream imagery as a path toward connection with the greater self and thus a way to reclaim soul.

Shorn of its narrative moorings, no longer coupled to one's life story or to the age-old myths, legends, and fairy tales that have contoured the heroic struggle for individuation, image no longer automatically opens up the window of imagination. Today, image is carried more by media stars than by poetry. Images have been dragged in the gutter, harnessed to the power to sell—films, television, or advertising. Creatures of studio manipulation, movie stars often hold together an image of glamour and fantasy, in which the desires of their fans can be mirrored. Sadly, however, this weight can become too burdensome for some to carry. Unable to separate her own desires from a thirst for love, Marilyn Monroe ultimately fell victim to all the projections of desire imposed upon her. With the incursion of electronic media, particularly omnipresent television, we are experiencing image manipulation to a heightened degree. The most successful multimedia superstars, those like Michael Jackson or Madonna, who understand intuitively the power the image incorporates, concentrate on the immediacy of visual impact—in other words, on the canned image. The orchestration of specially prepared images subjects the audience to a form of rapid fire shock treatment. This type of exploitation demands nothing of the viewer to complete the picture, thus denying imagination's proclivity for dynamic activity. It's all up there, out there. We can be fascinated or repelled—or both—but always we are riveted by the violent assault on our senses and titillated by the pulsations of exposed flesh.

Ever since *A Clockwork Orange* we have had a genre of movies that attract when they really should repel. Robert Sardello calls this "the outpouring of false imagination into the world," which he describes as "the force behind images that produce sensations contrary to the character of the images themselves. One need only to look at television or movies to see the repellant images producing the response of attraction."[7] Caught in this underworld of desire, we feel alternately battered and exalted, impotent and omnipotent. Increasingly in such a scatological society, the ob-scene (literally, off scene) image is center stage. Is this Eros's revenge because we have forgotten that desire is divine as well as human? Let us explore.

The Summons of Eros

Who, therefore, will doubt that Love immediately
follows Chaos, and precedes the World and all the gods
who are assigned to the parts of the World?
FICINO, *Commentary on the Symposium*

For those who love behold
The theophanic beauty of the world.
KATHLEEN RAINE, "Eros Remembered"

Any consideration of will must initially involve the Greeks, since many
of their original word definitions still apply today. Interestingly, there is
no single Greek word for will. One possibility, *thymos*, carries multiple
meanings that indicate how complex the notion of will is. *Thymos* means
"soul, breath, life," like the Latin *anima*.[1] Homer's use is akin to this
one. The *thymos* informs the hero what to do in all intense moments; it
insinuates feelings into his heart and words into his mouth. In what
seems like a contradiction, the word also relates to the Latin *animus*,
which carries another array of synonyms. (*Anima* and *animus* in Latin dif-

fer from the sense Jung gave to them.) One definition—"the desire for meat and drink"—seems to imply instinct mitigated by desire. *Thymos* also means "the seat of one's sorrow or joy," which implies an emotional content. Another subcategory suggests "mind, temper, will," as in "their mind or will was divided." The Greek language had far fewer words than modern English, and therefore individual words often had to carry multiple meanings. *Thymos* can mean "spirit or courage" and "manliness," but it is also "anger and wrath." Attributing a masculine connotation to will, etymologically, conveys that it is an activating principle. It is a carrier of agency and direction, and this is the way we often think of will—as a vector.

The etymological proximity of will to *anima* identifies it as a heart function, while its identification with *animus* classifies it as a spirit function. Spirit, including the collective *spiritus mundi*, traditionally falls into the masculine, or active, realm. This does not imply, however, an exclusive male enclave for qualities of spirit. As Shakespeare attests in so many plays, females can also embody will and spiritedness.

In earliest creation myths, Necessity, an iron-clad force of will, was the founding principle of the cosmos. As the realms of being evolved from the earliest turbulence, will then belonged exclusively to the gods, whose will, though sometimes subject to Necessity, was absolute in relation to humanity. The early Greeks focused attention on creation as a byproduct of will manifesting through the potency of desire. They were singular in recognizing that energy begins with Eros, that omnipotent compulsion to which even the greatest gods were subject.

In *The Theogony*, Hesiod proclaims Eros the prime generator of the cosmos, the force that brings the world into being. His procreative power could subdue a tumultuous mother earth. With Gaia he is the "first born" out of chaos:

> First of all there came Chaos,
>   and after him came
> Gaia of the broad breast,
>   to be the unshakable foundation
> of all the immortals who keep the crests
>   of snowy Olympos,
> and Tartaros the foggy in the pit
>   of the wide-wayed earth,

and Eros, who is love, handsomest among all
  the immortals
who breaks the limbs' strength,
  who in all gods, in all human beings
overpowers the intelligence in the breasts,
  and all their shrewd planning.[2]

The Greek will-to-order realizes itself through the instituting and reorganizing powers of Eros. This paradigm for civilization, unlike the current, dominant perspective, is not a process of slow Darwinian adaptation and survival, but rather a sudden theophany, a phenomenon of creation predicated upon desire. The will to bring-into-being is harnessed to desire, Eros's attribute, constituting a recognition of desire's supernatural strength.

By late Hellenistic times Eros, no longer the frightening swirl of creative energy described by Hesiod, was imaged as a youthful masculine figure. By late Roman times he had atrophied into a chubby, cherubic— and relatively harmless—boy. Even later, he devolved into a sordid symbol of concupiscence. What a contrast with those earliest creation dramas in which Eros was the force disciplining all the chaotic elements!

Today we make light of Eros's ineffable numen, if we think of this power at all, or fail to distinguish its multiple parts from erotic attraction or sexual hunger (libido). A few scholars are beginning to question the slight of Eros in the current emphasis on sex. Concluding his autobiography, Jung admitted that he had not sufficiently developed his thoughts concerning Eros. He faltered before the task "of finding the language which might adequately express the incalculable paradoxes of love." He mentioned the difficulty of encompassing the realm of Eros and suggested that another psychology could be built around understanding the irrational effects of Eros: "In classical times, when such things were properly understood, Eros was considered a god whose divinity transcended our human limits, and who therefore could neither be comprehended nor represented in any way." Jung adds that only through Eros do we reach greater awareness: "Eros is a *kosmogonos*, a creator and father-mother of all higher consciousness."[3]

Within the vast domain of Eros, will and desire are seminal forces, birthing forces, creators of the universe but also of one's own personality. Even Denis de Rougemont, always concerned about giving Eros too much sway, points out the animating power of the myths: "Great simple and organizing forms, active symbols and vehicles of the animistic powers of Eros, the myths can serve us as guides in the infernal, purgatorial, or sublime comedy of our desires, our passions, our love."[4] Later we shall examine how will and desire shape our individual personalities.

The mythology of the Homeric gods and goddesses augments the doctrine of the supernatural power of will predicated upon desire. In their celestial home, the Olympian deities present complex images of subtle differences in behavioral patterns. Greek polytheistic mythology provided image-pictures or magnified mirrors from which human beings could extrapolate the manifestations and consequences of will and desire. Greek religion was not stuck in stereotypes of narrowly defined gender traits; both gods and goddesses had areas of authority and control over human will. Homer provides many examples of human desire submitting to divine will. In *The Iliad*, Helen might have desired to remain with husband and child but was helpless to withstand the will of Aphrodite, who had promised her to Paris. As we know, either masculine or feminine deities might be the inaugurating force. Certainly Athena, Aphrodite, and Demeter were potent feminine examples of power and control over specific areas of life (although Homer downgrades Demeter's place among the Olympians).

Each of the gods and goddesses governs an arena of will that supersedes individual desire and the petty will of humans. Sometimes one supernatural will dominates, sometimes another. For example, Zeus provides a paradigm for the will to moral order in judicial judgment and in the treatment of strangers, while on the level of desire he exemplifies the creativity that can be experienced through multiple sexual encounters. Hera depicts the containment of will and desire within a monogamous relationship or within the continuity of community. Apollo conveys an image of the laser-like power of a direct penetrating thought; Athena, the martial virgin, manifests an image of insightful wisdom and persuasiveness bolstered by the will to fight for a belief if necessary. As Walter Otto says, "What Athena shows man, what she desires of him, and what she inspires him to, is boldness, will to victory, courage. But all of this is nothing without directing reason and illuminating clarity."[5] Demeter demonstrates the strength of the mother-daughter bond and the will to broach the downward pull of the underworld; Artemis embodies the desire for pure, virginal aloof moments and the chaste will of the chase. Again Otto explains: "Here there is nothing of the rapture which impels one to embrace, to the bliss of becoming one. Here everything is withdrawn and pure.... Her manifestation is...the loveliness that shrinks at the fervor of the lover and turns cruel if he approaches too near."[6] Hermes provides an image of the mercurial or shifty side of will, even though he gets away with his stratagems through charm. Aphrodite, goddess of desire itself, affords an image of the irresistible lure of sensual beauty, as Otto elaborates: "Aphrodite arouses the desires of love and vouchsafes their fulfillment."[7] Dionysus offers a haven for those desirous of ecstacy, wine, or rapture; Ares ignites the excitement of war. Hestia presides over the need for maintaining the center, the hearth. Hephaestus's desire for beauty manifests through his skills of craftsmanship, compensating for his physical ugliness. A corollary to these divisions of will and desire is acceptance of the fact that each is a separate domain, not to be shared by other gods or goddesses. We can identify with each of these deities when we are seized by overpowering desire or when will institutes a pattern of similar action in our own lives. In the structure of the psyche will has origins within the divine realm that are beyond our deliberate and rational employment of it.

The will of the gods, sometimes called Fate, would be ludicrous for mere humans to contest. With the gods or goddesses in a favorable mode, extraordinary feats of human will are possible. The prime definition of a "hero" is one favored by the gods. The classic concept of heroic will glorifies action and the dangerous deeds of leadership. Often it equates to a courageous stance, especially in battle or when confronting overwhelming challenges. Heroic will does not adhere to any notions of absolute law. Instead, and more subtly, it suggests a certain restraint associated with being alert to the warning of the gods concerning human limitations and the transgression of boundaries.

On a personal level, vital as it is to delineate one's individual will and desires, it is equally vital to discover how to live up to the best in oneself, always difficult, and how to speak up when a position isn't popular. It is also essential to discover how to curb excess will or willfulness, recognizing that hubris, then and now, always blinds. Agamemnon and Achilles demonstrate this point in their quarrel in the *Iliad*. Heroic will, being naturally expansive, invariably is tempted to overstep. When individual will becomes so powerful that it encroaches on the transcendent realm of the gods, it becomes blind to its own limitations. Oedipus, the classic example of inflated will, acknowledges his mistake and even initiates his own physical blindness, when he becomes aware of his previous lack of vision.

In the Homeric lexicon each pattern of supernatural behavior carries a special will to power and thus an arena of action, but each also carries its own shadow. Hillman calls this duality the "ontological distinction within the Gods themselves," in which "each God contains shadow and casts it according with how he or she shapes a cosmos. Each God is a way in which we are shadowed."[8] Mythology thus provides a stage for viewing the total theater of fundamental complexes with their attendant and visible strengths and also their unseen shadow-weaknesses.

Homeric mythology recognizes that desire obviously encompasses the demands of the physical body, but, less overtly, also embraces the needs of the soul and the longing of spirit. Each god or goddess, while rendering shades of differentiation of behavior, at the same time reinforces an inescapable, intimate relationship of the supernatural realm with the human through the sharing of qualities.

We find that addressing stubborn will and unruly desire is a problem all theologies face. Worldly desire has long been the greatest hurdle for those committed to a spiritual discipline, especially in the mystical Christian traditions and in many Oriental religions (i.e., in the yogic disciplines of India and Tibet, and the Zen training of China and Japan). Self-mastery is the goal, and, as explained psychologically by Esther Harding, it is accomplished only through "conscious control of energies that usually function autonomously. This is accompanied by certain psychic experiences described in the texts as being of the nature of an expansion of consciousness beyond the ego state, with a consequent freeing from the passions and desirousness that bind men unconditionally to the world."[9] In theologies based on reincarnation, desire chains one to the onerous wheel of time and misfortune.

For Hindus, the objective lies not in "the fruits of action" but in the pathway of knowledge. In India, the dominant religious teaching,

Harding points out, "is that the goal of life consists in loss of personal ego through union with or mergence into the All-Consciousness, the Atman. The doctrine is in contrast to the Western concept of the importance of the personal soul."[10] In the *Upanishads* the wise teacher Prajapati explains that behind human consciousness is the All-Knowing One:

> He who knows let me think this, he is the Self, the mind [consciousness] is his divine eye. He, the Self, seeing these pleasures (which to others are hidden like a buried treasure of gold) through his divine eye, i.e. the mind, rejoices.... He who knows that Self and understands it, obtains all worlds and desires.[11]

In Buddha's teaching, desire is an illusion, to be sublimated, and enlightenment follows adherence to the Four Truths. Much of Buddhist training is devoted to detachment from the pain that is a brother to being-in-the-world. The first Truth is the noble truth of pain: "birth is pain, old age is pain, sickness is pain, death is pain...in short, the five aggregates of grasping are pain." The second is the noble truth of the cause of pain, and this is "craving (*tanha*, thirst) that leads to rebirth, the cravings of the passions, the cravings for (continued) existence, the craving for non-existence." The third is the noble truth of pain's cessation, "the remainderless cessation of craving, its abandonment and rejection, emancipation and freedom from support." Knowledge of these three truths leads to the state of *arhat*, in which the perfected disciple has reached the goal of cessation of pain. The fourth Truth consists of the doctrinal means of arriving at these truths, the Noble Eightfold Path: "right views, right intention, right speech, right action, right livelihood, right effort, right mindfulness, right concentration."[12] In contradistinction, the cravings of desire are responsible for all man's woes and bring him nothing but misery.

The Buddhist concept of *Sunyata* refers to a search for the metaphysical void, that emptiness which only the All-Encompassing One can fill. Thus the banishment of personal desire—wishing, willing, desiring, seeking, which can only breed misery—is extolled. Personal will is properly exercised in opening the inner world, and in turning away from the misery of the exterior world which is *maya*, or illusion. Through renunciation of earthly longing, the faithful may realize *Nirvana*, the extinction of craving and passion. It is virtually impossible to pursue normal life and still be an acolyte. Long periods of probation, spiritual study with an informed guide, and much attentive waiting are required for masterhood, a course at odds with Western orientation toward action. Jung remarks that in the East "our cherished extraversion is depreciated as illusory desirousness, as existence in the *samsara*, the very essence of the *nidana*-chain which culminates in the sum of the world's sufferings."[13] Most Oriental religious practices stress study and training, mystic meditation (*samadhi*), with years of devoted preparation required to discipline will. This approach differs in emphasis from the Judeo-Christian inclination to promote forceful and independent action in schooling will power to subdue the internal demons.

The monotheistic religions, especially Islam, Judaism, and Christianity, are similar to Oriental religions in the sense that both denigrate human desire as the source of conflicting will and therefore the wellspring of all error. The West most often pinpoints the blame on sexual desire, which thus becomes the whipping boy, with will serving primarily as a curb. Ergo, disciplined will, necessary to control desire, is the only way to conquer our frailties. Stubborn, prideful, personal will clashes with the Will of God. Guilt occurs not only through deliberate acts of omission or commission but simply through human fallibility. The individual seeking salvation is sternly enjoined to align personal will with Almighty Will, a course in contrast with Homeric mythology, which has more sympathy for the contentious disparity between human and divine will, providing in its polytheism numerous image-pictures for the manifestations of will and desire. We, of course, are inheritors of both legacies.

To create the world, the Judaic God employed Logos, the word, a paradigm that seems more abstract to us (although not to Old Testament Jews) than the Greek image of the mating of Gaia and Eros. Almighty God and the arena of His Will became imageless. Yahweh's name could not even be spoken; his power could not be contained in any single image. From the viewpoint of imagination, this was a loss of specificity: no complexity of will-images here. The absolute, abstract nature of God's Will distances the deity from intimate association with human characteristics. Struggle becomes part of the equation when humanity's inclinations clash with God's. St. Paul laments: "I do not do what I will, but I do the very thing I hate.... I can will what is right, but I cannot do it" (Romans 7:15-25). In the third century St. Augustine also feels torn by this internal conflict:

> I was bound, not with another man's chains, but with my own iron will. The enemy held my will, and indeed, made a chain of it for me, and constrained me. Because of a perverse will, desire was made; and when I was enslaved to desire [*libido*] it became habit; and habit not restrained became necessity. By which links...a very hard bondage had me enthralled.[14]

The struggle centers around two points of view—first, that mankind is lured inexorably toward the sensual side of his being; second, that desire itself can coalesce and transform into an uplifting and therefore spiritual outpouring of love for God. Christianity has debated both sides of this equation, with ample Biblical precedents for each. Countering the stern admonitions of the Old Testament, the Prophets and the Song of Songs speak in lyrical voice of desire as the source of love and the impetus to enlightenment. As Louise Cowan elaborates, "The Psalms, the Song of Songs, Isaiah, and Lamentations quite overtly present the lyric eros in their yearning for the fullness of Yahweh's presence."[15]

As the chief objects of male desire, women have historically borne the brunt of desire's negative projections. This was never more savagely illustrated than during the years of the Inquisition. Demonstrating the incredible blindness that can grip those fearful of desire, the general populace (female, oftentimes, as well as male) and the established church colluded in mass torture and executions. Between the fifteenth and eighteen centuries at least one million and possibly as many as nine million people were immolated. Monica Sjöö and Barbara Mor provide this appalling picture:

> Of people punished for "witchcraft" in Europe, 80 percent of those accused, tortured, and burnt were women. Town records from Germany and France reveal that whole villages were emptied of their female populations during the peak of the fire-frenzy—including very young girls and very elderly women. Travelers of the time reported countrysides hideously littered with stakes and pyres. Large numbers of homosexual men were also tortured and burnt at the stake. In fact, this is the origin of

the term "faggot" to denote a male homosexual: Homosexual
men were bound together at the foot of witch pyres, their bodies used as "faggots" to kindle the flames.[16]

In the post-Puritan English world, sexual desire, always viewed warily,
became even more suspect, and again particularly with women.
Worldly desire in any form, whether of elaborate clothing or even the
love of a beautiful garden, raised suspicions.

In Dante's opposing view of desire, alignment of individual will to
the Almighty Will is only possible through the all-encompassing principle of love. This supreme vision persists, because no poet has defined
love as eloquently as Dante (even though secularists may be less inclined
to accept his theological beliefs). Attaining beatific vision in "The
Paradiso," the questing pilgrim exclaims: "Yet, as a wheel moves
smoothly, free from jars,/my will and my desire were turned by
love/the love that moves the sun and the other stars."[17] Love can thus
dissolve all separations, all dichotomies, all anguish between will and
desire, and this is an acceptable view today.

In the nineteenth century, will broke away from its religious moorings and became a secular force of singular authority, with Nietzsche its
foremost proponent. Extolling the virtues of the will, Nietzsche makes
every other feeling subservient. All our emotional affective states, he
argues, stem from the will in confrontation with the world: "My theory
would be that will to power is the primitive form of affect, that all
other affects are but its configurations."[18] If this contention is true, then
hatred, fear, anger, anxiety, envy, jealousy are all aspects of the will to
power.

Nietzsche frequently casts will as the dramatic struggle between the
forces of Apollo and Dionysus, those of structural coherence against
those of dismemberment. The muscle of will shines forth in combat
with the abyss or chaos, although the latter is never to be vanquished
because it is the source of all our challenges.

For Nietzsche the energy of life at its most primitive level is the energy of will. "This world is the will to power—and nothing besides," he
summarizes. "And you yourselves are also this will to power—and nothing besides. Will is not simply the energy that impels us into becoming,
it is the very being that results."[19] In other words, will is both the elec-

tricity that supplies the power and the light bulb that illumines and is therefore the product. It is "the nothing besides" that invites dispute.

Nietzschean will glorifies the raw struggle for domination. By this definition will is an instinct, or *the* primal power. Jung has a complaint about these assertions: "Nietzsche bases everything on power, Freud on pleasure and its frustrations."[20] That the will to power, like the life force itself, can be destructive we are well aware when we observe it in those determined to have their way, regardless of other's needs.

The misuse of personal will, or mixed, misunderstood motivations, is a central theme in much of Dostoevsky's writing. Individual will conflicts violently with Christian or communal morality. His characters often perform willful acts that consciously they seem to abhor. Dostoevsky's genius resides in his ability to render unconscious motives and then depict how they affect multiple lives, even entire communities, as in *The Brothers Karamazov*. Usurping God's function in choosing the right way and time to die is the issue with Kirilov in *The Possessed*. In many ways Dostoevsky alerts our attention to the fallacious ramifications of Nietzschean ideas when put into practice.

Will, like any energy potential, is not inherently destructive, dominating, or cravenly devoted to the enhancement of personal power. It can be put to creative use. Heidegger stresses this positive side: "Every willing is a willing to be more...enhancement and heightening are essentially implied.... To will is to want to become stronger."[21] Life is not just the drive to maintain itself, as Darwin thought, or a drive toward lessening of the tensions and seeking pleasure, as Freud seems to say. Will is also self-assertion. I like Abraham Maslow's term, "self-actualizing," or Roberto Assagioli's "self-realization," which highlight will's positive force.

Can we say there are measurements governing the amount of consciously directed will available at any time? Will can assume different forms, some more distorted than others. Willfulness or willing, as Nietzsche describes it, suggests that a greater amount of will is available to one person than to the next. It is primarily a life force, analogous to the libido in the sexual realm. Free use of the will can become more available to some than to others because of fewer entanglements, fewer conflicting complexes.

At some juncture will becomes exaggerated and causes us to step beyond the boundaries, blinded by our own sense of self-importance. At such moments we become Promethean, our only self-image being one of personal infallibility. At the other pole, the exaggerated opposite, the inverted will is manifested as a paralyzing *ennui*, no energy or imagination. T. S. Eliot, in "The Hollow Men," describes such moments as "paralyzed force, gesture without motion."

Such problems of apathy and hopelessness came into prominence as the orderly Victorian world began to fade. Logical rationalism no longer seemed adequate to explain aberrant events and behavior. For many, traditional religion offered only a nostalgic chimera of salvation. The Victorian perception suddenly shifted from a secure, dependable world to one hostile and unpredictable. In 1922 Eliot foresaw the coming tide of futility, followed by apathy. In "The Wasteland," "nothing again nothing," an apt description of the malaise, the impotent feeling of meaningless existence that disturbs the latter part of our century, seducing many into drug-induced numbness. Impotence, a frustration of desire and a failure of will, is characteristically followed by a consuming rage that finds its outlet in waves of violent crime.

In the soulless spiritual wasteland—where we view ourselves as creatures totally detached from the human continuum, from nature, or from spirit, only as egos living in mechanical bodies—we lose the intermediate soul realm through which love is filtered as the determining influence in our lives. Hillman says: "We have lost the third, middle position which earlier in our tradition, and in others too, was the place of soul," which he describes as a "world of imagination, passion, fantasy, reflection, that is neither physical and material on the one hand, nor spiritual and abstract on the other, yet bound to them both."[22] With this diminishment, with no secure niche in the chain of being, we can no longer think of ourselves as a little less than the angels.

By discarding the transcendental power of the gods, and the daimon Eros, we obliterate all the mysterious ways of awakening desire's image in the heart. Adolf Guggenbühl-Craig explains that "Eros gives meaningful involvement to the archetypal patterns we live. They are with Eros, not only inhuman forces that we suffer from, but also ways in which our soul is moved and our spirit kindled."[23] Those encounters of

Eros that rivet the soul require a sacred place. Without such *loci*, a vacuum is left for a complex of will to take over, exercising authoritative control over both people and situations. When this occurs, ego becomes identified with will and fixated upon management and manipulation. We lose what Allen Tate, in his "Ode to the Confederate Dead," called "knowledge carried to the heart," the wisdom of the soul as the guiding compass of our lives.

Since the decline of the forceful Eros image, love and longing desire no longer answer to the compelling call of soul or spirit. To counter this loss, to balance our obsession with needs, a reverse course is mandated. Recapturing a sense of reverence for Eros, accepting his unique and mysterious ability, would restore the splintered pieces of soul and connect us soul-to-soul. We can no longer continue to ignore his awesome aspect, with matters of yearning and desire marginalized or sloughed off as isolated, often trivial events. In the first century B.C., the intrusion of Eros was recognized: "The Love-God inflames/more fiercely/those he sees are reluctant to surrender" (Tibullus, *Elegies*).

Many today are exploring the existential longing for bridges between spirit, soul, and sensate realms of being. In this constructive search for new consciousness, Eros, the fiery partner of the psyche, stands ready and eager to ignite the soul's will-to-realization. Let us heed his summons, never forgetting that, through love of soul, connection is forged between spirit, as essence, and the soul's desire.

Eros, Psyche, and the Wings of Desire

Desire is reaching out for the sweet.
ARISTOTLE, *Rhetoric*

Love is a driver, bitter and fierce if you fight and resist him,
Easy-going enough once you acknowledge his power.
OVID, *The Loves*

All thoughts, all passions, all delights,
Whatever stirs this mortal frame,
All are ministers of Love
and feed his sacred flame.
SAMUEL TAYLOR COLERIDGE, "Love"

A probe of the basic drives of will and desire would be incomplete without a detailed examination of the role of Eros, for Eros is the essence of psychic energy—the great liberator and the great binder. Just as Eros, according to Hesiod, subdued the turbulent forces of original Chaos, creating the cosmos, so can his boundless energy subdue our personal emotional disequilibriums—our fears, our anxieties—and awaken the powers of transformation asleep in the soul. We can only discover soul with Eros as our helper.

According to the earliest Greek tradition, Eros, as god of passion, embodied awesome power. Too mighty to be actually seen, he was imaged as a frightening monster of nebulous shape whose four eyes continually shifted. With strength beyond the physical, Eros also held sway over those enigmatic realms in which spirit resides. He was "master of every movement of the spirit, of all things hidden," according to an ancient Greek papyrus containing *A Prayer to Eros*.[1] He provided inward form, invisible on the surface, and a reach that was beyond understanding.

A creature of the *mysterium tremendum*, a demi-urge, somewhere between angel and demon, Eros was sometimes called a god but, more often, a *daimon*. Generically defined by Sardello, the *daimones* are "imaginal, between-creatures who are simply agencies of action."[2] Eros was the binder or the loosener, always an unpredictable dynamo, unleashing primeval forces on a cosmic level and, on a personal level, propelling the hapless individual into engagement. In modern perception Eros has been reduced to the single dimension of sexual urge, simple desire, or erotica, and stripped of all the boundless grandeur of his original incarnation. In a recent publication, Noel Cobb recaptures the sense of Eros's initial all-pervasive reach: "a non-human force of devastating power, polymorphous and Protean in its shape-shifting complexity."[3] That is the aspect of Eros I wish to reinforce here.

In his major configuration—as passion—Eros introduces changes, disturbances, feelings that move us into connection. He causes us to join with something or someone other than our own introverted ego-ideal, enlarging our perspective beyond that of mere self-centeredness. He makes psychic movement within the soul possible, awakening sleeping parts of the personality to passionate involvement. He opens up the possibility of love, not only love that impels us toward another individual but love that impels us toward a life of alliance to the spirit.

Plato's definition of Eros offers the timeless standard to which we must return. The myth of Eros in the *Phaedrus*, stated in primer fashion, holds that the soul is divine and retains in memory, or *anamnesis*, the remembrance of its pretemporal state of union with the true, the beautiful, and the highest good. This longing moves us toward the realm of Ideas and beyond the sensual reality of physical existence. Eros is the magnetism, the upward attraction of the soul in its yearning to return to that divine realm. Plotinus, the foremost Neoplatonic philosopher, supplies this confirmation: "Love has from everlasting come into existence from the soul's aspiration toward the higher and the good."[4] The spiritual journey is launched by Eros who arouses the yearning to join with an ideal, a mate, or with the truth of one's soul. He is therefore a telic force, magnetizing us toward goals, toward possibilities ahead.

In *The Symposium*, in the famous discussion between Agathon, Pausanias, and Socrates on the nature of love, the argument is advanced that "Love is a longing for immortality."[5] Love is a longing to be remembered while at the same time a poignant remembrance of longing. To be held in the mind of a loved one is to achieve an augmented existence. With Eros as guide we can achieve that goal. We can relish every involvement that takes us out of narcissistic limitedness and increases our fervor. Socrates further differentiates the two forms of Eros—Vulgar Eros, who represents attachment to a sense object, and Heavenly Eros, who frees the soul from the tangible world to find release in ascent. In either case, it is Eros who sets the soul in motion, drawing soul out of its inadequate and isolated self-enclosure, freeing soul to soar.

Also in *The Symposium*, Aristophanes relates the playful allegory of how man once had a perfect round shape until Zeus, angry and jealous over his contented symmetry, split him into two pieces. He was thus doomed to search the world over, always looking for his missing part. It is Eros, of course, awakening us to attraction and adherence, who becomes the catalyst for finding those sundered halves and fusing them again—or, more cynically, luring us into believing that wholeness is possible. As Diotima, wise about love, said: "Human nature will not find a better helper than Eros."

It is as true now as then that we reveal the nature of our essential, secret longings through our love choices. It is almost as if our soul knows in advance what is essential. Otherwise how do we account for the dramatic "instant flash of recognition," so often experienced when we meet another whom we intuit immediately as significant to our future?

Rationally we may not understand why Eros engages us in seemingly contradictory ways. Perhaps only in retrospect do we realize we have been led into precisely those experiences that our psyche, or inner person, longed for, even though we may have been involved in distinctly contrary pursuits. In José Ortega y Gasset's perception: "The type of human being which we prefer reveals the contours of our heart. Love is an impulse which springs from the most profound depths of our being."[6]

Whether through bodily desire or spiritual longing or a combination of the two, Eros arouses us to seek those mysterious qualities that supplement completeness. In either positive or negative fashion, Lyn Cowan explains, "The work of Eros is to love and hate relentlessly, to drive us deeper into relationship with all the parts of ourselves and with others."[7] He is an agent of transport, a go-between not only between gods and humans but also, intrapsychically, between the physical and spiritual realms of each soul personality. As Hillman affirms, there is a spiritual component in all physical longing.

In early centuries Eros was the originating force of creation; he was not perceived as a personal god until the third century B.C. He is therefore the oldest and the youngest of energies, in much the same way that Venus is the earliest planet viewed in the evening twilight and the last to evanesce from the morning sky. In some myths Eros's mother is impoverished Penia (Need) and his father Poros, translated as Resourcefulness, reinforcing the duality of his nature. "As his mother's son, Eros is poor, coarse, and squalid, a vagabond, who 'takes after his mother in always keeping company with want.' But he is like his father in always having designs on the beautiful and the good, and in being bold and enterprising," according to Anders Nygren.[8] The mythologem in *The Symposium* goes something like this: When Need (Penia) came begging at the door, Metis's son (Resource) wandered out in the garden and conceived a child (Eros) by her. It continues:

> As the son of Resource and Need, it has been his [Eros's] fate to be always needy; nor is he delicate and lovely as most of us believe, but harsh and arid, barefoot and homeless, sleeping on the naked earth, in doorways, or in the very streets beneath the stars of heaven, and always partaking of his mother's poverty. But, secondly, he brings his father's resourcefulness to his designs upon the beautiful and good, for he is gallant, impetu-

ous, and energetic, a mighty hunter, and a master of device and artifice—at once desirous and full of wisdom, a lifelong seeker after truth, an adept in sorcery, enchantment, and seduction.[9]

Eros always intensifies the feeling of lack, and the reason for the close association with want and resourcefulness is clear: energy flows when Need can trigger Resourcefulness. In the realm of image, we call this response "imagination."

When Eros enters we become needy, only too aware of our isolation, only too frightened of the possibility of betrayal. Hillman says that what gets activated with Eros are both the arrow and the wounds, but actually the wounds are already there. They draw the arrows. We imagine that the other person will heal the wounds.[10] Ann Carson explores the etymology of the name, a reminder that Eros brings awareness of deficiency: "The Greek word *eros* denotes 'want,' 'lack,' 'desire for what is missing.' The lover wants what he does not have."[11] Thus Eros was called "sweetbitter" (*glukupikron*) by Sappho—sweet when all goes well, but with the potential bitterness of loss always a poignant, incipient threat. The longing goads us into preempting the sweetly desirable as our own, even with the possibly attendant bitterness. Carson makes the significant point: "Eros' sweetness is inseparable from his bitterness, and each participates, in a way not yet obvious at all, in our human will to knowledge."[12]

More than any prominent figure of mythology, Eros bridges into the contemporary world because his dictates afford the most effective solution to modern day dilemmas. When heard and followed, his call offers a way of joining turbulent emotions to spiritual longings, gives knowledge that can be taken to the heart. The Jungian psychologist Raphael López-Pedraza recognizes to a unique degree what we can draw from mythology: "In our culture, the pagan gods, and the forms of life they personify are the most repressed; that is why they are the very gods who trigger our deepest psychic movements."[13] Jung, at the end of his career, offers the suggestion in his autobiographical *Memories, Dreams and Reflections* that a new approach to psychology could emerge by following the irrational pathways of Eros, conceivably superior to his own method of reflecting on soul.

No better illustration of this approach exists than the myth of Amor, or Eros (henceforth I will use the Greek form), and Psyche from Apuleius's *The Golden Ass*, a later classical Roman story that is still vital for us. It is our only recorded story of Psyche and is therefore very important for psychology. The centerpiece, the myth of Psyche and Eros, has attracted so much attention that the rest of Lucius's adventures (the man who desires magical knowledge is transformed into an ass for having curiosity without the requisite discipline) is generally overlooked. At the core of the book's meaning is the soul's awakening through magical attraction to what it secretly (or we might say unconsciously) loves. The tale of Psyche and Eros is the focal point of the larger tapestry that depicts the suffering and humiliation required for the soul to begin the journey of transformation—from torpid, primitive animal (ass) to a novitiate of Isis, who is the eternal female principle. Through multiple layers of meaning, the myth demonstrates how each major figure (including Aphrodite herself), despite previous avowals, awakens to new, unimagined potentials. Eros unwittingly affects all.

In the beginning the young Psyche, a mortal, is worshipped for her beauty as if she were Aphrodite. Donald E. Kalsched says the story "begins in a situation of unbalanced desire," because "desire is too identified with the human realm when its proper object is the Divine."[14] However, she finds it impossible to make intimate, human connections, and so she feels useless, passive. She gathers destructive energies around her. She is called a bride of death, because no human will associate with her or mate with her. At the insistence of the oracle her father consults, she is sadly escorted to her doom on an abandoned rock. At this point Fate shifts, an indication that love comes to the soul when it feels most abandoned. Eros rescues her, defying his mother's injunction to destroy her by making her fall in love with the lowliest of creatures.

Initially Psyche accepts living with Eros in the isolated luxury of a crystal palace, in a state of blinded bliss as she receives only nocturnal visits from her lover. In real-life experience this translates as the blindness and deafness that initially envelops any love object. We don't want to acknowledge the flaws, we prefer to see selective rose-colored realities. Enjoying the demigod's nightly visits, Psyche doesn't question his appearance or disappearance. From the practical point of view we might wonder, if she had full use of her sensual faculties, why she was unable to distinguish between a feathered god and a human in the darkness. Of course, that would spoil the tale.

Prodded by the envy of her sisters who come to visit her and tell her she might be married to a dragon, her compulsion to see her mate is aroused. The sisters are not merely spoilers of the paradise of love. They are the cynical side of Psyche, but they move her toward knowledge of herself. Psyche lights a candle and searches the dark void to make visible Eros's form, discovering the youthful god of love himself.

While gazing with fascination on Eros, Psyche picks up one of his arrows and is pricked. Love in the dark is transformed into specific love of Eros. At this moment she moves into the realm of the connected. Eros is no longer the god on one hand, the terrifying monster on the other. One of his names is "the very God of the Flame."[15] Apuleius's tale says that at the sight of him (Eros) the light burns cheerfully higher. Psyche, by taking up his element, gathers some of his fire, assumes the active role, takes on his aspiring nature, and becomes the searching one. His fire brings Psyche new vitality and awareness. She can no longer remain coolly detached from the process of living.

Psyche, unknowingly in service to the principles of Aphrodite, has been shunned as too beautiful to be human. A creature of the watery, ephemeral side of Aphrodite, she has been in danger of dissolving until exposed to the fire of Eros. In return for what the god of connection gives her, she cools down his fire, quiets his yearning for union. The joining of soul with passion is an end to destructiveness for them both. It is the quintessential alchemical transformation when water and fire combine together.

This paradigm indicates that on the personal plane psychic development begins when the soul ceases being only passively attentive (when it is no longer enough just to be admired as beautiful by Eros). When we begin to assume an active role of differentiating the individual aspects of our longings, of distinguishing what we love and desire, psychic life stirs. Or, concurrently, when receptivity no longer satisfies and energies begin to flow outward, then Eros responds.

An important feature of Eros not accentuated in other gods and goddesses is his wingedness. Carson recalls how Socrates forms an image link between the growth in awareness of soul and the physical likeness of the wings of Eros: "When you fall in love you feel all sorts of sensations inside you, painful and pleasant at once: it is your wings sprouting. It is the beginning of what you were meant to be."[16] The wings of Eros stir desire for knowledge of identity.

Psyche must discover her strengths and weaknesses, her heroine and her shadow sides. Pursuing the tasks that Aphrodite assigns her to win back Eros's affection, which she lost by disobeying his injunction never to gaze at him, Psyche has many moments of total discouragement. At the beginning of each impossible, inhuman demand she contemplates suicide and is saved only by her sensitivity to the lowly voices of the insects (ants) in the first task, plants (reeds) in the second, and the knowing tower of intellect (the aspiring spirit) in the third. All these demand getting in touch with herself on basic levels of being.

The final chore sends Psyche on a mission for Aphrodite to seek a box of eternal beauty from Persephone. It is a tradition for heroes or heroines to face a descent to the realm of the dead. It is only in contemplation of death that the soul discovers its eternal nature. The water of the river Styx, which three times surrounds the underworld, represents the deep, black hatred that must be broached for psychic differentiation to take place. Psyche must traverse the valley of the dead, while carefully following instructions so that she avoids contamination or any identification through pity that would compel her to remain with the lifeless souls.

Having faced hell and returned, Psyche is at last free, but she can't resist opening the box of eternal beauty. She is rendered helpless and must be rescued by Eros from the deathlike trance that flows out of the box. Healed from the molten wax wound on his shoulder, Eros is now aware of his undying love for her. He is able to choose this course of commitment only because he has matured and outgrown his slavish service to a possessive mother. Though our first love is given to mother, only when we move into a wider circle of caring can we find love of soul.

As demonstrated by Aphrodite's need for renewal from the underworld, the eternal beauty of love is linked to acceptance of change and of death. One of the enduring truths of the myth is that for soul to sustain substance, for love to be eternal, death has to be broached. Thomas Moore explains that the soul needs intimacy with death: "The psyche is at home in the underworld. Love may seem to offer benefits to the ego and for life, but soul is fed by love's intimacy with death. The loss of will and control one feels in love may be highly nutritious for the soul."[17] The marriage vows, in which we say somewhat casually "Till death do us part" emphasize the soul's longing for the depth of connection found only in death. The myth testifies that love and soul, passionately joined, can survive death. Or that given love, soul becomes immortal.

After many trials Psyche and Eros reunite in a mystic union, an *heiros gamos*, a holy wedding of young lovers straining for individual completion but also for surrender to connection that Eros initiates. Kalsched explains that the "ultimate symbolic aim of desire [is] a divine/human marriage." Their child, Joy, is gathered, together with Psyche, into the realm of the immortals as a recognition that transformation through love is possible. Kalsched adds that the resolution solves the paradox about desire: "It says that Joy is both human and divine, not either/or, and that the way to this Joy is a passion of ecstasy and humiliation in which both the human and divine are transformed, through the agonies of human relationship, into love."[18]

Psyche and Eros attain the immortal plane only after accomplishing those hard tasks that overcome their individual drawbacks. Psyche has authenticated her identity by pursuing her desire to the end, no matter how painful the journey. In tandem, Eros, to achieve his full stature, must acknowledge openly his passion for Psyche and assume responsibility for defending her from his mother's jealousy. Again Kalsched's point is important—that the divine Eros accepts limitation in order to enter the human realm: "Desire does not want unlimited expression (discharge). It seeks human limitation in order to transform itself."[19]

In some mythical renditions, Eros remains a baby until the goddess Themis is consulted and warns: "Love cannot grow without passion." Hence Eros can flourish only as long as accompanied by his brother Anteros, god of passion; whenever separated from Anteros, he reverts to childishness. This indicates that passion *must* accompany any endeavor that moves the soul to new awareness. Eros's involvement calls forth soul; Psyche comes to life through passionate attachment.

On an individual level, when desire awakens the soul into a love relationship, we are forced into an extension of awareness, not only of the other but of ourselves as well. When awakened by erotic desire, the very essence of the soul's longing is for more, for the beyond, for what might be, but isn't yet. We come to know our separate identity in being able to form a connective link with the other. Rilke elegantly describes this expansion in consciousness:

> Loving does not at first mean merging, surrendering, and unit-ing with another person (for what would a union be of two peo-ple who are unclarified, unfinished, and still incoherent—?), it is a high inducement for the individual to ripen, to become something in himself, to become world, to become world in himself for the sake of another person; it is a great, demanding claim on him, something that chooses him and calls him to vast distances.[20]

In our rationalistic modern age many, including psychologists, have concluded they could ignore the mysterious power of Eros. We cannot blame Freud unduly for an erosion that occurred over many centuries. Early Freudian theories only recognized the loss by subsuming Eros under the rubric of libido, according sex the dominant role in the dynamics of psychic structure. Jung admitted that Eros had been demeaned: "It [Freud's sexual theory] commits the imprudence of try-ing to lay hold of unconfinable Eros with the crude terminology of sex."[21] Later in his life Freud partially corrected this oversight by admit-ting Eros's importance as the life-seeking principle: "Eros operates from the beginning and appears as a life instinct."[22] In *Beyond the Pleasure Principle*, one of his last volumes, Freud conceded that, contrary to libido or sexual pleasure that seeks discharge of tension, Eros is the increase of tension within us. Eros has the significant role of compensat-ing the Thanatos or death impulse, the seeking of a decrease of tensions consonant with the death instinct. This new configuration places Eros in opposition to both Thanatos and libido. Confusion exists because Eros and Thanatos are Janus-faced energies, actually never entirely separable.

It is difficult but essential to make the distinction between sex as a physical need and Eros as a deep and fateful desire, a longing. A strong compulsion drives us into erotic encounter, and it won't let go until soul is satisfied. Lust, which is of the eye, is momentary and quickly dis-bursed; Eros enraptures the soul in committed engagement. Rollo May began the revival of Eros by naming him "the power in us yearning for wholeness, the drive to give meaning and pattern to our variegation, form to our otherwise impoverishing formlessness, integration to counter our disintegrative trends."[23] In thus acknowledging the significance of psychic development, May gives a sense of the wonder and power of Eros:

> We are in eros not only when we experience our biological, lustful energies but also when we are able to open ourselves and participate, via imagination and emotional and spiritual sensitivity, in forms and meanings beyond ourselves in the interpersonal world and the world of nature around us. Eros is the binding element par excellence.[24]

As an agency of interaction, Eros has a special bond with imagination, although the energy of Eros will always remain unimaginable, because it is the forming principle of imagination itself. Kerényi connects Eros—somewhat inscrutably—with the necessity of image-making, explaining that the spiritual side of Eros is "the memory of determinative primordial images." He emphasizes the joining-together aspect of Eros: "Even the spiritual part of Eros...flows into bonds and ties." [25]

In another linkage, Jung portrays Eros as psychic relatedness, still a limited and rather cold perceptual definition, with Logos, as the word or intellect, the function that clarifies and defines. Jung characterizes Logos as the mode of operation of masculinity, with Eros more akin to female functioning. (In spite of being considered generally a friend of women, Jung in this instance angered many of them.) Did he sufficiently appreciate the power of Eros? I question whether he did, and obliquely he acknowledged that lack at the end of his autobiography. Eros is infinitely belittled if we think of him as only relatedness or if we forget the longing urgency, the acute delight, the agony of potential loss, all generated by Eros.

None of Jung's followers have fully developed the awareness of Eros as the fateful psychic force he is. Hillman, however, acknowledges that force by making Eros initiator of the individuation process (Jung's term): "The individuation impulse that rouses personality out of its inertia and toward its development would then be Eros who is born of Penia, need, acute necessity."[26] Most Jungian interpretations of the myth of Psyche and Eros in the last twenty years limit it to only one aspect of growth toward consciousness—the thrust of male contrasexuality is the anima (Robert Johnson)—or as levels of female initiation into the masculine component (Eric Neumann and Ann Ulanov). Without denying the validity of any of these amplifications, since the myth sustains all such multiple meanings, I argue that transformation is the essential core—transformation that can only begin with the singling out and honoring of soul. Only through this primary attention can soul awareness then expand into love of spirit. We must know soul not only through Logos but through Eros as our guide. Even the doyenne of Jungian analysts, Marie-Louise Von Franz, views the myth as an incomplete accomplishment because Psyche and Eros are taken back to Olympus and depart the human realm, indicating that their union is beyond human comprehension. I prefer the interpretation that a connection with the spiritual realm is permanently forged whenever soul and Eros are joined.

Denis de Rougemont offers an opposite point of view by criticizing Eros's devastating but unsuspected impact on Western mores. In his two books, *Love Declared* and *Love in the Western World*, he brilliantly elucidates the import of the Tristan and Isolde fable on Western morality since the Middle Ages. As inheritors of this tradition, we secretly, he believes, strive for ecstasy by capitulating to adulterous liaisons—even to risking the anguish experienced by the lovers in the legend. To de Rougemont, Eros symbolizes this pagan notion of love in contrast to the Christian idea as embodied in Agape and Caritas. It is thus the thrill of falling in love that counts, even against our better instincts, in the same way that: "Tristan and Iseult do not love one another.... *What they love is love and being in love*."[27]

While de Rougemont acknowledges the power of Eros, he disapproves of the behavioral impact. He discredits Eros by relating "romantic love" to passive desire, while categorizing authentic love as more active and demanding: "To be in love is a state; to love, an act."[28] He observes the way passion ensnares and blinds us, but he literalizes the worship of Eros and fails to see the many possibilities that Eros opens other than erotic or profane love. Passion's power does require understanding, for the bewitching pull of Eros can indeed overpower the will to resist. De Rougemont denigrates passion as merely the seeking of pleasurable excitement, without acknowledging the learning, growing, transformative process that coincides with any deep involvement.

De Rougemont associates Eros with tragic death, the consequence of passion overriding convention. The rupturing of rigid societal codes in Shakespeare's *Romeo and Juliet*, Racine's *Phèdre*, Byron's *Don Juan*, Flaubert's *Madame Bovary*, or Tolstoy's *Anna Karenina*, to name a few, seems to support de Rougemont's main contention that erotic love disrupts and destroys lives, thus implicitly damning Eros as a transgressor of social mores. In some instances, however, only such a transgression can move us from complacency and lassitude. A visitation by Eros is invariably invited whenever humans set up rigid constraints on personal behavior and fail to understand the nature of desire. Frequently this lesson is driven home through community-imposed straitjackets aimed at almost any prurience or licentiousness. Here de Rougemont ignores the message Eros bears from the gods that we, who in our ego-oriented way believe we can control all the contingencies of life, are in fact, in certain circumstances, helpless. We do not always, as Pascal points out, understand our heart's desires: "the heart has reasons which the reason knows not of," another way of saying that we cannot dictate to Eros what path our passion will take us in revealing the soul's yearning. Eros is stronger than Logos. Love is stronger than will.

Just as he can impede all direct, willful actions, so can Eros connect to the unexpected. Within his sphere, what we thought would happen, doesn't. Action moves into the sphere of the gods, or destiny. The course of life is altered, twisted, renewed, made indirectly quixotic and imaginative by Eros. "Our wills and fates do so contrary run/That our devices are overthrown,/Our thoughts are ours, their ends, none of our own," Shakespeare's Hamlet says. As mediator between spirit and human realms, Eros can lift us out of either a mundane or a fractured life and give new meaning to it. Something within us responds and is compelled to answer the call.

Eros is all encompassing and always unexpected. Through the ages, under his luminous lodestar, love has been dissected in all its aspects in literature and poetry. One of the most moving among countless examples is by the great Sufi teacher, Jalal 'Uddin Rumi, who emphasizes the animating characteristic of love in "Odes from the Divan Shams-I-Tabriz":

Those who don't feel this Love
pulling them like a river,
those who don't drink dawn
like a cup of springwater
or take in sunset like supper,
those who don't want to change,
let them sleep.[29]

Love draws us into awareness of soul qualities, then into an awakening of the nature of spirit. Ultimately Eros not only makes patent hitherto unrecognized layers of being, but also leads us into awareness of the Divine Image in another human being. Cobb chastises psychology for failing to understand the compelling nature of love: "Psychology pays far too little attention to the theophanic nature of love."[30]

Today, in the self-absorption of our tumultuous, material-oriented world, Psyche and Eros are increasingly shunted aside. Some part of our humanity is lost in the modern equations of personal conduct. With the gods in effect banned from our secular world, Eros has lapsed into a banal, powerless Cupid. We smile naively at the dimpled, baby boy who shoots his arrows at the heart once a year on Valentine's Day. Soul today is preoccupied with food or music, not the eternal verities. Discussing the etymology of the word "psychology" in a class, an irate student resented hearing that psyche means soul and that one of the prime purposes of psychology is to recover the speaking of the soul.[31] Even when we accept the spiritual aspect of soul, we tend to confine it to church, just as we limit love to sex, forgetting that the two are mates—soul mates, if you will. We experience *angst*, the Age of Anxiety, to borrow W. H. Auden's phrase, as a consequence of disregarding soul and her helpmate, Eros.

We can revitalize this dormant Psyche/Eros connection through attentive awareness to our deepest desires and longings. Granted we may never fully know the needs or dimensions of soul, since we may never penetrate its mysterious realm. While we sometimes act as though answers will inevitably be forthcoming, there is no assurance. We cannot directly pursue soul, for then it vanishes; we can only stumble into soul knowledge. We can encourage psyche to emerge by bestowing attention on her. Invisible Eros, the initiator of connections, is like language. He makes things appear, makes a world appear. Sardello makes an important observation:

> The gods are strewn throughout the world as the emotion in things, awaiting to be re-membered. The re-membering cannot take place directly; it must take place through Eros who alone can connect each thing with its god. That is, the emotion of each thing needs to be given back to Eros who connects it with its appropriate divinity. Eros, in this sense, is the image maker.[32]

We must continue probing to discover what soul is asking of us, what our problems want of us. All the things, all the people that excite us, solicit our attention, our response, our passion. When we reflect on and strengthen these attachments, we deepen soul through Eros.

Finally, the ubiquitous Eros can awaken the creative spirit, and it's not always a pleasurable summons since it can jolt us out of self-contented lethargy. Sardello calls Eros "the will of imagination," correctly attributing the involvement of passionate will in adherence to any image as the supplier of energy. Will and imagination sometimes act in tandem, may sometimes spar in contention, with will interfering, denying, but each always entails the other in any action. As passionate desire, far more than rationalistic persuasion, Eros forges a synchronization, saving us from the searing separations of the supposed opposites. Eros as imaginative connector broaches pain and pleasure, delight and disorder, form and chaos, present and future, life and death. He is the enticement to form the unexpected linkage.

To discover our unconscious volitions or intentionality, we must get closer to the passions of our souls, both the longings and their movement in our psychic lives. As the active, fiery god, Eros ignites both imagination and will in the soul, bringing them to form. If Eros carries the will-to-image and Psyche carries the desire-for-experience, can we say that the joining of Eros and Psyche is the willingness to experience the images of our desires? The myth claims this marriage is the way to the fulfillment of soul.

Sulphur and the Fury of Desire

The soul is often described as the
hidden part [*occultum*] of the sulphur.
THEOBALD DE HOGHELANDE, *"De alchemiae difficultatibus"*

Venus is undoubtedly the *amor sapientiae*
who puts a check on Sulphur's roving charms.
JUNG, *Mysterium Coniunctionis*

From desire I plunge to its fulfillment,
where I long once more for desire.
GOETHE, *Faust*

To fathom those conflicts that scourge the individual personality both internally and externally, an understanding is needed of the relationship among aspirations, desires, and demands, and of how they commingle to initiate the engagement of the will. It is rare to experience aspirations in pure form; normally, they are meshed with a potpourri of desires. Whether a personal wish or compelling need, these desires, fueled by various complexes, can frustrate even a strong will. Needs cannot always be viewed as matters of choice; often, they are experienced as matters of emotional survival.

When we speak of the "feeling-toned complexes," as Jung defines them, or of individuation, we are using conceptual language. To the lay person these words can seem abstract, too radically simplistic to circumscribe the infinite complexity of our humanity. Having habitually grounded his psychology in myth, folk tales, art, religion and its icons, Jung, during the latter part of his life, gravitated toward alchemy, those paradigms rich in symbolic imagery, better to understand psychological dynamics. He came to this conclusion: "Alchemy is not only the mother chemistry, but is also the forerunner of our modern psychology of the unconscious."[1]

As Jung moved deeper and deeper into understanding the mysteries of the hermetic traditions, he initiated alchemical analogies to understand the unconscious unfolding of individual soul personality. He acknowledged the excitement he felt upon discovering these historical analogies:

> The experiences of the alchemists were, in a sense, my experiences, and their world was my world. This was, of course, a momentous discovery: I had stumbled upon the historical counterpart of my psychology of the unconscious. The possibility of a comparison with alchemy, and the uninterrupted intellectual chain back to Gnosticism, gave substance to my psychology.... I now began to understand what these psychic contents meant when seen in historical perspective.[2]

In three massive and scholarly volumes, Jung focused on the alchemical process as his model for individual development that extended beyond the merely physical. The imaginative drawings and etchings that alchemical symbolism had inspired through its long history excited him. He agreed with the basic tenet of alchemy that "one can only hold fast a mood of the soul by means of a concrete picture."[3]

Jung believed that the real search of the alchemists was not for the metal gold, but, symbolically, for the imperishable, eternal soul, the "pearl of great price." The alchemist held that the lapis, the philosopher's stone, revealed the essence of God as the core of all matter. Jung concurred that the goal of transformation was the awareness of the divine in human nature: "In the image of Mercurius and the lapis the 'flesh'glorified itself in its own way; it would not transform itself into spirit but, on the contrary, 'fixed' the spirit in stone, and endowed the stone with all the attributes of the three Persons. The lapis may therefore be understood as a symbol of the inner Christ, of God in man. I use the expression 'symbol' on purpose, for though the lapis is a parallel of Christ, it is not meant to replace him."[4]

Alchemical symbolism also intrigued Yeats, who saw it as "the gradual distillation of the contents of the soul, until they are ready to put off the mortal and put on the immortal."[5] He sought the transformation of the ephemeral into the essential by forging simple words into lasting poems and by concentrating images so that they could render a single theme. He often utilized alchemical imagery, as in "Byzantium" with a "Miracle, bird or golden handiwork,/More miracle than bird or handiwork," that is made "In glory of changeless metal," and that will remain beyond "All that man is,/All mere complexities,/The fury and the mire of human veins."[6] He spoke reverently of the alchemists who "sought to fashion gold out of common metals merely as part of a universal transmutation of all things into some divine and imperishable substance;…the transmutation of life into art, and a cry of measureless desire for a world made wholly of essences."[7]

In Medieval times alchemical processes were often purposefully obscured. Theophrastus Paracelsus, the sixteenth century physician, and a cryptic alchemist, expanded the division of work, or opus, into three primary elements—mercury, sulphur, and salt. For earlier alchemists it had entailed only the first two. In this enlarged version, analogies were drawn between mercury and the imagination (quicksilver, flashes of insight), between salt and memory (bitter, wrung out of tears, sweat, urine, blood), and between sulphur and will and desire. Thus one way of approaching will, which is called "part of all things," is by following the alchemical symbolism of sulphur. In the *Mysterium Coniunctionis*, Jung calls the element sulphur "the unconscious will." This was a fundamental shift in perspective, a profound innovation, for his earlier work dealt with will only as a conscious volition.

Symbolically, the alchemical process is divided into six steps that refine the desires, emotions, and will of the body and the soul so that they form a proper vessel for embodying the spirit. The first three tasks are called "the lesser work" and involve an upward move, a making lighter of body, the refining and distinguishing of soul, a taming of the instincts and spiritualizing of the body. The other three, "the greater work," involve a descending motion of this embodied spirit into the specially prepared soul and body. It is important to note that neither body nor soul are transcended. The aim is to bond body, soul, and spirit together, thus freeing them from intrapsychic conflict.

Of alchemical agents, Sulphur is most prevalent in nature. It is called the active principle, because it makes things happen in the opus, in nature, in all spheres of life. Intense and fulminating, it burns and consumes. It is that which catches fire, all that flames up, any sudden blazing leap. Through this imagery we can apprehend the closeness of will to that desire which burns in us all. Whatever compulsively attracts, whatever glints, there will and desire are magnetized. In discovering our heart's desire, we begin to discover what galvanizes our will into engagement with the world.

Will, as volition, is closely involved with compulsions. Coupled with desire, it stirs them. It is both a captive and an enforcer. In the chemical process, sulphur is the enforcer, seizing loose radicals. Think of iron sulfate making blue rings on the tub, or copper sulfate. Think of the bilious yellow color and stench of sulphurous water. Sulphur, the corruptor! Jung affirms and expands this assessment: "Sulphur...is the active substance of Sol and is foul-smelling. Sulphur dioxide and sulphuretted hydrogen give one a good idea of the stink of hell."[8] Sulphur symbolically signifies the drive toward involvement, the rage to live. It is *the* motivating power, the relentless drive toward consciousness. In Jungian terms:

> Sulphur represents the active substance of the sun or, in psychological language, the *motive factor in consciousness:* on the one hand the will, which can best be regarded as a dynamism subordinated to consciousness, and on the other hand compulsion, an involuntary motivation or impulse ranging from mere interest to possession proper. The unconscious dynamism would correspond to sulphur, for compulsion is the great mystery of human life. It is thwarting of our conscious will and of our reason by an inflammable element within us, appearing now as a consuming fire and now as life-giving warmth.[9]

Thus to the extent we are aware of our motives, we would be aware of will.

Here Jung emphasizes the burning aspects of will and the bewildering conundrums of compulsion that thwart conscious choices. Sulphur embodies the natural or primitive will, automatically and autonomously engaging whenever desire or need is present. Will that is conscious would have to become less hot and solar, more lunar, subjected to some reflection. The work refines sulphur so that it becomes more stable, less inflammable.

Compulsion has two sources: the shadow and the Anthropos,[10] defined by Jung as "the preconscious state from which the individual ego arose."[11] As the preconscious state is difficult to access, it is best to begin unraveling compulsions by looking at the shadow. It is often only the pain of our repetitive compulsions that motivates us toward the difficult task of discovery and delineation of the shadow.

Will and desire are scarcely separable at a basic level, and both are enveloped in the sulphur symbolism. Herbert Silberer regards sulphur "as a symbol of the expansive power, as individual initiative, as will."[12] Hillman defines it as the principle of "combustibility...the flammable face of the world...its aureole of desire." He likens alchemical sulphur to the heart's desire:

> That fat goodness we reach toward as consumers is the active image in each thing, the active imagination of the anima mundi that fires the heart and provokes it out.

> At the same time that sulphur conflagrates, it also coagulates; it is that which sticks, the mucilage, 'the gum,' the joiner, the stickiness of attachment. Sulphur literalizes the heart's desire at the very instant that the *thymos* enthuses. Conflagration and coagulation occur together. Desire and its object become indistinguishable. What I burn with attaches me to it; I am anointed by the fat of my own desire.[13]

Focusing on consumption, Hillman sees the object of desire and the subject who desires as synonymous. He also suggests the importance of recognizing that will is activated by desire and in turn ignites a desire for action.

In alchemy, sulphur is a masculine element, the active one, a solar quality that joins with quicksilver, a feminine one, the receptive one, a lunar quality. Feminists may resent this differentiation until they understand more acutely how alchemy honors the feminine in the fullest way. Only by a successful joining of what has been separated as quintessential masculine and feminine can the crowning of the androgyne be achieved, the marriage of the red king and the white queen. A reciprocal dependence exists between the active and the passive elements. In psychology this is true within the individual psyche as well as within any gender relationship. This would indicate the need for a deep understanding of our masculine and feminine qualities before expecting to find a happy meld.

Sulphur confers form and color to the process. Oddly it is not whiteness that is the final color of the alchemical marriage but red, the red of blood that is never left behind. Sulphur is primal essence and fixes the volatility of quicksilver. It hinders sublimation, which means that it prevents forgetfulness. The end product sought is an "incombustible sulphur," which has all the strength that sulphur contributes without the obsessiveness of inflammable sulphur.

In alchemical symbolism sulphur has an affinity with the dragon, who is called by Jung "our secret sulphur and the still unredeemed power of nature."[14] The hero's way is to attack the dragon directly, to kill the unconscious desire and crush the instincts of the body. The better way is not to repress or slay that which draws us into engagement but also into self-knowledge. As impossible as it sounds, we can learn to enjoy the desire without having to have the object itself. Whenever this detachment is possible we drive a wedge between desire and its will-to-realization.

In Christianity sulphur is the devil. Through his stench we know his proximity. He is luring us into the world, drawing us into the tinsel and glitter that dazzle the eye. Sulphur is Lucifer on one hand and Phosphorus, the light-bringer, on the other. Power drives, under the aegis of Lucifer, are part of being alive, but they lure us into trouble and force us to confront our compulsions. Of course, we can't hide them anyway. Indeed after we have gained some skill in handling them, we might remember to say: Thank God for our compulsions! They force us to face problems that otherwise might be avoided for years with convenient forgetfulness.

Without our power drives there would be no sense of vitality, no excitement. They compel us to reflect by always demanding our attention, always wanting the wrong things. Robert Grinnell explains it in a direct way: "Sulphur is a hot demonic principle in life;...from man's birth, it kindles an inner warmth; from it comes all motions of will and the principle of appetition. It is a 'vital spirit' having its seat in the brain and its governance in the heart."[15]

Our rampantly desirous nature is sometimes depicted in alchemy as the great lion with large mouth and insatiable belly, or as an image of the yellow lion with yawning mouth, never sated, always slavering for more. Very graphic! In our era we see it in manic activities, in compulsive consumerism, the wanting-it-all syndrome. In "The Vision Seminars," Jung links the lion to the Promethean urge:

> The lion obviously represents the will to power, which is identical with the royalty of man, in that man's will is a weapon which he superimposes upon nature. That is the difference between man and animal. The animal is obedient, pious, he obeys the laws of nature; but he can *only* obey the laws of nature, his power extends only that far; for the animal's power is not his own, it is the power of nature manifesting itself through him. But man has real power because, in his disobedience to nature, he has succeeded in wresting away, or abstracting, a certain amount of energy from nature, and has made of it his own will power. The danger lies in the fact that this was originally animal power which may still assert itself and run away with him. He has stolen something from the Gods, and is therefore punished by them, as in the myth of Prometheus.[16]

This leonine power of the passions and the harnessing of it are vividly illustrated by Hillman:

> Our way through the desert of life or any moment in life is the awakening to it as a desert, the awakening of the beast, that vigil of desire, its greedy paw, hot and sleepless as the sun, fulminating as sulphur, setting the soul on fire. Like cures like: the desert beast is our guardian in the desert of modern bureaucracy, ugly urbanism, academic trivialities, professional official soullessness, the desert of our ignoble condition.[17]

In the alchemical imagery, the male substance, the sulphur, rides the lion of power, while the more reflective quicksilver, with moon qualities, rides the griffin of imagination. The former suggests that informed will is upheld by, but can also tame, the power of desire. Another image of intense desire is the green lion with paws cut off. Green relates to the natural world and is also the color of hope and optimism. Green is the color of Venus, who is important to the opus. We are not to kill the lion of our desires, only to cut off the talons of his grasp, to curtail the necessity to be satisfied, to tame desire but do not forfeit the capacity to desire. The goal is to relate to emotion enjoyably, to experience desire without compulsion. This sounds hardly possible but, as Paul Kugler explains, the paradox is resolved by "looking to see the image in the fire. The difficulty is in taming the sulphur without putting out the fire."[18] As Gertrude Stein might have said: The point of desire is desire is desire. It can remain as strong as ever, but only so long as its outreach is curbed.

Sulphur is linked to Eros and Aphrodite. In *The Theogony*, Hesiod calls Eros and his helper, Himeros, "the geniuses of love and longing." Like sulphur, Eros and Aphrodite embody desire. Like sulphur, Eros is enraptured of the mother. Similarly, sulphur becomes Mother Earth's captive by making itself too malleable. In the same metaphorical sense, can't each of us be imprisoned by being too obliging to others? Eros's mythological mother, Aphrodite, the goddess of beauty, is also dangerously involving, yet mythology cautions that we can't slight her. She embodies seductive beauty that often cloaks an unconscious attraction for the unknown treasure that draws us into intimacy with others and into self-authenticity and soul knowledge.

Psychology in the twentieth century has not paid sufficient heed to the warning that we ignore Eros or Aphrodite at our peril. In a diminished, aberrant form, Eros enters into the Freudian notion of libido or psychic energy, but even in Jungian psychology, where Eros assumes the broader role of relatedness, he is not adequately acknowledged as the mysteriously powerful connector and initiator of the soul's journey. Aphrodite in her manifest role of making beauty visible is not acknowledged at all.

Oddly, while Aphrodite is extremely feminine in representations in Greek mythology or as the planet Venus, her element, copper, carries a masculine valence in the alchemical process. She governs the first, and sometimes the second, of the greater alchemical tasks, postulating love and beauty as ever-motivating factors. While the stages are separated for clarity's sake, in actuality neither of the two movements, the upward "spiritualization of the body" or the downward "embodying of the spirit," can be sundered from the other.

Venus dominates the fourth stage. "In her sign the sun of gold and the spirit, incombustible sulphur, appears above the tree of the cross. The sun swallows up the moon, and its form-giving power imprints anew the cross of the elements,"[19] Titus Burckhardt obliquely explains. The form-giving aspects of sulphur are important in terms of achieving "an active descent of the Spirit into the lowest levels of human consciousness, so that the body itself is completely penetrated by the 'incombustible sulphur.'"[20] Burckhardt adds that the final completion is "the transformation of the body into Spirit-become-form."

Sulphur provides the *prima naturae* and, linked with Venus, the radiant gold of Sol, the sun. In Grinnell's view, "Gold owes its red color to the presence of Copper (Cu) which he [the alchemist] interpreted as Venus, the Cyprian, which is also a transformative substance."[21] Venus, or Aphrodite, rules over transformations and therefore we understand her significance to the work of changing base matter into gold, or changeable nature into the eternal philosopher's stone, or the pearl of great price.

Sulphur is also linked to Mars and to iron, Mars's predominant component. Jung details the unlikely combination of Venus and Mars, who in some tales fathers Amor, or Eros: "Mythologically, the personified Amor is a son of Venus and Mars, whose cohabitation in alchemy is a typical *coniunctio*."[22] It is surprising, startling even, that unruly Mars would govern the second of the greater tasks, the next to the last. The conclusion seems inescapable that only those strong passions of loving and warring bring the soul to its fullest knowledge of itself. Among others, Erich Fromm refers to this effect. A long letter of the English alchemist John Pordage, explaining the spiritual instructions concerning the *opus,* is worth quoting, because it explains the importance of the inner marriage of extreme opposites and the product of new consciousness:

> The father of this child is Mars, he is the fiery life…. His mother is Venus, who is the gentle love-fire…Mars, or the husband,

must become a godly man, otherwise the pure Venus will take him neither into the conjugal nor into the sacred marriage bed. Venus must become a pure virgin, a virginal wife, otherwise the wrathful jealous Mars in his wrath-fire will not wed her nor live with her in union; but instead of agreement and harmony, there will be naught but strife, jealousy, discord, and enmity among the qualities of nature....

You must see to it that they lie together in the bed of their union and live in sweet harmony; then the virgin Venus will bring forth her pearl, her water-spirit, in you, to soften the fiery spirit of Mars, and the wrathful fire of Mars will sink quite willingly, in mildness and love, into the love-fire of Venus, and thus both qualities, *as fire and water,* will mingle together, agree, and flow into one another; and from their agreement and union there will proceed the first conception of the magical birth which we call Tincture, the love-fire Tincture. Now although the Tincture is conceived in the womb of your humanity and is awakened to life, yet there is still a great danger, and it is to be feared that, because it is still in the body or womb, it may yet be spoiled by neglect before it be brought in due season into the light. On this account you must look round for a good nurse, who will watch it in its childhood and will tend it properly: and such must be your own pure heart and your own virginal will....[23]

Walter Burkert reminds us that the odd conjunction of Mars and Venus is the basis of musical harmony: "The daughter of Ares and Aphrodite is Harmonia, Joining, which at the same time denotes musical euphony, sprung from the conflict of war and love."[24] In Greek mythology and Neo-Platonist philosophy, Love and War were born together from the eggs of Leda.

The Olympian triadic of Venus, Amor, and Mars and the Homeric one of Aphrodite, Ares, and Hephaestus are rich in symbolic connections. Bed to battle, battle to bed; always there is a strong correlative link, reaching to the present with "All is fair in love and war." Recall in the *Iliad* when Aphrodite spirits Paris from the battleground and deposits him in Helen's bed chamber. The goddess becomes furious because Helen finds it distasteful to make love to Paris in such an abrupt transition from battlefield to boudoir. Aphrodite reminds Helen of her tremendous power to endow her favorites or to destroy her enemies.

Similarly in the story of Phaedra, her stepson Hippolytus, thinking he could ignore Aphrodite, brings about the calamitous downfall of the entire household. The message is clear: love, beauty, and desire cannot be ignored. We cannot scorn their life-enriching and soul-enhancing qualities.

The gods and goddesses of Greek mythology mirror the ambivalence of human behavior. In essence, they are like us, only more so. Mythology is rich in imagery, in stories that dramatize our human passions on a canvas broad enough for us to be able to comprehend the magnitude of these passions, both heroic and base. In Virgil's *Aeneid*, Nesus asks Eryatus the core question, "Do gods give this eagerness to our hearts or does each/Man make a god of what is his own fierce desire?" By becoming aware of our Aphroditic nature and heeding where Eros leads us, we can achieve a revelation of our heart's desires and the way that the will responds.

Alchemy, like mythology, provides instructive links, connecting the macrocosm to the microcosm, the planetary world to the individual body and soul, making both nonlocal and less singular and personal. The blessings and the diseases of the individual, or collectively of society, relate to the cosmic rhythms of the supernal world. The metals we mine in the earth, the sulphur, the copper, and the iron, are also—as Sol, Venus, and Mars—planets in the sky. Mastery of personal desire and will requires recognition that we are creatures of a vast and complex interdependency system, one in which the will of the gods has a place too. Only hubris could make us suppose that we are totally stand-alone creatures. We can only respond to the world that presents itself to us. By doing so, we become able to take responsibility for choices based on awareness of our conflicting desires and knowing engagement of will. In alchemical imagery, our sulphur and quicksilver are always poised on the back of the lion and griffin, waiting to begin the journey toward wholeness and the mysterious crowning and marriage of the red king and white queen.

Aphrodite and the Ensouled World

The soul is always an Aphrodite.
PLOTINUS, *Enneads VI*

Things give themselves generously to aesthetic
apprehension because the world is ensouled
thanks to the presence of Aphrodite, the
Goddess of sensual fantasy.
JAMES HILLMAN, "On Mythical Certitude"

From Aphrodite, glorious Aphrodite, comes the gift of beauty itself. To awaken desire, to capture and hold our attention in the sensual world, she touches all things, rendering them visible and arresting. Her enchantment bestows brilliance on even the most mundane, and her gifts extend beyond the individual to all living beings. Walter Otto describes her beneficence as "not so much the ecstacy of desire as the charm which kindles and propels it.... Not only men and beasts but plants, inanimate images and appearances, even thoughts and words, derive their winning, moving, overwhelming sweetness from her."[1]

Thus we are indebted to her for making us see the world as both beautiful and desirable. When the first space travelers looked back and saw the world's lovely configuration, perhaps we ushered Aphrodite, long diminished, back into our lives.

Mythology holds that Aphrodite emerges with the pearlescent dawn, clothed in hues of pink and aqua, an ephemeral beauty visible for a few radiant moments as darkness lingers at the cusp of the heavens, soon to be eclipsed by the incandescent light of day. She is always on the margin—of day and night, of sea and shore. She is the misty fusion of water and air in the luminescent sea foam or morning dew. The four elements of nature are her domain, with one never exclusively dominant. Even her earthiness partakes of an airy lightness. In gods and humans she quickens pulsations of rapture and the lyric voice. To embrace Aphrodite is to embrace joyous excess.

Aphrodite has many prototypes, among them earlier Mideastern goddesses such as Ishtar, Astarte, and Innana. Her name is not Greek, and yet she is the most Greek of goddesses. She is the embodiment of fertility, procreation, and prosperity. She is the essence of the life of the senses, and yet she transcends the purely natural world. She is the spirit of beauty in nature; in alchemical terms she is *lumen naturae*. Jung never lets us forget the nature/spirit connection: "Nature is not matter only, she is also spirit. Were that not so, the only source of spirit would be human reason."[2]

Aphrodite's special range of powers emerges from her diverse origins. Two very distinct stories of her birth are recorded in mythological lore, both highly sexually oriented. In Hesiod she is related to the oldest generation of the Olympians. She emerges (as Aphrodite Urania) full-grown from Uranus's genitals, which bobbed in the sea after Kronos castrated his father for the rape of Gaia and for burying their children in the earth. A violent beginning for such a beautiful creature!

Aphrodite is coupled to two sides of the father, the exalted spiritual side, but also to the senex, the seedy, seminal stuff of masculinity. She is his sole creation, reawakening fantasies of youthful energy, puer fantasies. Hillman explains this rapport between fantasy and disillusionment: "Without Kronos and the senex-despair of the complex, Aphrodite and her illusions might never float in off the foam."[3]

Hesiod relates in *The Theogony* that she came ashore at Cythera and "grass grew up beneath her shapely feet." But Cythera was too small an island for her, and she quickly departed for Cyprus which henceforth she called home. Her companions, whom she is rarely without, play significant ancillary roles. Love (Eros) accompanies her, the great magnet, the motivator. Longing (Himeros) is in her entourage, symbolizing the unslakable thirst that propels one ever onward toward the object of desire.

Her birth as Aphrodite Pandemos in the alternate version is less violent. She has a mother, Dione, an immortal sea nymph, making her less singularly a father's fancy. She is the offspring by natural means of Zeus, who in the *Iliad* (Book 5) refers to her as his "dear daughter."

Whichever version we accept, Aphrodite appears as strongly solar, her radiant goldenness a dominant feature. She is persuasive, hard to resist. Paul Friedrich points out the linguistic associations of her goldenness with gold and honey, gold and speech, gold and semen; all are linked symbolically in her appeal.[4] Jean Shinboda Bolen suggests that procreation and verbal creation have a common nexus.[5]

Although not lunar like Artemis, Aphrodite does relate to the rhythms of the tides, and she has astral features as well. As Venus, she is the evening planet appearing first in the twilight sky and nestling near the new moon. As the morning star, she is the last to leave the heavens. Keith Critchlow, in *Islamic Patterns*, draws a remarkable pentagonal diagram of the planetary pattern that the planet Venus's pathway takes in the heavens, entering and leaving. Aphrodite is always betwixt and between places, both spatially and emotionally. Her proximity signifies a possible turning, a moment of change, a transformation.

Aphrodite is predominantly procreative; all nature bursts into bloom in her presence. "She draws forth the hidden promise of life," as Ginette Paris describes it.[6] She is the essence of summer and she favors all manner of fruits, flowers, and fragrances. Her fertile beneficence stimulates the maturation of apples, peaches, and pomegranates. Among flowers she is particularly associated with the rose, but she also likes the daisy and the lily; she is always described as "garlanded." She is a favorite of small animals and birds; swans and doves circle about her and do her bidding. In her presence fierce animals are tame and gambol in the sun in pairs. She is wafted by Zephyr, the west wind, or rides on the dolphin, a pink scallop, or a cockle shell. Botticelli's *Birth of Venus* immortalizes her wispy veiled figure emerging from the sea on an open-faced scallop shell.

From the moment of her appearance she is involved in dressing, undressing, and perfumed bathing. "The Hours received her happily and happily put ambrosial garments around her," the "Hymn to Aphrodite II" records. Her garments possess the power to enchant. In Book 14 of the *Iliad,* the goddess Hera, usually at odds with her over the sanctity of marriage vows, borrows a magic girdle from Aphrodite in order to seduce Zeus and to lure him away from the battlefield. It is described as a curiously embroidered girdle in which all her magic resides. "There is the heat of Love/the pulsing rush of Longing, the lover's whisper,/irresistible—magic to make the sanest man go mad."[7]

Aphrodite's domain also embraces jewelry, and of course she is lavishly bedecked. The pearl imitates her power to transform ugliness into beauty: irritated by a bit of gritty sand, it emerges from the sea as a luminous gem. In other applications, her beauty and magic are more ephemeral, of the present, of transient sensuality. Clothes illustrate this phenomenon. They are not meant to last forever. Cosmetics, another of her areas, have to be reapplied endlessly.

Among surviving cult statues, those of Aphrodite are more numerous than any other deity. The collections of the Louvre verify this. In classical times she was always portrayed clothed, if only barely, often with a wet, clinging garment but never in a stiff pose. Her body is usually twisting and full of movement. She is perpetually changing, the goddess of turning. She is described as having "sparkling eyes" and a "beautiful backside" (*callipge*). When Praxiteles fashioned a naked statue of her, fourth century B.C. Athens was shocked. In our time, contemplating a copy of this sculpture known as the *Cnidian Aphrodite*, Kenneth Clark precisely summarizes the eyes of "innocence" that the modern world seems to have lost:

> Perhaps no religion ever again incorporated physical passion so calmly, so sweetly and so naturally that all who saw her [Aphrodite] felt that the instincts they shared with beasts, they also shared with the gods. It was a triumph for beauty.[8]

As one of the Olympians, Aphrodite had for the Greek world supernatural and religious import. Yet ever since her early prominence, she has raised a conflict; at its crux is whether her distinguishing feature is merely earthly consciousness "exalted to the highest purity" and therefore merely human—or whether sensual beauty has deeper inherent psychic or spiritual value. According to J. J. Bachofen, Aphrodite represents "the intermediate stage that in the cosmos marks the position between *nous* and *soma*."[9] Otto affirms her reach: "Her enchantment brings into being a world where loveliness moves toward delight, and all that is separated desires blissful fusion into oneness. In it all possibilities and desires are included, from dark animal impulse to the yearning for the stars."[10]

Appropriately for one who is an admixture of water and air, of ocean spray and morning dew, Aphrodite often mediates across the chasm that divides mortals and immortals, perhaps because she is effective in both realms. Her liminality is an important aspect of her crossover identity. The liminal, being on the edge, always challenges the ethical societal norms of the middle and therefore is adjudged perilous. In modern political parlance, she would be labelled an extremist of either right or left because she threatens the comfortable status quo. Either by awakening unrealized desires for aesthetic beauty or by repelling those who value crudeness, she breaks down barriers to create openings for new experiences. Through an eruption of novel attractions, she challenges the entrenched ego.

Aphrodite is the goddess who makes unions possible, whether brief or enduring, even unlikely ones. The complexity of relationships attracts her, and particularly those in triads, whether male or female. She is accompanied by the three Graces, the three Hours, or involved with the three Moirai. In one of her guises, as *Urania*, she is deemed the eldest of the Moirai, linking her to the cycle of birth, life, and death.

In two of her manifestations (Epitymbidia and Tymboychos), she is directly involved in mortality as goddess of tombs and of the dead. Persephone is often called Aphrodite's underworld aspect, which startles. How can such an earthly, lively creature connect with the pale, shadowy world of the dead? This nexus suggests that wholehearted acceptance of Aphrodite yields knowledge of both life and death. Rejection of Aphrodite implies two shadows: a belittlement of the sensual world and an avoidance of the uncomfortable awareness of life as inherent part of death and death as part of life. Perhaps this paradox explains the animosity she can arouse in those wishing to avoid full-hearted confrontations with both aspects of the living process.

The animosity is perhaps engendered by her attitude toward marriage, with which she is frequently at odds. Having possessed many lovers, she of course encourages love affairs. Yet with each of her own amorous liaisons, a virginal aspect is manifested. In a curious sense, she is a perpetual virgin, meaning she is never permanently attached, not *virgo intacta*. The word *parthenos* as applied to Aphrodite describes a feminine figure who is "one in herself,"[11] who does not need another to be complete. She is not the half of any pair. She is never raped, because she is the teacher when it comes to lovemaking.[12] For Aphrodite, the act of love is an art and never hasty, as opposed to Dionysian sex, which is more animalistic, more like a hunger—a compulsive urge, demanding quick gratification.

Aphrodite is a nonconformist, cut from a different mold than any other god or goddess. She takes a lover with no regret and yet those who serve her are apt to feel helpless, even masochistic. Even in her choice of companions there is paradox. *Ananke* (necessity) and *Aidos* (shame) join her entourage, and in odd ways they belong. Necessity is the core of all complexes, of which she is a great evoker. Shame exhibits itself in everything from a simple blush to extreme humiliation. John Sanford and George Lough examine this connection with the goddess:

> Indeed, the language in which Aphrodite is described is the language of masochism. For Aphrodite was said to "ensnare people's hearts," to inflict people with the "lashes of longing," and to "chain" people with her charms. She herself was often pictured in Greek art as Aphrodite in chains. For hers is the power that binds; she binds the soul to her, people to themselves, lovers to each other.

> For this reason, masochism also serves the feminine. Its strange power, its delight in the darkness, its irrationality, its appeal to the soul, its circuitous route, its erotic arousal, its passion, its stirring to love—all of these emanate from the great feminine archetype that Aphrodite is part of. And all of this compensates in many men an ego development that has gotten too far away from its roots in the world of the feminine.[13]

In exploiting passion and ecstacy Aphrodite can trigger some very uncomfortable combinations. She is the essence of pairing, but frequently the dyad enlarges to become an uneasy love triangle. Allowed to choose her own husband, she picked Hephaestus, even though all could predict that she would never remain faithful to this lame but highly skilled god. Although seemingly unequal, this bonding affirms that beauty and craft have an affinity, a need to enhance one another. We understand the connection if we appreciate that ephemeral, aphroditic beauty can be rendered into manifest, durable form through hephaestian craftsmanship.

In her other major relationship, her long affair with Ares, the attraction is again an association of apparent dissimilarities that actually belong together. A haunting association exists linguistically between the closeness of *Eros*, Aphrodite's child, with *Eris*, the goddess of strife, and *Ares*, god of war, indicating that beauty and the martial arts are never as remote as we might expect. Her pairing with Hephaestus produced no progeny; yet with Ares came three diverse children—a girl, Harmonia (Harmony), and then in disquieting opposition, two sons, Phobus (Fear) and Deimos (Terror). Even in her affair with Hermes, who is sometimes called the father of Eros, similarity and difference reflect the powers she repeatedly draws to herself.

Her volatile nature bears more kinship to Hermes than to most other Olympians. Both are forever changing, unpredictable, always unreliable. Both lie, both steal, and both like to laugh when caught in delinquencies. The offspring of this union is an hermaphrodite, sharing equally in both of their names and both sexual natures. In alchemical literature, Aphrodite by herself, as Venus, has an androgynous nature, containing both masculine and feminine energies.

Aphrodite has Eros as both companion and son. Sometimes she is vying for his attention; sometimes she is sending him on missions that further her causes. This bond exemplifies the problem confronting the young son who struggles to release himself from erotic attachment to the mother, or the older woman hungering for a handsome youth.

In the personal realm the closeness of the tie between Aphrodite and Eros is apparent: "She is the active principle of Eros which enables us to be related to our own emotions, and also to touch the emotional substance of another," Nancy Qualls-Corbett explains.[14] Relationships under her aegis are so intense that even the Olympians had difficulty extricating themselves from emotional attachments that came under her governance.

Aphrodite herself cannot always escape the complex emotions she arouses in others. Occasionally she is ensnared in a painful affair of the heart. Her relationship to Adonis is post-Homeric, but illustrative of the love of the mature woman for a youthful man. Here she is forced to share Adonis with Persephone for part of the year, even though Persephone suffers a division—an attachment to her mother and to Hades for part of each year. Priapus, the vulgar manifestation of sexual urges, is the son of Aphrodite by either Dionysus, Hermes, or Adonis. Ultimately, she abandons him, perhaps because his nature is too compulsively sexual for her more refined taste.

Beyond her involvements with the deities of the pantheon, Aphrodite has a propensity for human relationships. Some say that Zeus, envious of her power over immortals (except Artemis, Athena, and Hestia) and wanting to pay her back for her provocations, caused her passions to be aroused by the human herdsman, Anchises. "The Hymn to Aphrodite I" describes this fateful encounter in these words:

> And when she saw
> him, Aphrodite, lover of laughter, she
> loved him, and a terrifying desire seized
> her heart.[15]

Instead of leaving Anchises after a brief affair, she remains bound to him, unusual for her, and this union produces a favorite child, Aeneas.

When summoned by mortals, Aphrodite often responds. The tenth book of Ovid's *Metamorphoses* tells how King Pygmalion falls in love with a naked ivory statue that he has carved. When he prays to the goddess of love, Aphrodite fulfills his fervent desire that the statue come alive. Galatea, brought to life by Pygmalion's longing, is the mirror image of desire. In another example, on the eve of his foot race with Atalanta, Hippomen prays to Aphrodite, and she gives him three golden apples. Atalanta sacrifices the race when she stops to pick up Aphrodite's apples, but she wins a husband.

In another mythic encounter Myrrha falls in love with her father and tricks him into sleeping with her. When he is about to kill her, Aphrodite transforms Myrrha into the fragrant myrrh tree. Her trickery, her enticements, ensnare both sexes, but more frequently women are the victims. Perhaps this is because she does not easily tolerate competition from her own sex in the realm of beauty—as Apuleius's story illustrates. Psyche's beauty makes mortals forget Aphrodite. Furious, Aphrodite wants Psyche destroyed. Instead of crushing her as he is commanded, Amor takes Psyche to a secluded paradise where he only appears during the night. In retaliation, Aphrodite sets arduous, even perilous trials for Psyche to surmount before she can win acceptance as his mate.

This spirited goddess can also be harsh on males attempting to bypass her. In Euripides's tragedy *Hippolytus*, Aphrodite brings first devastation and then death to Hippolytus because he ignores her in swearing allegiance to Artemis and celibacy. His stepmother, Phaedra, is used by the goddess to avenge his neglect. Phaedra, trapped by her passionate feelings for her stepson, commits suicide. In the play, Aphrodite says: "Those that respect my power I advance to honor, but bring to ruin all who vaunt themselves at me."

Aphrodite not only stirs emotions, she intensifies them, both in oneself and in one's feelings toward others. Her very nature is the embodiment of passion and desire. Using the subjective voice of unfulfilled longing that she inspires, Sappho, her devotee, sings of the power of love:

> Let the depths of my soul be dumb
> for I cannot think up
> a clarion song about Adonis
>
> for Aphrodite who staggers me
> with shameful lust
> has reduced me to dull silence,
>
> and Persuasion (who maddens one)
> from her gold vial
> spills tangy nectar on my mind.[16]

None are ever neutral toward Aphrodite, and many fear falling under her aphroditic sway. Ninety-five percent of Sappho's poetry, which encompassed Aphrodite's realm, was destroyed, much of it willfully, first by Greek Orthodox fanatics and later by French and German Crusaders in the Fifth Crusade, revealing the harsh depth of emotional reaction that Aphrodite stirs. A long passage from Friedrich focuses on this tragic obliteration:

> On several occasions her [Sappho's] poems were publicly burned by the orders of popes and bishops or by mobs of zealots.... This compulsion to burn Sappho indicates that her vision threatened the Christian foundations of patriarchy, hypocrisy, and puritanism.

> What survived chanced to be illustrative material tucked away in technical works on grammar and style or, weirdly enough, served as the papyrus ingredients of the sort of papier-mâché used for coffin cartons, mummies, and the stuffing of stuffed crocodiles! Her hymn to Aphrodite—perhaps the greatest lyric in Greek—was preserved as part of a syntactic treatise by Dionysius of Halicarnassus as an example of "finished and brilliant composition." Of her five-hundred-odd poems, there survive to this day between six and seven hundred lines. Her work was extirpated from the Greek-speaking world just as ruthlessly and almost as successfully as the image of her persona, Aphrodite. [17]

Despite critics like Martin Nilsson who dismiss the goddess of desire as merely a natural instinct, and others who deplore her vanity, her tendency to dawdle, and her hedonism, I am convinced that Aphrodite's sway, then as now, is the most potent of the twelve Olympians. Not even Homer's efforts in the *Iliad* to make her a figure of ridicule and to dramatize her ineffectiveness on the battlefield are persuasive. It is mockery aimed at mitigating Aphrodite's terrible power to turn lives upside down and change destinies. Homer allows only the remotest recognition of her might. Yet after careful evaluation, I believe she emerges as the dominant force in the *Iliad*, casting her shadow over the panorama of the Trojan War and its far-flung consequences. Perhaps, in the patriarchy that Homer exalted, it would have been difficult to acknowledge directly the strength of female sexuality that Aphrodite embodied. It was easier to accept multiple acts of lust by males (e.g. Zeus).

Aphrodite's commanding power over events leading to the Trojan War begins with Paris's decision to give her the golden apples, inscribed "to the fairest of them all." Eris, goddess of Discord, had found the perfect way to disturb the world when she brought the apples to the wedding of Thesis, to which she had not been invited. Paris's decision initiates the action that is responsible for Helen's leaving a respected position in a noble household with a beloved husband and child to follow Paris to Troy. Aphrodite makes clear her power to enhance or destroy her favorites. Her influence is never far from the vortex of action.

In the song of the poet Demodokus in the *Odyssey*, it might seem once again that Aphrodite is being ridiculed. The story relates how Hephaestus traps Aphrodite and Ares with golden chains while they are making love. But even this occasion, which might have ended badly, is turned by Hermes into a cause of merriment when he mentions that he and many others would be happy to take Ares's place, even at the risk of being caught. When released, Aphrodite quickly skips off to Cyprus to be renewed and refreshed and to continue her endeavors. She is simply fulfilling her nature.

Her character is replete with contradictions and complexities. She may be a "lover of laughter," but her operating mode does not necessarily produce "an unbearable lightness of being," to borrow a phrase from Milan Kundera. Beauty itself, and those rapturous interludes it stimulates, are by nature evanescent. But after all, Aphrodite is not the guardian of longevity. She wistfully symbolizes the fact that excruciatingly beautiful or passionate moments are ephemeral. Bachelard says it well: "All departed love ushers the soul into Purgatory."[18] The poignant awareness of abandonment, loss, and finally death as part of the ever renewing cycle of life are also Aphrodite's province. She quickens living, while bringing awareness of the nearness of death. What is life-enhancing one moment can be life-threatening the next. At the dark perigee of her sexuality cycle, Aphrodite can be both castrating and man-eating.

Yet, in contradistinction, she exemplifies that esoteric and little-understood link between sophisticated sensuousness and civilization. In the Sumerian epic, when Gilgamesh wishes to tame the barbaric Enkidu, he sends the goddess of rapture. The half-man/half-beast is domesticated to civilized life after eight days of lovemaking with the goddess. Perhaps out of exhaustion!

Aphrodite bridges the extremes between dynamic opposites. Her great power is this special attribute, a subtle force that can govern the most severe, excruciating tensions, acute and polarized dissociations, often resolving them into new formations. Every archetypal configuration holds together dissimilarities, but she is the prototype of all archetypes, as she structurally unites extensions and subtleties of dimensions of being that only derive from passion. Karl Kerényi puts it nicely:

> Shining in golden purity, Aphrodite, the male-female wholeness, makes pale every sort of partialness. She is present when wholeness emerges from the halves and when the resolved opposites become the indissoluble goldenness of life. [19]

Christine Downing has this to add: "We may learn from you [Aphrodite] a way of knowing ourselves and the world that comes only through turning in love toward another."[20] Ginette Paris relates her power to bind cultural as well as personal contradictions: "She [Aphrodite] revitalizes the tension between opposites and yet permits union between them: nature and culture, body and spirit, sky and ocean, woman and man."[21]

Friedrich observes another of the contrasting characteristics that make Aphrodite so potent and so dangerous: the combining of sex and sensuousness with maternity and motherliness. Together these qualities bestow on her an intimidating concentration of power intended, as Friedrich puts it, "to threaten the male's image of his authority by bringing into the open the sexual and emotional power of the female."[22] The exposure of this tensile bond reveals the dangers inherent in the incest taboo, perhaps accounting for the blanket repression of Aphrodite's influence in our world.

In our day, which barely concedes the soul's existence, we find it hard to accept a philosophical precept obvious to the Greeks—that beauty is purposeful to the soul's destiny. Ron Schenk makes a cogent point: "For us to recover the psychological value of beauty, we would need to restore the 'metaphysical dignity' it held for the Greeks."[23] Ardent feminists in the 1960s may have added unwittingly to this prohibition by striking out against ornamentation and alluring clothes as antifemininist and merely another aspect of the patriarchal structure that dictates that women must strive to please men. Appreciation of any act of adornment—putting on earrings, arranging a bowl of roses on the table—evokes the Aphrodite in all of us. Would today's poet dare to attempt to captivate our interest by describing his lover's clothes with such mellifluous lines as those of seventeenth century poet Robert Herrick in "Upon Julia's Clothes:" "Whenas in silks my Julia goes,/Then, then, methinks how sweetly flows/that liquefaction of her clothes?" The nineteenth century English Romantic poets did attempt to restore a measure of appreciation for the beauty of worldly things, as Lord Byron's euphoric line suggests: "She walks in beauty like the night." Sadly, in the latter part of the twentieth century we are often more focused on the unseemly than the decorative.

To single out beauty and call it a grace is a hurdle for many. Even more disturbing is the uneasy connection between beauty, sexual attraction, and the desiring nature that yearns for a connection with the gods. Through studies of Sufi mysticism, Henry Corbin reaffirms that human beauty has sacred meaning, "a divine manifestation, the theophany *par excellence*."[24] This close alignment infers that a longing for beauty will lead to the knowledge of the radiant individual soul and to the awareness of the reach of our desires. Plato's point.

On the individual level, we may sometimes intuit that those who attract us sexually offer us an insight into soul-making. John Donne's words capture the feeling that love has a preordained quality: "Twice or thrice had I loved thee/Before I knew thy face or name" ("Air and Angels"). In today's psychological parlance we say that our passions for another are projections of our fantasies. We look favorably on them as reminders that it is possible to stay some of the projection and develop those sought-for, missing qualities of soul in ourselves. The quickening of interest, called an anima or animus response by Jung, is a vital initiation of the individuation process. Transformation of sexual attraction into lasting love only follows when beauty is discovered as an inward as well as an outward grace. Qualls-Corbett affirms this point: "Aphrodite embodies not just instinct, but also the soul's desire. In a mature alliance, the partners realize both the erotic and the spiritual potential of the relationship."[25]

In the West, commencing with Hesiod and Homer and continuing with Christianity, the realm of Aphrodite has been diminished.

Whatever vestiges that might have remained were exorcised by Puritanism in its rejection of sensual pleasure. In the Islamic world today, women with Aphroditic qualities are considered seductresses, deserving of punishment. The basic schism lies in the acceptance of a disjunction between the mind, the body, and the spirit. Rejection of the body, especially the female body, as the temple of the soul/spirit produces a total distaste for any connection between sexual and religious urges. The resulting loss brings terrible splits in the psyche and threatens the nonbeliever with the violence of fundamentalistic fervor.

The mystery and magic of sexuality and spirituality are not so dissimilar, since each draws us out of our exclusivity. The Tantric tradition in India openly accepts the *mysterium tremendum* involved in both realms of being. The connection is obliquely acknowledged in the imagery of the church or nun as bride of Christ and in such expressions as "the passion of Christ." Donne accepts this symbolic connection through such phrases as "batter my heart," "ravish me," "enthrall me," "imprison me," as he beseeches the Holy Spirit to take charge of his soul. We need to be reminded that the white dove of Aphrodite is also the dove of the Holy Spirit.

The prevailing debasement of Aphrodite's gifts prompts females to dislike their bodies and to suffer perpetual dissatisfaction in trying to live up to some abstract standard of beauty, with little awareness of individual appeal. Women despair about beauty, frantically seeking to take the ugliness out of their bodies, some even resorting to the extreme emaciation of anorexia. Under Aphrodite's aegis, beauty is a state of grace (*charis*). So is sexual attraction. The Judeo-Christian tradition of the last two millennia makes all sexuality that is not potentially procreative a condition of sin, causing confusion and lack of appreciation for an entire spectrum of our humanity.

As early as the fourth century B.C., Aphrodite was beginning to receive short shrift, as the Eros myth superseded the Aphroditic. In Plato's *Symposium*, attention is often focused on love between older men and young boys or impersonally on the soul rather than on the multiple spectrum of creative relationships that Aphrodite inspires. Unruly Eros was reintroduced into our time by Freud, more as a concept than as an image. We might ask: why Eros and not Aphrodite? Classically he is the errand boy, but she is the power behind him. If we replaced the erotic with the aphroditic, modern psychology would be very different. Hillman points out this discrepancy and its lacunae for archetypal psychology:

> She [Aphrodite] appears in Freud's hermeneutics of symbols understood by their genital shapes. She appears in Freud's notion of libido, whose etymon refers to lips, sexual desire and liquid like the sap of life. Again, instead of referring libido to the *person* of the Goddess of insemination, desire, fruit, flowers, and the visible beauty of soul, it was translated into a Promethean concept of psychic energy. How different our depth psychology would have been had we let the Goddess emerge within the psychoanalytic disease. [26]

Erich Fromm contends that Freud's extreme patriarchalism "led him to the assumption that sexuality per se is masculine, and thus made him ignore the specific female sexuality." Fromm's criticism of Freud's theory is "not that he overemphasized sex, but his failure to understand sex deeply enough."[27] Both male and female sexuality is lived out in our time in maladapted ways. Bachelard suggests that we honor both maleness and femaleness and that our goal should be "to live at both poles of our androgynous being."[28]

Jung acknowledges the power of Eros is foundational, contrasting it to Logos, but he does not go far enough in recognizing the manifest aspect of beauty and desire to further Psyche's journey. Again Hillman reminds us that Jung, in separating psychology from aesthetics, failed to appreciate the importance of manifest beauty, with unfortunate consequences for the validation of images:

> Approaching fantasies in terms of their causal antecedents side-steps the impact of the image. It is deprived of its appeal, the claim of its immediate body. Something more important lurks behind—the psychodynamics by which it can be understood. The same devaluation occurs when we look at images for their symbolic contents, thereby putting in second place the form of their containment. By ignoring these formal and sensate aspects of psychic materials, we force Aphrodite to return only via her diseases—transference, sensualism, naturalism, concretism, and the flesh as sheer superficiality.[29]

Perhaps the neglect of Aphrodite stems from what one writer calls "our decadent Puritanism," which robs our culture as well as our personal life of multiplicity. Ginette Paris points out that "real cultural poverty is expressed by the total absence of Aphrodite" and that the "lack of Aphrodite brings frigidity in all interpersonal relationships."[30] Slighting Aphrodite makes us search for beauty in aberrant ways, in pseudo-pleasures, in ever more glossy surroundings, and in rampant materialistic consumption. Is this punishment for demythologizing her glorious gold, allowing it only commercial value, thus limiting us to a rapacious and sterile search for it in a debased form? Celebratory pleasures are undervalued in our time, replaced by weird forms of sensationalism and hedonistic rituals. Is this also her revenge? The empty search for sensual satisfaction, the trivializing of our desires, the working out of them in undercover ways have followed in her vanishing wake.

All of this adds up to failure to acknowledge the mysterious power of change inherent in sexual attraction, to a total misunderstanding of the profound spiritual nature of our sexuality. A culture that spawns rampant pornography or rape as a ritual of manhood provides poor substitutes for the exalted and pure passion that a loving encounter can bring. By confusing the basic human need for beauty, we end up seeking transformation or escape from twentieth century sordidness through drugs. If we cultivated Aphrodite's attributes, the missing elements in our thirsting search for beauty might emerge again. If we made this eclectic goddess more welcome in our midst, we might recapture and honor those images that illumine the constructive aspect of our desires.

Agape and Eros

Love is an endless mystery, it has nothing else to explain it.
RABINDRANATH TAGORE, *Fire Flies*

Where love reigns, there is no will to power; and
where the will to love is paramount, love is lacking.
C. G. JUNG, *Collected Works*, vol. 7,
The Problem of the Attitude-Type

Will without love is manipulation.
OTTO RANK, *Love and Will*

Both words, *Eros* and *Agape*, mean "love" in Greek, but many—including Platonists, Neo-Platonists, Orphics, and early Christians, among others—have long argued about subtle gradations of the definitions. Plato allegorizes Eros in *The Symposium*, reflecting the range of love's power to move the soul. "Heavenly Eros" is classified as the soul's yearning for ascent to the divine. In contrast, "Vulgar Eros" is merely physical appetite. Eros, of either sort, invokes a yearning to join with an object or quality that captivates desire. Eros inflames an ever-present sense of felt need, always reminding us that whatever we have is not all there is.

Greek mythology, an inexhaustible source of wisdom in generating images for complex emotions, portrays Eros both as a beautiful youth and a childish archer. Both facets foreshadow his budding potential. He seems perpetually to verge on flowering, as though waiting to burst into full-blown maturity. When he appears as a youth on Attic vases, three companions appear with him—*Himeros* (physical desire for love grasped in the moment), *Pathos* (longing for the unattainable), and *Anteros* (responding love)—suggesting that each is an accompanying part of desire. In every instance, the common characteristic of Eros is his reach, his stretching—like his arrow—toward connection. He thus epitomizes the urge to capture, to pull that which is desirable toward us.

Along with the Greek tradition, which still guides us in unseen ways, we are also inheritors of the more-acknowledged Judeo-Christian vision that shifts the focus of love away from something sought for, tilting it toward its giving nature. This is *Agape*, and to understand its complex evolution requires diligent desire, learning, and consistent attention, because to give love is far more demanding than to grasp it.

In simple terms, *Agape* is the gift of life, of creation, a gift offered whether merited or not. Agape arises out of its own magnanimity, since giving is its essence. It is distinguished by being indifferent to merit, offering a total extension of love, even to the unworthy sinner. God, our Heavenly Father, provides the perfect example of an Agapean outpouring of life and love to His creatures. The gift of His son, Jesus, points the way and proves the amplitude of His caring. Philip S. Watson has this explanation: "Both creation and redemption, therefore, are the work of `grace' or of free, generous Agape."[1] In this formula the role of humankind continues to raise questions: Is our place only to give love or is it wrong to seek love? Speaking philosophically, Watson makes this helpful separation:

> In Eros-love man seeks God in order to satisfy a spiritual hunger by the possession and enjoyment of the Divine perfections. But the love of man for God of which the New Testament speaks is of quite a different stamp. It means a whole-hearted surrender to God, whereby man becomes God's willing slave, content to

be at His disposal, having entire trust and confidence in Him, and desiring only that His will be done. This love is not, like Eros, a longing and striving after something man lacks and needs, but a response of gratitude for something freely and bountifully given.[2]

Thus in theological thought, Eros-love is generally—although I would argue not entirely—centered in the individual. By contrast, Agape is theocentric. Some have explained this as the difference between need-love and divine-love. Rilke captures the subtlety of difference: "To be loved means to be consumed in the flame; to love is to shine with an inexhaustible light" (on a note in *The Notebooks of Malte Laurias Brigge*).

Eros always embodies a duality, an in-betweenness, which emerges from his semi-divine nature, not entirely a human but yet not a god, both earthly and godly. Eros is not merely sensual love, in Andres Nygren's interpretation of Plato, but "a love that is *directed upwards*; it is the soul's upward longing and striving toward the heavenly world, the world of Ideas."[3]

Otto Rank joins Nygren in favoring Agape over the earlier Eros concept: "The difference between the love-philosophies in Antiquity and the Christian era can be stated as the difference between coercive possessiveness versus yielding." He believes that the God of the Old Testament depended upon punishment and revenge, which was altered in the New Testament by a Christian God of love and forgiveness. Rank explains how this move affected individual attitudes toward love:

> The religion of hatred changed into the religion of love, which in turn changed the individual's attitude from will-ful wanting into a desire of being wanted, that is, loved. In this sense, the personality of man changed from the will-ful into the loving type; psychologically speaking, the will to want turned into the will to be wanted (loved).[4]

A resemblance is sometimes asserted between Agape and the *Anteros* aspect of Eros, but de Rougement, in *Love in the Western World*, vehemently denies any likeness. He argues that Agape is an agent, activist to the extreme, while *Anteros* is merely responsive. He particularly warns of the fateful consequences of Eros-dominated love in the Western world, emphasizing instead the need to develop the non-possessiveness of Agape. He profoundly distrusts Eros as the epitome of a desire for something more ecstatic than life, of a pagan death-seeking drive. He urges that any love relationship be attuned to more life-enhancing aspects, in emulation of God's supreme love of humankind. Similarly, Rank explains: "No attempt to overcome neurotic fear of death by sex can ever be successful, because sex implies death and its acceptance. Agape, on the other hand, can overcome the fear of death, for it is the most positive expression of it."[5]

Yet in the search for Agape, it is not, in my view, necessary to forgo Eros. In many ways, this beautiful youth remains our best helper, even though we have difficulty understanding him. Simone Weil correctly claims: "Only desire brings God down into the heart" (*Waiting for God*). Too often we have tried to equate Eros with sex, thereby oversimplifying the nature of both. Again, I emphasize that we have come close to trivializing and destroying the *mysterium tremendum* of erotic love.

Let us not forget that love of another human soul in all its majestic dimensions, the God-infused image of another, is often Eros-inspired, and through it we are able to expand and find universal or divine love. Dante attests to this in *La Vita Nuova* and *The Divine Comedy* by insisting that his only path to salvation opened through his love of Beatrice, which was inspired by a childhood vision of her and which was sustained throughout his life without any physical consumation. As an avid follower of the *Fedeli d'amore*, as a servant of love, Dante recognized that the soul achieves access to the spiritual realm only through the portal of active earthly love. From his fateful, youthful meeting with Beatrice, his guiding soul-image blossomed. This brief encounter cataclysmically changed his life, ultimately expanding and transforming into a beatific vision of eternity and the supreme love of God. As no poet before or since, Dante illustrates that universal love commences with love of a single soul. W. H. Auden wittily provides a twentieth century twist:

> For the error bred in the bone
> Of each woman and each man
> Craves what it cannot have
> Not universal love
> But to be loved alone. ("September 1, 1939")

Falling in love is, of course, a romantic, highly charged process. In the first phase, it is a palpitating summons to one person and one alone. It signals an event of transcendent importance—*amor fati*, Nietzsche calls it. In subsequent phases it can be quirky and unpredictable, as when we discover that the object of our sublime passion is an inappropriate person, temperamentally or otherwise. From the socio-biological point of view, our tribal ancestors proved that this tendency to be drawn to some non-genetically related person favored development of the species. The attraction for opposites, or unalikes, promoted tribal diversity.[6] Of course, there were terrible fears to overcome, as there still are. The excitement of the challenge and the image of future possibility (Eros) goads us on, then as now.

The real challenge is how to evolve from that early moment when the cosmos distills into two lovers, each sufficient unto the other, into a realization of a fullness of involvement in which each nurtures the development of the other without intrusion and without denial of any essential expression of individuality. It is not only a challenge but a conundrum, with no agreement from the most profound minds.

In essence, the process of falling in love requires letting down one's ego boundaries and permitting another person access to our secret places and intimate body spaces. This willingness to allow such innermost core contact offers enormous possibilities of hurt but also of expansion. It is the connecting power of Eros that makes us able or eager to take this risk. His arrow seeks our weak spots, our wounds. But the place of our hidden longings, our special needs, is also the place of soul possibilities. We might never allow this openness to pain but for the ecstasy it brings, even if only initially. Such an encounter promises, as Leslie Farber explains, "the exciting possibility of receiving and offering a range of perceptions and sensibility whose othernesss can be uniquely and surprisingly illuminating."[7] Jesse D. Geller and Richard A. Howenstine provide this clue: "We are affirmed and come to know ourselves in the process of disclosing ourselves to our lovers."[8] There's a newness and freshness to life that balances the trauma of opening ourselves up.

One of the pleasures of falling in love is the manner in which it alters our perception of linear time. Life takes on new meaning and seems to begin again, with all past history telescoped into a fresh beginning in a joyous present. In the tenets of Buddhist mysticism, acute awareness lived in the current moment is the recognized source of contentment and joy. In the presence of an adored other or, in the objective world, in moments of appreciation and identification with the earth's abundance, we live in an intensity of presentness of perception. Time is compressed. We are bound in a web of personal bliss and the unshared past evanesces as unimportant. Even though the future may be blighted by fading love, the here and now, in all its anguish and ecstasy, is everything for lovers. Beyond its delicious novelty, the moment of falling in love provides a marking of time, and events predate or postdate this crucial turning point, offering the opportunity to rewrite one's narrative history.[9]

Eros plays an instrumental role in first commanding our attention, but we are responsible for what transpires afterward. Initially, what we thought was physical desire for love grasped in a moment, what seemed like simple sexual yearning, leads us into the most labyrinthine pathways of discovery. Love for a unique individual involves seeing the essence, seeing beyond the stereotypical image of standardized beauty or handsomeness or conventional social posturing. A third eye is needed for seeing inner beauty. It may require acceptance of even undesirable aspects of the other, subsumed in a lovable whole. It takes time, often years of diligent attention, plus willingness to listen and to adapt to another's needs. In our world we sometimes resist the expenditure of energy needed to understand and totally love another. Rollo May states it this way: "Hate is not the opposite of love; apathy is."[10] Paradoxically, realization of the utmost return from our love partnership in terms of self-exploration and self-completion is possible only when we also educate ourselves to understand Agape, the outpouring of love.

Often, consumed by our passion, we assume our partner will be willing to change to suit our needs, but this adaptation is not an automatic, reflexive process. Certainly some alterations are possible, and these may turn out to be very rewarding in expanding our mutual horizons. Still, we always want to clarify our expectations (very difficult for many to express), because we can't assume our mate possesses intuitive, mind-reading powers. It is far better when the need for change is understood and freely elected by our mate, not demanded by ourselves.

Many relationships deteriorate into mutual accusations of inadequacy because, either through fear or timidity, there is little attempt by either mate to comprehend the needs, however quixotic, of the other.

Romantic love may have more than a little narcissism at its core. Often an attraction is an extension of one's own needs, or dreams, rather than a recognition of the uniqueness of the other. The essential nature of a partner may be submerged in the excitement of encounter. The prime motivation may be an appeal to our longings for self-magni-fication or aggrandizement. Viewed through this prism, the mate becomes a prize, a trophy, rather than a multidimensional human being. Some writers find women more practical and less romantic than men in their choices—they possibly sense the need to weigh economic issues, since they often lack financial independence, even today. Geller and Howenstine describe a male's need to find a partner who matches his dream image:

> In early adulthood a man's preoccupation tends to be with him-self and the creation of his dream. Other people tend to be involved from what they contribute to his quest. The special woman helps to animate that part of the self that contains the Dream. She shares it, believes in him as its hero, gives it her blessing, joins him on the journey and creates a 'boundary space' within which his aspirations can be imagined and his hopes nour-ished...the special woman can foster his adult aspirations while accepting his dependency, incompleteness and need to make her into more than (and less than) she actually is.[11]

The search for matching soul images is largely an unconscious one, an involuntary reach for completion, seeking those personality qualities in the other that we find lacking in our own. Ann Carson summarizes this need: "The self forms the edge of desire."[12]

In Jungian terms we seek an image to match our inner soul *imago*, the anima (in a man) or the animus (in a woman). We could call this attraction fatal, because it invokes our fate. Hillman provides this account of the feminine anima, personified as She, who is:

a) the personification of our unconsciousness...

b) a particular personification appearing in a particular moment...

c) the feeling of personal interiority...

d) personalized existence...

e) that person by means of whom we are initiated into imaginal understanding, who makes possible experiencing through images, for she embodies the reflective, reactive, mirroring activity of consciousness.

Anima has a major role in translating the imaginal to us as well as providing the place for love fantasies to alight. Hillman explains this complex:

> Functionally *anima* works as that complex which connects our usual consciousness with imagination by provoking desire or clouding us with fantasies and reveries, or deepening our reflection. She is both bridge to the imaginal and also the other side, personifying the imagination of the soul.[13]

What is implied by Hillman but not acknowledged directly in traditional Jungian thought is that anima images are not confined strictly to the masculine psyche. Women carry not only contrasexual masculine images but also feminine imprints, a point often overlooked. Otherwise women would have no interiority, no fantasies, no reveries, if these emanate from the anima that women don't possess. In a complementary way men also carry animus images. Tom Moore clarifies this point: "Fatherhood of the soul is a face of what Jung called animus, which can be father-spirit in man, woman, family, organization, nation, or a place."[14]

Archetypal images are cross gender in character, as such Olympian paradigms as Athena and Zeus apply intra-psychically to the interplay of male-female in an individual. Despite the recent work of Robert Johnson, Robert Bly, Jean Shiboda Bolen, Christine Downing, and Sam Keen, we still have insufficient knowledge of masculine and feminine imagery as lived out in women's and men's lives. While the reaction of males to the regressive pull of the negative mother, for instance, may be more intense, women respond to her manifestations as the witch, Medusa, Pandora, or Persephone with much the same mixture of ambivalent fear and fascination that men bring to these figures.[15] Women feel the regressive pull toward the unconscious as acutely as do men. On the positive side, the soul image in its highest form for women is a female Sophia, just as she is for men. Sardello writes of the regeneration and renewal of the world soul through Sophia.[16]

The early stage of a personal relationship often depends heavily on each partner's being able to embody the fantasies of the other. Yet there are realistic limits. As we approach marriage the query might be: how much of what we call "love" embodies unalloyed appreciation of our partner? To what extent do we really know our partner's needs and dreams? To what extent are we projecting on a partner the burden of our own desires? Not that it's a mistake to believe in the capacity of the other to fulfill our dreams; indeed, it can hardly be avoided when Eros intrudes. It is prudent, though, not to overwhelm the other with too much responsibility for our own personality debits. It is too much to ask the man to carry entirely the responsible, dependable profile or the woman to be the sole custodian of the feeling values. Such a division of labor will result in a diminishment rather than the potential for expansion the relationship offers.

When our instinctual longing for love does not find adequate reciprocity in a partner, our energy flow often reroutes into a control pattern. Then, even though we may not discern it, the will to power or to dominance may supplant the instinct of love. Jung repeatedly warns against the negative effects of misunderstanding Eros: "An unconscious Eros always expresses itself as will to power."[17] This power play takes over not only in partnerships but also between parent and child. Referring to the way a mother can unknowingly seek to dominate her child, Jung says: "the less conscious such a mother is of her own personality, the greater and the more violent is her unconscious will to power." Esther Harding has this to say about the connection between the maternal instinct and the power complex:

> The mother's sense of I-ness is enhanced through her children, either directly by reason of their number or beauty, or in relation to her power over them, or an account of their devotion to her, or more indirectly because of their achievements in the world.[18]

Adolf Guggenbühl-Craig elaborates the way in which the will to power can contaminate the mother-child relationship:

> The mother archetype appearing without Eros is merely over-protective, smothering her child in materialistic securities, over-concerned with food and warmth. There is an absence of morality, no ideals, no spirit; there is just her child in the center

of her world, a tool used for power and dominance, like a biological increase of the mother herself.[19]

Many well-intended parents are shocked to discover that their
impulse to love has hardened into a will to control. If, in our imperfect
way, we could simulate the example we are given of God's love, then
love for our children would involve a gentle outflowing of affection
rather than the narcissistic desire for self-mirroring that it often
becomes.

This will-to-power floods into the vacuum whenever the full nature
of love is underdeveloped. Intimate relationships, even those projecting
into other aspects of life (political, social), can be derailed when getting
is uppermost, when giving and forgiving are abandoned. Whenever
Agape is eclipsed in parental or sexual love, a continuing clash of wills is
invited. A constant jockeying for position ensues with one person dominant at one moment and the other acquiescent, then flip-flopping as
circumstances differ. On the surface it may seem that one mate has
achieved total command with the other pliantly submissive, but this is
rarely the case. When one partner does achieve a dominant role in decision-making, excluding the other, then the defeated one will respond
with such tactical maneuvers as frequent illness, perpetual lateness,
slowness in acting, overspending, not paying bills—anything that sabo-
tages the will to dominate. The ways of silent revenge are many.

Many modern relationships carry high expectations in some areas,
but are undervalued in others. The love union is expected to satisfy our
full range of emotional needs even though we may recoil from total
commitment to the responsibility, anxiety, and care of another. In such
instances, we trivialize passion, even scoff at it. By not acknowledging
the power of love to change us profoundly, by not accepting that love
may involve a long-term commitment, continuing even after divorce or
separation, we subvert its transcendent power. Strangely, this denial of
the possibilities and potentialities of loving can be a method of avoiding
anxiety. It seems easier not to care too much.

Through excessive materialism, undue emphasis on the accumula-
tion of wealth, power often supplants love as the most prized of life's
commodities. Sexual conquest becomes a mode of ego enhancement, a
glittering bauble of power. As Viktor Frankl attests, the desire for titil-

lating but transitory pleasures now often preempts the ageless quest for enduring love.[20]

This cynical approach explains why, as difficulties mount or romantic love wavers, Americans tend to toss the whole thing. Opportunities for deepening experiences, for increasing understanding of both ourselves and our mates, are impatiently cast aside. As legal and moral barriers weaken, it seems more expedient to wipe the slate clean (an impossibility) and fashion a fresh future. Forgotten are the cherished joint recollections (having children together, facing difficulties together). Americans seem perennially more attracted to future prospects than to history. We tend to superficiality in our connections, not only with lovers but also with friends. And yet we still hope that these relationships, however tenuous, will be a harbor from all the turbulence, the inanities of our world, offering a sense of security, while all else storms around us.

With its sense of sophisticated and ironic detachment, today's younger generation has particular difficulty acknowledging romanticism. A cynic recently claimed that the half-life of romantic love is eighteen months. Easy access to sexual satisfaction on one hand and doubt of the need for longevity on the other makes commitment, in the old-fashioned, whole-hearted sense, problematic. The agape aspect—the extending, giving part of a relationship—requires devoted effort, tenacity, and continuity so that each person can know and appreciate the other. We tend to forget the nurturing love requires. We think coupling should take place more naturally. Friction-free love becomes thematic. Hence the vast increase of single-parent families.

Erich Fromm's *The Art of Loving* reminds us that in reality loving is an art. We do not simply "fall" into it. We may consider a relationship desirable as long as it continues in reasonably tranquil fashion, but fail to realize what is required to further its progress. This discipline demands that we probe into the dark interstices of our own inadequacies, rather than reproach our partner for failure to supply the necessary ingredients of stability. In the same fashion, we often set up, through an overdeveloped need-to-be-needed syndrome, artificial ways of capturing attention. By thus focusing on this singular and selfish imperative, we create a convenient excuse for becoming excessively demanding.

Loving relationships require prolonged willingness to concentrate one's attention. An infusion of energy into the mating ritual encourages psychological and spiritual growth on both sides. It is no simple task to esteem and to comprehend the infinite hues and complexities of the human psyche. We are each full of intriguing diversities, like Shakespeare's Cleopatra, of whom Mark Antony says:

> Age cannot wither her, nor custom stale
> Her infinite variety; other women cloy
> The appetites they feed, but she makes hungry
> Where most she satisfies. (*Antony and Cleopatra*, 2.2.243-246)

Romantic love does not automatically atrophy in a protracted relationship. While we live in an age of cynicism, signs of change are afoot. A number of books with titles such as *Living, Loving, and Learning* (Leo Buscaglia) have made the best-seller lists. It is becoming acceptable again for a film to fade out with the hope of lovers living happily ever after—an antipodal digression from the black comedy of the past decade or so.

Scott Peck's *The Road Less Traveled* has enjoyed many years of popularity, even though its message is not an easy one. He emphasizes the spiritual aspects of love: "the will to extend one's self for the purpose of nurturing one's own or another's spiritual growth." This teleological definition sets forth a goal, hard to achieve, of loving both self and others. "Not only do self-love and love of others go hand in hand, but ultimately they are indistinguishable," in Peck's view.[21] This linkage is self-evolving and circular in its beneficial results. In someone's facetious adage, when we send our bread out upon the waters, it comes back buttered.

Peck claims that the reason we don't learn to love is mostly sheer laziness. But if apathy is part of love, then the will to keep trying must also be part of the process. Peck sees love as purposeful but requiring diligence, a continuing reach for emotional understanding, and only achievable through a sense of devotion. A disciplined will enters into the formula, a steady hand on the tiller:

> By the use of the word "will" I have attempted to transcend the distinction between desire and action. Desire is not necessarily translated into action. Will is desire of sufficient intensity that is translated into action.... Love is an act of will—namely, both

an intention and an action. Will also implies choice. We do not
have to love. We choose to love.[22]

Whereas the irrationality of romantic attraction in the initial stage may
cause will to feel powerless, love and will become partners in the
achievement of Agape-type love.

Accepting this thesis makes me argue that Peck, like Fromm and de
Rougemont, underestimates the irrational, mysterious ways in which
Eros, as agent of our psychic longings, draws us into one experience
and not another. To deny the imaginal stirrings brought by Eros, the
unconscious connector, who often uncovers what psyche wants, even if
previously unrecognized, is a serious omission. Rollo May gives a significant place to Eros and has drawn some criticism for doing so. Hillman
supplies a pertinent image: "Eros is always in the psyche just waiting to
burst into fire. At any moment you can catch fire. The French call it a
'coup de foudre,' a lightning flash."[23] Eros, as lord of the flame, can
strike suddenly and violently or turn any existing flame up higher.

Hillman criticizes traditional psychology for not finding a proper
place for Eros. What Eros excites is both the heart and the image-making faculties, and this latter aspect may be as important as the personal
appeal. Hillman makes explicit the connection: "When we fall in love,
we begin to imagine; and when we begin to imagine, we fall in love. To
this day, depth psychology is caught by the necessary connection of love
and imagination which it has not yet had the philosophy to place." [24]
When imagination functions, we are awakened to potentiality and to
the future, not only on the physical but on the spiritual plane of being.
Hillman laments the isolation of imagination when its role as accom-
plice to love is not recognized:

> By personalizing the heart and locating there the word of God,
> the imagination is driven into exile. Its place is usurped by
> dogma, by images already revealed. Imagination is driven into
> the lower exile of sexual fantasy, the upper exile of metaphysi-
> cal conception, or the outer exile of objective data, none of
> which reside in the heart and all of which therefore seem heart-
> less, mere instinct, sheer speculation, brute fact.[25]

We want to retain Eros, and thus imagination, and still acknowledge
the gift of God's love—and of the celestial creation that completes the

circle of love, from the heart and back to the heart. Agape, in early definitions, was called "love's feast," finding a rightful place as the celebratory
part of the Eucharist. The feast of love is the joy of the bountiful heart.

In a literary mode, Louise Cowan describes an outpouring of love as
the essence of the lyric voice. This movement of soul, though it may not
be called Agape, transposes pain and anguish miraculously into joy. It is
evident in Dostoevsky's novels (*Crime and Punishment, The Idiot, The
Brothers Karamazov*) and the best of today's works, such as Toni
Morrison's *Beloved*, Isabel Allende's *The House of the Spirits*, and much of
Eudora Welty, that the worst in human frailty is redeemed through love.

The recognition of the physical universe as God's special gift produces a
"felt change of consciousness" (Owen Barfield's term). As Kathleen Raine
reminds us: "When the sun rises, when a flower opens—all of these are
immediate communications of spiritual reality."[26] The poet Gerard Manley
Hopkins masterfully envisions the joy of "the dearest freshness deep, down
things." In "God's Grandeur," for instance, he writes: "The world is
charged with the grandeur of God,/It will flame out, like shining from
shook foil." In his "Pied Beauty," thankfulness is expressed for the natural
wonders of the cow, the trout, and the country landscape:

> Glory be to God for dappled things—
>> For skies of couple-colour as a brinded cow;
>>> For rose-moles all in stipple upon trout that swim;
> Fresh-firecoal chestnut-falls; finches' wings;
>> Landscape plotted and pieced—fold, fallow, and plough;
>>> And all trades, their gear and tackle and trim.
> All things counter, original, spare, strange;
>> Whatever is fickle, freckled (who knows how?)
>>> With swift, slow; sweet, sour; adazzle, dim;
> He fathers-forth whose beauty is past change:
>> Praise him.[27]

Richard Wilbur also reminds us that "Love Calls Us to the Things of
This World." This is not simply a secular viewpoint of love but an
acknowledgement that nonpersonal, universal love is roused when we
participate in and celebrate the world's magnificent creativeness. It
might be rephrased this way: Love is invoked in a heart responsive to
the soul of this world, the *anima mundi*. We can verify this by letting
things affect us, taking time to absorb their particularity and beauty: the

obvious but often overlooked pleasure in observing a sunset or a moon-rise. How surprising we pay so little attention to things we don't have to pay for: observing on which side the moon appears to grow or diminish when the great silver sphere is waxing or waning. Slowing down the pace might allow us to study the nuances of nature, to appreciate such milestones of creation as planting and harvesting, changing colors, the positioning of the sun on the horizon as it travels from winter to summer solstice, cloud patterns in the sky and on the landscape, the first star seen at night. Like Samuel Coleridge's Ancient Mariner, who first saw the creatures of the deep as slimy and ugly, in bestowing our attentive gaze we may ultimately comprehend the beauty of all God's creatures, and "bless them unawares."

Love in Agape radiates out, extends from the heart as a ray of love that triggers the possible transition from the petty insularity of personal desires to the sweeping awareness of joy and wonder, that frees the imagination to do what it is intended to do, inventing images and thereby transforming and redeeming ugliness and pain. In the heart's probing reach, moving outward to join the celebration of creation, will rests for a moment. This hiatus allows a synchronization of will with image, an alignment that initiates the unfolding of psyche's secret wisdom.

To sum up, we can say it is with Agape that desire and will come together, where there is no longer any conflict or opposition, for here will and desire are exactly the same. They are bonded. The conflict between love and desire is resolved when love is the singular lodestar. As St. Augustine says: "Love God and do as you will."

Image and Will

Nothing can be known unless it
first appears as a psychic image.
C. G. JUNG, *Psychology and Religion: West and East*

The imagination has some way of lighting up the truth that reason has not, and...its commandments, delivered when the
body is still and silent, are the most binding we can ever know.
W. B. YEATS, *Essays and Introductions*

No human action is possible unless galvanized by image, imagination's
tool. It is only when will and imagination fuse that we can execute even
such a simple operation as opening the door. And in this basic pairing,
imagination is by far the stronger partner. Because we feel its onrush,
we may believe will is dominant: yet image is the originator, not the
passive follower. More than the product of desire, image embodies
desire, gives form to desire, which can subsequently be translated into
action. If imagination tells us the wall is solid, no amount of will power
can push our bodies through it. Thus, contrary to popular supposition,
imagination precedes rather than follows will's initiatives.

Jung insists that *all* psychic processes are initiated by an image: "Everything of which we are conscious is an image, and that image is psyche."[1] Images surround us, envelop us, like the layers of atmosphere that encircle our planet. We ourselves are always in images, but often unconscious of their vital role in our existence.

Jung maintains that image is of comparable importance to instinct in the psyche's organization. Across the archetypal spectrum, instinct is the red terminal and image the bipolar blue. The crucial role of the image is defined by Hillman: "[I]nstinct acts and at the same time forms an image of its action. The images trigger the actions; the actions are patterned by the images. Thus, any transformation of the images affects the patterns of behavior, so that what we do within our imagination is of instinctual significance."[2] In a comparable dialogic schema of will and image, we can consider will akin to the red, the instinctual end, while image is the blue. Yet they remain, as in the example Jung developed, differing expressions of the same force field. Will is triggered by images. Will cannot claim priority over image.

Everything that rises to conscious awareness emerges as an image. Scientifically, we know that all of our thoughts, all of our sensory experiences originate from energy patterns that consciousness translates into image. We are not aware of the neurological pathways of our synapses. Phenomenologically, images seem intuitive in appearance, or to Bachelard like "a sudden salience on the surface of the psyche."[3]

In understanding the relationship of will to image no one provides better signposts than Bachelard. He posits image and concepts as opposites, not image and will: "Concepts and image develop along divergent lines of spiritual life."[4] Many of Bachelard's aphorisms stress the dominant role of imagination. He turns upside down the conventional way we think of will through such statements as: "The will must imagine too much in order to realize enough."[5] Once imagination and will are joined, there is always an excessive quality, which gives us an exaggerated sense of power, a headiness, and this is what we register. Imagination is, by definition, dynamic and expansive. It is imagination that confers upon will the grip of expansive possibility.

Bachelard is explicit in stating that these essential human faculties— imagination and volition—are the two principles of psychological functioning: "Imagination and will which at first glance seem to be opposites are in fact the same. One only wants what one imagines."[6]

Will then emerges as a junior partner of imagination when stirred by desire. "People desire intensely only what has been imagined abundantly,"[7] Bachelard declares. This assertion is contrary to the general assumption—that will decides and then engages or utilizes imagination. Bachelard claims that imagination is matched by will, thus making image the initiator.

Edward S. Casey provides a profound and richly detailed phenomenological description of imagining: "To `image' is to form an imaginative presentation whose content possesses a specifically sensuous—an `intuitive' or `imagistic'—form.... To image, then is to imagine in a sensory-specific way."[8] We generally think of images only in a visual dimension, imagining coinciding with visualization. Actually images carry auditory and even olfactory characteristics. We are often only visually perceptive, thereby limiting the depth of our awareness.

Hillman verifies that all images carry a piece of soul: "We cannot get to the soul of image without love for the image."[9] We might twist this to add: We cannot get to the soul without image. The psyche hungers for images; indeed, far more than for words or abstract concepts. Eligio Stephen Gallegos puts it this way: "Paradoxically, written language has done perhaps the most damage to imagery by providing the impression that words are concrete verities and that concepts are eternal. This idea moves us into linear time and removes us from the aliveness and immediacy of imagery."[10] Though many words originally carry images, with habitual use we lose awareness of this underlying imaginal content. How often are we aware of the rich mythology behind the words for the days of the week, for example? Do we remember the Norse gods on Wotan's day (Wednesday) or Thor's day (Thursday)? Do we recall Saturn on Saturday? Our lives are enriched whenever image is wed to language.

Poets revitalize language for us (Owen Barfield). Participating with the poet in the amassing of word-pictures into a coherent image cluster is an imaginative act of joyful re-creation. To concretize images, to clarify them, is the work of *poeisis*, "the imagination at work projecting an order onto reality" (David Miller). Poetry is the *exact* joining of will and image, which explains why total absorption in a poem is such a healing experience. To transmit an image, to convey it to another, is the meaning of art. Opaque images, often held in dim awareness, are vivified by artists, poets, writers, or speakers, for communal sharing. Goethe understands this mission of the poet in a letter written in September 23, 1827, concerning his work on *Faust*: "Since so much from our experiences cannot be plainly stated and directly communicated, I have long since chosen the method of revealing the more hidden meaning to the attentive by means of images placed in juxtaposition to one another and, so to speak, mutually reflecting one another."[11] Poets in particular can educate us into appreciation of the creative image.

Will invents its own image, Leslie Farber claims. While essentially correct, his assertion juxtaposes the two elements, placing an undue emphasis on will. We might say that will develops from an image, an interior "negative," like a photographic negative. In a corresponding reaction with a "positive," a picture given us is in confrontation or interaction with the world. We bring our individual image lenses to bear on the way we view this picture and how we see our place in the ongoing projection. Imagination then supplies intermediate steps, like a film of successive takes, to reach a match-up with the picture we have made of the *telos*, or the end result we seek to achieve. If the image of a goal is fleshed out, will is summoned in response.

Will is involved in a multi-stage action, in responding to the image and then charging it with the energy to manifest its implied potential. Will thus supplies the psychic force to move toward the end product through the required successive stages. In this sense will is experienced as or through the energy of accomplishment. Energy is released and renewed in the process of transformation from potential to realization. Success reinforces will's intention to try again.

Often this sequential process is followed by productive people without any analysis of the detailed steps. It is commonly assumed that all it takes to succeed is, first, to have a well-defined goal; second, to muster the determination to persist until the goal is achieved. What is not given sufficient attention is the galvanizing power of the image (of what we consider desirable) to summon will to follow through. The energy of will, experienced as a surge or jolt, receives more than its proper share of credit.

Fears and fearful images, if overwhelming, can thwart or alter our resolve. On the other hand, we can be energized by mild challenges or obstacles that must be confronted. Tell a child: You are not yet old enough to do that. This assertion is likely to inspire an immediate attempt to prove you wrong. Many productive people attribute their success to someone they respected, often the father figure, who said they lacked leadership capacity, or who questioned generally their strengths and abilities. However, repeated frustration or failures will discourage even the most tenacious.

All modes of ego personality functioning can be experienced through the will's dynamism. Jung emphasized will power as a developer of consciousness. Jolande Jacobi elaborates:

> Many psychologists regard the will as a basic function; in Jung's view, however, the will is a freely available psychic energy, present in each of the four basic functions. It can be 'directed' by an intervention of consciousness. Thus the scope and intensity of the so called willpower are closely connected with the breadth of the field of consciousness and its degree of development.[12]

Jung's four modes of operation serve to illustrate. While I concur with Hillman that the attempt to categorize people narrowly through simple tests carries the theory of function-types to far more literal lengths than Jung ever intended, here the separation may be useful. Jung's typology divides the primary functioning aspect of personality into these categories: *Thinking* types, with *Feeling* the opposite; *Intuition*, with *Sensation* the underdeveloped function, or the other way around. Jung added that Thinking and (surprisingly) Feeling are rational functions. Intuition, which gives flashes of understanding, and Sensation, which gleans information from sensate reactions, are irrational. This distinction is important when we consider decisions that we make consciously or those realized in a twinkling, of which we are only vaguely conscious of the intermediate steps.

Each archetypal way of functioning involves an imaginal mode with which we identify. Images gather around our initial choice, but also limit them. Thus if we see ourselves as a single-minded person, we may resist any attempts to experience complexities. Each specific type evolves images of experience that vary with topology. The images chosen determine what we perceive and what we value. We do not all see the world in the same way.

Thinking

(In this section I will capitalize "Will," treating it as the Greeks often did, giving to an abstract quality an isolated, individual personality.)

When we operate in the Thinking mode we are conscious of the energy of Will as an essential ingredient in a definitive series of acts in time. For example, when we decide to learn a sport or a language or accomplish any other goal, we are able to construct mental images of what it requires. Both willing and feeling may influence the Thinking mode. What moves thought from one thought to another in some kind of order, that is Will in the mode of Thinking.[13]

The disciplined use of will power is most commonly associated in our minds with Will. We experience it as determination: "I won't give up or give in" or "I will stick to my plan." We may have reinforced our ego strength in the past by taking on projects and employing Will to keep us on track, to avoid procrastination, and to drive through to success. We are able to school Will to aid the thinking process. Though discipline has been downgraded as a virtue in our permissive culture, though it is not part of our religious or aesthetic training, it remains a priority of Will to be constant—not to desert us at the first hint of discouragement.

The more success we experience with Will in the Thinking mode the more confidence we gain in our ability to force Will into conquering *any* situation, even some that may be inappropriate. For example, we may attempt to assert our will power over those around us, feeling that a show of determination will compel capitulation to our wishes. Will can thus manifest itself as an implement of control. Thinking types who believe they can master any situation through assertive Will often develop a power complex.

Any interference in the Will's direct vector toward realization of intent will come from the opposite mode, the Feeling mode. Unconscious or semiconscious complexes can undermine a goal pursuit by questioning its worth or our capacity to achieve it. Still, we operate in the conscious area of willful choice when in the Thinking mode. In the post-Puritan era, this mode has become the most favored, although recent studies suggest that intensely creative people, including many heads of corporations, are more often dominantly Intuitive.

Feeling

At different times we engage Will in each mode, regardless of our primary mode. If, however, as Jung says, we suffer most unconsciousness in the function opposite the primary, then if Thinking is the dominant mode, Feeling gives the most trouble in areas of either will or desire. In the Feeling mode, inner dialogue might flow somewhat like this: "I feel drawn to him, I'm positive we could get along well if we just get to know one another better." As in the Thinking mode, we can postulate those steps needed to reach our get-acquainted goal. Of course, when actuality does not match feeling, desire is frustrated.

Rather than treating feelings, especially the most hurtful or negative ones, as isolated phenomena, it is more effective to recast them by searching for an image that simulates the expression of emotion. When we can remove painfully acute feelings from the personal realm, when we can filter them through myths or literature, we gain a clearer, more expansive perspective. They functioned in that fashion in less literal times when the oral tradition held sway. According to Hillman, when image prevails "then the feelings become a kind of necessary quality of the image, rather than being obsessive in themselves. The image gives you an imagination of the feeling. The image frees you from your obsession with feelings."[14] In other words, those images we summon to capsulate feelings, and even those presented in dreams, can insulate us from thralldom to those emotions. A changed image changes feeling, once again evincing the dominant power of the image. In either the Feeling or Thinking mode, images of nascent desires, while perhaps not totally conscious, are more discernible than images of Sensation and Intuition, which present themselves generally as the completion of a process. The intermediate images of the latter two remain part of a more unconscious operation, which explains why Jung calls them irrational modes.

Sensation

The Sensation mode provides the most direct access to the physical body, which absorbs the world through sensual perception. In this osmotic mode we decide without much fuss to get up, have breakfast, and drive to town. Images in the Sensation mode have body, kinesthetic qualities. They are not merely visual, although that is the most common way we conceive of them; they can carry smell, taste, or touch as a concomitant to memory. Hillman speaks of the common ground we share in this realm: "We are all sensation types as soon as we are seized by an image."[15]

The body mode works best without excessive interference from the Thinking mode. For example, when we think about a tennis stroke while playing a match and concentrate excessively on the technique of hitting the ball, it becomes very difficult to win the point. Tim Gallway in *Inner Tennis* demonstrates how much more effective it is to follow the beauty of the ball's arching trajectory than to concentrate on what we want to do. Thus we allow the body to move with fluidity and without fear of failure or apprehension over style. We engage imagination as well as will power. The grace of the image of movement plus the exhilaration of possible improvement spur engagement in any activity. Will alone becomes ponderous, a heavy-duty, bodily endeavor that largely fails. Techniques such as SyberVision[16] demonstrate how much it can help to view repeated images of the proper strokes on the television screen before starting play and then letting the body take over. The retained images are free to pattern the stroke effectively.

William James offers an apt description of how, in the simplest act, body and Will can either argue about what to do—thus producing paralysis—or can cooperate in effortless action:

> Probably most persons have lain on certain mornings for an hour at a time unable to brace themselves to the resolve [to get out of bed in a cold room]. We think how late we shall be, how the duties of the day will suffer; we say: "I *must* get up, this is ignominious," and so on. But still ... resolution faints away and postpones itself again and again just as it seemed on the verge of the decisive act. Now how do we *ever* get up under such circumstances? If I may generalize from my own experience, we more often than not get up without any struggle or decision at all. We suddenly find that we *have* got up. A fortunate lapse of consciousness occurs; we forget both the warmth and the cold; we fall into some revery connected with the day's life, in the course of which the idea flashes across us, "Hello! I must lie here no longer"—an idea which at that lucky instant awakens

no contradictory or paralyzing suggestions, and consequently produces immediately its appropriate motor effects. It was our acute consciousness of both the warmth and the cold during the period of struggle which paralyzed our activity....[17]

As James demonstrates, once we engage desire and imagination, we have no trouble visualizing ourselves at the end of an act. We can respond with alacrity. It is the image of the goal that galvanizes uncomplicated action, seemingly a natural unfolding. If there is not too much negative argument, these acts seem effortless. If we are severely hampered by fears or conflicts, every act, even getting out of bed, can be a problem. In this area of wavering Will, of lack of clear, purposeful endeavor, even the simplest act can evoke endless deliberation.

It is axiomatic that more can be accomplished when repetitive, daily requirements are made routine and not subject to inner negotiation. Brushing our teeth, for example: we needn't question this decision or force the Will to decide whether we shall or shall not. Yet, in our fevered time, unfortunately, even simple decisions are often divorced from body connection and fall into a purgatory of conflict. The only resolution is to perform these simpler actions by rote. By clearing the path of mundane matters, by assigning them to the realm of habitual regularity, we will be better able to tolerate the suspended judgment required for more profound choices.

Certain complex decisions will always be troublesome. The most involved aspects of consciousness will always remain to a degree unresolved and in flux. William Sheldon argues that a well-rounded Humanist must live with deep-lying human conflicts subject to continual reassessment. Over a lifetime we need flexibility to approach the hurdles that living presents. We will need to reexamine current life goals; we will have to face the ultimate perplexity of how to approach our death. Bombarded as we are by so many exterior sensations in our time, our often restless minds need periodic cleansing to permit time and space for counterbalancing, for doing the inner work necessary to coalesce our thoughts into enduring, meaningful patterns.

The definition of "character," a word with less positive emphasis today, relates to decision-making and predictability in immediate, personal matters. It also suggests a dependable elasticity and toleration of conflict at the periphery of consciousness. Without such traits of adaptability contained within a consistent, stable structure, any disquieting thought can throw the mind out of balance. With so many distractions impinging on us, it becomes difficult to establish a hierarchy of discriminate insight into the relative importance of contending desires. Every temptation of the moment can become a diversion, producing chaos and frustration. The best palliative is to subdue concerns involved in our routine activities and free the mind to confront broadly gauged problems with imaginative energy. This amusing ditty (author unknown) is apropos:

> The centipede was happy quite,
> Until the toad in fun
> Said, "Pray which leg comes after which
> When you begin to run?"
> This wrought his mind to such a pitch
> He lay distracted in a ditch,
> Uncertain how to run
> ["The Puzzled Centipede", author unknown]

Intuition

The suprarational role of Will is best illustrated in the Intuitive mode. Here we can make decisions almost without knowing we have made them. A sympathetic group of people, a congenial thought, or some intriguing circumstance can magnetize our interest, often without our perceiving any connection. Or we focus on a particular person. Why? Is it because we intuitively sense that he or she offers an experience compatible with our need or desire of the moment? Such decisions spring from recognition that some blend of circumstances—perhaps an amalgam of people and places—is exactly attuned to what we seek. Our inner pictures (especially in encounters with the opposite sex) are governed by what Jung calls our anima or animus needs. The word *anima* means soul in Latin; our soul choices lie in this domain. Intuitively, we know that not every person, nor even very many, match our precise emotional configuration. The discovery of a special person is like a summons to an arcane experience that our soul covets. Richard Wilbur describes the idiosyncratic urge in this way: "When we fall in love, we are powerfully drawn by something, but we do not yet know what it means."[18] In a more sardonic way, Gore Vidal suggests: "The rocks in his head fit the holes in hers." An article in the *New York Times Magazine* touches on the quirkiness of the movements of the romantic heart:

> What attracts people to each other seems to be coincident by luck with what keeps them together for the long haul. Combining the two happens flukily. That it happens at all makes me believe in Cupid, if not in God.... Love comes by chance. The timing must be fortuitous.... You can hardly articulate, much less ask for, the things that turn out to count most. Lovers have to smell right to one another. My next true love will be someone interesting, confirming, admirable, familiar—which are, of course, the most idiosyncratic and personal of traits, the ones that allow any lovers to declare that their partners' ordinariness is fetching.[19]

The inner soul images that we seek to replicate are byproducts of our desires. Somewhat reductively and pejoratively, psychology calls this dynamic "projection," implying that these inner images are simply placed upon any available image-hangers we encounter. Actually seeing into our projections is a *via regia* for seeing into our soul's yearning. When we discern the qualities that attract us to others, we discover where our soul finds a home.

Will and Image in Dream

Dreams are treasure troves of images. Those who have learned to appreciate this component of life value sleep time for the opportunity to achieve rapport with feelings, with soul messages. Response to a daily activity often will arouse memories of similar emotions in a comparable earlier situation. Connecting with these images through the portal of dreams will open buried emotional life. Sometimes dream imagery will focus on the individuation process and give indications of the psychic place we inhabit or of a pathway to pursue. Images of failing health or death are not always an expression of fear of their occurrence. They may be actual warnings that we ignore at our peril. In one of my few serious encounters with ill health, I received rather explicit signs in dreams for two weeks before collapse finally forced me to a doctor. Occasionally we receive what native Americans and Jung call a "big dream," one that conveys a sense of totality or wholeness, a mandala or four-cornered image, for example. It may take an abstract or mythological form. These rare images may be the summation of a process that has been going on for a long time, or they may signal a moment of pause and integration before the next conflict gathers on the psyche's horizon. Whenever such a dream presents itself, we wake up in the morning feeling exhilarated.

Marion Woodman explains why getting in touch with the world of imagery has such a restorative effect: "Image reaches out to the imagination, and the imagination brings both the physical and spiritual world together.... It [the imagination] bridges the world between the body and the psyche, so it activates both the visceral and the psychic dimensions."[20] In a dream image, even a frightening one, will and desire are evidenced. Casey speaks of "the intrinsic *completeness* of imagination," and adds, "Imagination's uniquely self-completing, self-enclosing, self-transparent character has no counterpart—not even a forerunner—in perceptual experience proper."[21] Images, being whole in themselves, are a form of holistic medicine.

Images are the building blocks of dreams, but how does will influence them? During daylight, when we visualize a goal that seems capable of fulfillment, we are aware of the throb of will as feeling energy. In daydreaming, or reverie, when we open ourselves to imagery that drifts up from unconscious depths, we perceive will as entering our image world in intermittent fashion. For awhile we may allow images to carry us along, to unfold in their own pattern. Unconscious will may come into play, as the customary conscious will lies dormant. As we engage with imagery, or start to direct these images into action channels, we feel an investment of energy in the outcome, which brings will into the picture. Due to their nature, as Bachelard says, "images are incapable of repose."[22] I agree with Sardello's belief that we are never entirely conscious of will: "We can be conscious of the mental image that guides the will to carry out the action. Or we can be conscious of a feeling that guides the will to carry out the action. But we are totally unconscious of the will as such."[23]

Whatever daytime consciousness we have of will goes to sleep at night, as felt-will leaves the body. The dream ego, over which we have even less control than the waking ego, comes to life. Imaging eases our passage into the dream world, since that is its natural environment. Hence the process of going to sleep is facilitated by such techniques as visualizing sheep jump-ing over a fence or a passive pastoral scene that requires little willed action in response. By stilling the free-floating anxieties that surface when night encroaches, and by releasing the will-to-control that blocks access to our dreams, we allow ourselves to slide peacefully into the world of images. Some people are not able to give themselves fully to the deep sleep that nourishes the dream. But, for those who are, images are free to express, unabashedly, unconscious will and desire.

In the image, desires or fears—the desire to avoid—are reflected; in the image, will is revealed. Jung says that the image "portrays its own meaning"—in other words, "image and meaning are identical; and as the first takes shape, so the latter becomes clear."[24]

The following rudimentary dream, while oversimplified, illustrates the point: The dreamer is a woman. In her dream, a male friend (not lover, or romantic interest), the husband of a next door friend, carries the dreamer's baby on his shoulders into a school auditorium. My inter-pretation: A new idea has come into being, something close to her, a new creation. This particular man, painfully shy, has difficulty articulat-ing his thoughts. So something newly born and important, a potential change of consciousness, is having a hard time making itself known. The dreamer's desire to see it supported is revealed, along with her concern that it is not yet strong enough to stand on its own.

Some individuals, in a technique called "lucid dreaming," claim to be able to redirect their dreams, at least partially. The only way to effectu-ate this change is by substituting one image for another (for example, by implanting an image of flying for one of falling, if that is a recurring nightmare). We can ask a dream to continue on a subsequent night, and often we will be rewarded, but this probably would happen anyway, if the dream process is working out an important aspect of soul aware-ness. However, our desire to persevere sustains our interest, and there-fore we are more apt to be alert to the sequel on future nights. Since our culture places such emphasis on rational consciousness, many refuse to allocate the time needed to capture these brief vistas of another realm of being that are available when we seek to unravel the labyrinthine pathways of dreams. For those who do succeed in sampling the richness of attending to dreams, an aperture of discovery opens in the direction of unconscious will. In recalling our dreams, we tap a source of great energy, even if we make no effort to interpret them. We become aware of the soul's desires and become buoyant witness to spirit infusing our lives, because, as Hillman says: "Dreaming is the psyche itself doing its soul-work."[25]

Will and Image in Health

Will, image, and desire all become part of the equation of illness and recovery from it. In current medical studies, attention is increasingly focused on the psyche, or the soul, as well as the soma. Thanks to Bernie Siegel, Larry LeShan, Larry Dossey and other pioneers, patients are now encouraged to take charge of their diseases, to ask questions, to seek answers, to assert an empowered role, and thus refrain from automatically assuming the worst and passively accepting a victim's fate. Fear is always the dominant factor in any illness. Seeking ways to block that fear from surging into panic is vital to restoration of health. The key ingredient in getting well is the loss of fear. Depression saps the immune system at a time when T-cells are most needed to fight the lethal intruder. The loving involvement of those around the patient often alleviates the fear and despair and can even tip the scales in a life-and-death struggle by reinforcing at crucial moments the will and desire to survive.

As contradictory as it may seem, illness can cloak a secret desire for revenge toward intimates, perhaps because we feel unappreciated in some way. Like a petulant child, the symptoms may be a disguised appeal for attention. An internal check is helpful to weigh hidden motivations in order to determine if illness carries an attempt to punish oneself or to punish another for some grievance. An unacknowledged grudge can block the pathway to recovery.

In a positive light, illness can sometimes be seen as a period of expanding awareness. Larry Dossey provides pointers in his book *Space, Time, and Medicine*. Through the forced constraint of immobility, time slows down and it is possible to achieve an extended sense of self-realization, and even nurturing love that is unattainable in the usual rush of daily living.

In the field of healing, biofeedback demonstrates scientifically that the power of visualization can affect physiology, by, for example, raising the temperature in the fingers or lowering blood pressure. Imagework can improve health or augment a cure, particularly when used with meditation practices that bring us in touch with higher alpha energies.

Carl and Stephanie Simonton's early work on imaging techniques to conquer cancer demonstrates a decidedly positive effect on the prognosis of disease. Despite these proven successes, a cautionary word is needed. The sick can be cast in the role of valiant conqueror in such scenarios as imaging disease as an enemy and attempting to quell its army of invaders. But Raphael López-Pedraza warns of the one-sidedness of this scenario in that it can block access to unconscious healing.[26] A heavy burden of responsibility, a feeling of blame, may result when the technique fails, for whatever reason.

Martin Rossman believes that illness affords the opportunity to tune into the higher purposes of living. He advocates imaging, "getting in touch with the inner advisor," to direct one toward the soul's intention, and then "listening to your symptom:"

> This consists in focusing on a symptom, allowing an image to represent it, and then engaging the image of the symptom in dialogue in order to find out why it is there, what it wants, and how you can meet what it represents.[27]

This method honors the will of the soul and recognizes a purpose that may not be apparent in our haste to find a cure.

Religious mystics and native shamans are experienced in the healing fields, possessing wisdom we could well incorporate in standard medical practices. Shamans have traditionally known how to confront disease not as an isolated occurrence at a specific site in an individual body but as part of the entire environment surrounding the patient. The health of a community affects and is in turn affected by any disease of any patient. In ancient rituals, restoring the body's innate desire for harmonized balance is the aim, rather than merely removing the depleting agent. Jeanne Achterberg elaborates: "The treatment for all ailments first emphasizes augmenting the power of the sick person and only secondly counteracting the power of illness-producing agents." These methods, which we often dismiss as primitive, display an intuitive knowledge of how the autoimmune system functions. The shaman long ago sensed what traditional medicine is proving now, as Achterberg points out: "The so-called primary causes of major illness—viruses, bacteria, and other invisible elements in the environment—are a threat to health only when a person's natural protective mantle develops a weakness."[28] Western medicine traditionally concentrates only on the bullet of pharmaceutical cure without sensitivity to the body's warning message about its distress.

In the shamanistic traditions, avoiding death or prolonging life is not the critical issue. It is far more important to secure one's soul, because what would life or afterlife be without a soul? Combining the ancient knowledge of healing with modern scientific medical techniques would impel us toward increasing the preventive methods for staying in healthy balance rather than focusing entirely on the intervention that becomes necessary when the disintegration processes of illness approach terminal severity.

Achterberg, whose recent discoveries in the field of imaging will undoubtedly change traditional medical practices, describes two emergent modes through which healing can take place:

> In the first mode the imagination acts upon one's own physical being. Images communicate with tissues and organs, even cells, to effect a change. The communication can be deliberate or not. It is preverbal in the sense that it probably evolved much earlier than language, and uses different neural pathways for the transmission of information. The second type of healing imagery is *transpersonal*, embodying the assumption that information can be transmitted from the consciousness of one person to the physical substrate of others.[29]

The two modes indicate that imagery works both in deep cellular communication and as a medium of transference of mental or emotional thought patterns. Images carry telepathic messages. While much work remains to be done in this area, at least it is no longer considered to be in the over-the-top realm of the occult.

Images ground at a fundamental level, because they determine not only *what* we see but the *way* we take in the world (Casey's dictum). From the image springs the desire and the will to manifest it. Hence we do well to look to the image. When value is bestowed on it, will is engaged. Will infuses an image in response to desire, or, as Aristotle says in *De Anima:* "Will moves through desire."

Desire is an imprint on the tablet of our personality. Our soul, seeking expression through desire, makes us known to ourselves. Desire can be carnal, as we usually think of it, but it can also be spiritual—in beatitude, for instance. By nature, desire is always reaching for the beyond, never appeased. Desire clings to soul images in order to manifest itself—although, as evidenced in Eros, desire is winged and will always surpass any single image. In *A Midsummer-Night's Dream*, Shakespeare offers a poignant image: "Love looks not with the eyes, but with the mind,/And therefore is winged Cupid blind"(1.1.234-235).

The awakening of Eros, whether in response to a person or an aspiration, engages imagination and summons will to cooperate in the realization of desire. Eros is the bearer of image. Ann Carson illuminates this point poetically: "Imagination is the core of desire.... The reach of desire involves every lover in an activity of the imagination."[30] In another instance, she adds: "Imagination prepares desire by representing the desired object as desirable to the mind of the desirer."[31] Thus will is galvanized by the image of desire.

Will is a potent engine bearing us up and down the hills of life. It is also the fuel. The engineer who charts our course, who pictures the ultimate destination and then pilots us to it, is the imagination. Thus, the goal, the end, the place to which we want to travel is a product of our image-making. When will works in a smooth and almost effortless way, manifesting soul images rather than as a power or action drive, we have the perfect marriage of will and image.

Reappearance of Will

Ever since Freud we know what goes on in the heart
is neither truth nor history; it is desire and imagination.
JAMES HILLMAN, *The Thought of the Heart*

The role of the will and, in general, of the mind,
is not creative, but merely corrective.
JOSÉ ORTEGA Y GASSET, *On Love*

With the advent of the twentieth century, will, long a subject of consuming
interest, moved into being a non-subject, perhaps through the belief that
everything about it had already been said. After Nietzsche and William
James, will virtually disappeared from psychology. As it became obsessively
Promethean, will faded into obscurity or unconscious inattention.

None of the three giants of early twentieth century psychological
inquiry—Sigmund Freud, C. G. Jung, or even Alfred Adler—under-
took a full-bodied investigation of will. While studying the broad
domain of human behavior, Freud found that many of the processes that
had always been considered rational were buried in obscure beginnings,

the memory of them long suppressed. Freud thus altered the very concept of will, replacing the rational will of earlier centuries with an obscure will driven by repressed, irrational motives. Choice became clouded by unconscious urges, thus relieving the individual of much of the decision-making responsibility. The result was increased emphasis on determinism and necessity. The primary act of libidinal will became the Oedipal elimination of the parent. With motivation and behavior controlled by the unconscious, the strong will admired by the Victorian Age became the culprit for repressing emotional spontaneity.

While skirting a direct discussion of will, Jung includes it as one of his seven basic urges. Most of his references concentrate on its conscious functioning:

> I regard the will as the amount of psychic energy at the disposal of consciousness. Volition would, accordingly, be an energic process that is released by conscious motivation. A psychic process, therefore, that is conditioned by unconscious motivation I would not include under the concept of the will. The will is a psychological phenomenon that owes its existence to culture and moral education, but it is largely lacking in the primitive mentality.[1]

Jung thus equates will to the rational thrust of the ego, denying its unconscious aspects. The subsuming of will under ego is a typical twentieth century approach, and Jung later expands his views. Never accepting that any exploration is exhausted, he returns repeatedly to the same material, but adds new, thoughtful dimensions. He favors imagery, rich in history and myth, over a purely conceptual approach. In the latter part of his life he draws more closely to the alchemical tradition for his analogies. Jung qualifies earlier statements by insisting that will pushes toward the Self as its ultimate aim (to me, this means away from the ego end of the axis), implying a non-rational impetus, the dynamic thrust of will to differentiate us.

Adler contends that will is a protest against the parent, but in an opposite sense from Freud. Instead of the urge to replace the father or the mother, Adler's will asserts itself as a desire, the will to be different from one's parents. Though Adler's contribution in the will-to-dominate area is formidable, a thorough exploration is still needed of the differences between consciousness and unconsciousness in the domain in which will operates.

Why have these disparate points of view not been further reconciled by scholars? The answer, it seems to me, is that after the nineteenth century, will became identified with will power and thus coupled with rigidity, repression, denial—and all those negative energies that the twentieth century sought to liberate. The emphasis on individuality caused will first to be subordinated and then fused with ego, useful only in the further pursuit of egomania. The entire arc of will from spirit phenomena to instinct became narrowly confined. Desire, which initiates the action of will, also became confused, limited to bodily needs primarily, but to the ego as well.

Followers of Freud, Jung, and Adler have made sporadic efforts to bring will back into the central focus it has lacked since the nineteenth century. Otto Rank, Leslie Farber, Rollo May, Francis Aveling, William Sheldon, Victor Frankl, Roberto Assagioli, Silvano Arieti, and Gerald May, to name a few, have updated the subject, once the province of philosophy, with current psychological knowledge. In the latter part of our century, will once more begins to emerge as an important human factor, although not in the deterministic mode of Freud.

Science has taken a different direction by gradually revising rationalistic notions of a strictly mechanical universe. Einstein introduced relativity whereby the observation of a phenomenon differs from one observer to another, depending on their relative states of motion. The year 1927 signalled a momentous alteration in the theory of determinism when Heisenberg unveiled the Uncertainty Principle, postulating a finite limit to the precision with which phenomena can be known. Thus the objectivity of scientific exploration fell to the relativity of uncertain determinants. This shift produced tremors in many fields not directly related to physics. Psychology encountered difficulty defending the absolutism of some of the theories of Freud and Skinner. Henceforth all scientific studies that laid claim to certainty would come into question: To Donald Cowan it meant that "the imagination has free play, as it did not in a strictly predictable universe."[2]

In 1929 two books by the eminent German-American psychoanalyst, Otto Rank—*Will Therapy* and *Truth and Reality*—brought Freudian terminology again into the psychological spot light, expanding some of his original concepts, even though moving away from

Freudian determinism. Rank stresses the personal aspect of will and the possibility of choice (within limits). He shrugs off the strict determinism implicit in Freud's theory of the instincts; yet he still equates will with will power as it impacts the environment. How identity is established through will concerns him: "The human being experiences his individuality in terms of his will and this means his personal existence is identical with his capacity to express his will in the world."[3] He is particularly interested in how the creative person fashions his or her personality through the will. "The average person yields to the inevitable; the neurotic fights against it; the artist wills it actively,"[4] a Rank disciple explains.

Rank favors recognition of the importance of will's role, though not in the exuberant manner of Nietzsche's exaltation of its creative energy. Rank offers certain caveats that he feels Nietzsche omits: Will originally has a negative character, a "not wanting to," which creates both positive and negative poles, a will and counter-will; will is "only so strong or is willing as such when it is used to assail outer and inner resistances."[5] He thus equates will with ego power and casts it in the heroic mode. He also sees it as a descendant, a representation of the biological will-to-live made conscious. One of his most perceptive observations is that will is the conscious *expression* of instinct, which is closely connected to emotions which in turn are the conscious *awareness* of instinct. Will expresses emotional necessities, the stimulation to acting, thinking, and feeling. Without claiming that will is entirely conscious, he believes we are aware of it through consciousness. "Consciousness itself is probably a will phenomenon,"[6] he elaborates.

If we accept will as an ego function in this model, then to the extent that we are conscious of our egos, will is a conscious function. Basic instincts experienced through the ego by consciousness equal the power of the will. Will evolves an ego ideal, not solely on the basis of genetic inheritance or on past experiences. We also make goal choices, which are not predetermined, but for which we consciously strive. In Freudian terms, Rank sees the ego in conflict with the id, or instincts, and the super ego. Ego, then, is strong to the degree that it is representative of the primal force of the will.

Rank believes that sexuality challenges the will, especially at puberty. Sexual urges are such a compelling force that they threaten to subvert the equilibrium of the personality. Thus we develop a counter-will to defend against the domination of sexuality. The assertion of this counter-will strengthens the ego at puberty, pushing us toward singularity or individuality. And yet I feel Rank gives insufficient recognition to the areas in which ego is diminished at the time of puberty. This period involves major choices in terms of identity. Will can be turned inward, against the self, annihilating the ego through self-hatred. For example, in anorexia or bulimia, will is reversed into a conquest of appetite, an attack on the body resulting from an inward sense of inadequacy rather than an outwardly directed impulse to conquer the world. Desire for singularity is certainly strong in the adolescent at the time of identity crisis, but will takes a destructive bent if the only way to express individuality is by punishing oneself. As informative as his ideas are, Rank doesn't address the negative aspects of introverted will, turning back on itself.

Ultimately the assertion of personal will is, in Rank's view, in direct opposition to God's will. Willing therefore opens us to existential guilt. Jesus symbolizes the defiant son, who becomes a paradigm of the conquest of personal will by rebellious human nature. He does so not by asserting his will, but by submission. Physically he fails; spiritually, he triumphs. Yet today the Christian concept of submission, as espoused by Jesus, conflicts, in Rank's view, with the will-to-success in the Western world. He therefore links will to guilt, the handmaiden of increased self-consciousness. Guilt results when ego-centeredness assumes a dominant personality role, but then realizes will cannot always have its way. Isn't this the lesson learned by every mythological hero (e.g., Achilles, Odysseus) who accepts responsibility for his actions?

In 1960, in *The Ways of the Will*, Leslie Farber took exception to many of Rank's contentions, endowing will with a positive character but making it less a function of ego. Farber calls will "the responsible mover." He delineates two spheres of the will, one unconscious, the second conscious. In the unconscious sphere the thrust is often in a direction that we hardly recognize. It might be called an intuitive decision to take a certain direction or make a choice. It is often only later, after the experience, that we can look back and recognize there was something important or crucial about a choice that seemed incidental at the time. W. H. Auden places this type of choice in a metaphorical framework: "I had very little sense of the seriousness of what I was doing and only later did I discover what had seemed an unimportant brook was, in fact, a Rubicon." The sense of freedom falls in this area. Choices are easy when they are spontaneous and not conflict ridden. They feel like part of a seamless whole, the most revealing part of our essential selves.

In the second category, conscious choice dominates those moments experienced as isolated events, such as a decision to move toward some object or goal. It can be an objective we visualize in advance, even though plans do not always work out as expected. Such decisions are primarily utilitarian. Achieving, winning, possessing, competing, owning—all fall within this realm. Paradoxically, the choices of the second application of the will may turn out to be less useful, as I have indicated, than those of the first, which were considered neither purposeful nor highly motivated at the time. Farber contributes significantly by defining the importance of choices, often only dimly perceived, that can be more vital to our essential well-being than those we make with all the fanfare of conscious decision-making.

One question we have asked is whether will is psychological or psychic energy. Francis Aveling, while emphasizing the importance of concentration or attention, claims that will is not necessarily effortful. He makes a distinction between willing (often easy) and striving: "A volition ensuing, even in difficult action, may be absolutely effortless. Will is not itself effort, though it may initiate effort of an extraordinary kind."[7] How surprising it is that the same action can require a great effort one time and very little the next! It would be informative to distinguish when, how, and why this is true. The difference has to do with how desires and emotions are lined up and engaged or opposed to will. Desire is always the stronger partner.

Silvano Arieti, who defines will as "the capacity to make and implement choices...the culmination of all psychological functions,"[8] contributes some cogent distinctions to the enduring argument over whether humans are autonomous, endowed with freedom of choice. To paraphrase Arieti, if we look at the child whose first sense of volition is curbed by the "no-no" of the parent, we might say that life begins by submission to the will of others. Therefore, if we are not to be passive conformers, identity becomes a challenge of sorting out and defending our desires against the will of others. Even after childhood, this hostility to conformity can linger, particularly in those who confuse will and desire. Some adults establish identity, indeed a whole personality, around protest against parents—procrastinating, always arriving late, never wearing a raincoat, or similar acts of latent rebellion. The grown person is never totally autonomous, Arieti feels, but the options available to adults allow greater freedom of latitude than Skinner, in particular, would accept.

Rollo May, a substantial contributor to the literature of desire and will, feels that will has not been given full exposure: "Something more complex and significant is going on in human experience in the realm of will and decision than we have yet taken into our studies."[9] He makes the eyebrow-raising observation that "Freud developed psychoanalysis as an antiwill system." Because he blames repression for mankind's entrapment in neuroses, Freud sees will as purely negative restraint, according to May, as "an implement in the service of repression, no longer a positive moving force."[10]

In the area of Willing and Wishing, May offers these distinctions: "*Will is the capacity to organize one's self* so that movement in a certain direction or toward a goal may take place. *Wish is the imaginative playing with the possibility of* some act or state occurring."[11] May discusses desire in other terms than need and gives will a proper place, while recognizing its tendency to overbearingness. He explains that at times when will is in crisis, it is often less complicated to know what one is *against* than what one is *for*, hence it is easy to protest or to blame: "*But if will remains protest, it stays dependent on that which it is protesting against.* Protest is half-developed will." In blaming, "We see here an example of the self-contradictory effect of all psychological defensiveness: *it automatically hands the power over to the adversary.*"[12]

In his scholarly examination of the will, Roberto Assagioli emphasizes the intimate connection between self and will in achieving psychosynthesis, or harmony between the disparate parts of the personality. He describes a dual role for the will: first, as a powerful adhesive force, to give us the sense of our individual identity by putting the splintered pieces together; second, and contrarily, as a quiescent force needed to attain a sense of wholeness—a feat only possible in moments of transcendental experience. Assagioli asserts that "will becomes easily submerged by the constant surge of drives, emotions, and ideas."[13] Today it is particularly difficult to rescue will from the distractions and sensations surrounding us. Assagioli seeks to elucidate these gradations in acts of will (I am summarizing here):

1) *Strong will*—frequent misconception that the strong will constitutes the whole will. Strength is only one of the aspects of the will, and when dissociated from the others, it can be, and often is, ineffectual or harmful to oneself and other people.

2) *Skillful will*—Obtaining desired results with the least possible expenditure of energy. (This is what I call optimum use of the will, requiring the image of desire to be consonant with will.)

3) *Good will*—learning to choose the right goals, so as not to bring harm or umbrage on oneself or others.

4) *Transpersonal Will*—similar to Abraham Maslow's "higher needs."[14] (This tack elevates will to the position of supporting partner on the pathway to expanded dimensions of being, taking it beyond the self-centeredness of personal demands.)

In summary, Assagioli joins will to a value system and suggests a hierarchy of steps in its utilization.

Viktor Frankl's search for the meaning of will comes from his intense search to comprehend the horrors of the Holocaust. He concludes that the function of the will is to seek order and meaning out of the shattering experiences encountered in a world of senseless pain. In addition, he cautions that "sometimes the frustrated will-to-meaning is vicariously compensated for by a will-to-power, including the most basic form of the will-to-power, the will-to-money."[15] Ergo, when existence is lacking in purpose, life's meaning can deteriorate into a monolithic will-to-money. In *The Doctor and the Soul,* Frankl contends that in this century we are almost totally involved in satisfying a will-to-power and will-to-pleasure, leaving a great void in the third of the primary functions of will, the will-to-meaning. Without it, the very reason for life itself comes into serious question.[16]

To Gerald May, will is a spirit function that can be schooled to contemplative concerns by those who truly wish to connect to their deepest layers of being. But, May theorizes, human nature gravitates to willfulness: "It is a sign of our addiction to willfulness that in the absence of demands placed upon us from the outside, we create them for ourselves."[17] He contrasts two opposite methods of employment of will: WILLFULNESS or WILLINGNESS. May claims that too much WILLFULNESS results in "spiritual narcissism, ego's ultimate ploy," with ego unable to surrender and enter WILLINGNESS. One aspect of ego can often fight with another. He insists—and this is the whole premise—that when "an internal battle is waged between willpower and personal desire...when willpower is all there is, desire wins."[18] With omnipotent will thus humbled (no contest) by desire, the only recourse is to concede powerlessness, and admit defeat, somewhat akin to the first three steps of Alcoholics Anonymous. Will power fails in any contest with desire.

May is particularly helpful in detailing ways to reach the Unitive Experience (similar to Maslow's "peak experience"), when will surrenders its desire to control and becomes WILLINGNESS. Not everyone wants to surrender will-control long enough to accept metaphysical, or beyond physical, experience. Lack of control can feel very threatening. Even if we desire transcendental experience, we cannot call it up at random or tap into it automatically. We can only prepare ourselves for the Unitive Experience, which is described by May as the feeling of being outside of one's temporal limitations.

Stage One: Being at one. Time seems to stop. No sense of controlling anything. Necessary to give up self-defining thoughts. Will is an essential part of identity, yet self-identification is the sacrifice we must make if we want to experience deepest meaning.

Stage Two: Awareness open.

Stage Three: Ecstatic reactions occur (awe, wonder, joy, reverence). We may only articulate these euphoric states afterwards. To try to put the experience of the moment into words, a logos function, chases away the transcendental.[19]

W. B. Yeats describes such a transcendental moment in his poem, "Vacillation," when there is heightened perception, a loss of the sense of time as linear, and a brief mystical state of ecstasy:

> While on the shop and street I gazed
> My body of a sudden blazed;
> And twenty minutes more or less
> It seemed, so great my happiness,
> That I was blessèd and could bless.[20]

Willingness to surrender control can be a liberation, an opening to higher realms of being. To Bachelard the contemplation of beauty always has therapeutic value: "Aesthetic contemplation alleviates human sorrow for an instant by detaching man from the drama of will."[21] Without writing directly on the subject of will, Bachelard contributes many phenomenological definitions of its attributes. In one instance: "Beginning is the particular privilege of the will."[22] He places will at the source, an initiator, as did Kant, who held that will is the capacity for beginning.

Bachelard believes all lessons in life are learned from the challenge of matter. Our imagination is attracted to the primary elements—to earth, air, fire, water—according to our natural disposition, and will seeks engagement with these objects we desire. Through emphasis on images created by interaction with the sensate world—images that motivate us to action—Bachelard forges the connection of will to imagination. Together they are the molders of existence.

In this interplay with the material world, will becomes the formative impulse, molding even the organs of the physical body: "The primal consciousness of the will is a clenched fist."[23] Bachelard likens primal human instincts to those of the animal. Risking sudden, aggressive movement, an animal demonstrates the will-to-attack, "dramatic and uncertain" when compared to the more diffuse and universal will-to-live that all creatures share. His definition of will penetrates into all realms of being and renders a picture of its manifest presence. Will becomes the directive aspect of all bodily engagement.

The French philosopher correctly moves toward reconnecting will with desire and hence the image. In essence, Bachelard's precept of will is a response to the world that challenges us to make something of it and of ourselves. It calls forth our individual creativeness, summons us to the path of individuation. It functions on levels of consciousness and unconsciousness, much like the ego complex, although not identical, as it embodies the deepest layers of the self.

Will, then, spans the entire human spectrum. At the most instinctual level, it is the will-to-live. Developing from this primal base it can become the will-to-power when not ameliorated by love. At a conscious level, a well-trained will keeps us focused on the goal in mind. In any task, will's responsibility is to sustain concentration, to keep the heat on. Imagination, naturally expansive, envisions the whole and embodies desire, and thus will strides with it *pari passu*—a partner in the task of realization. Will's pathway may be quite intuitive or suprarational in the realm of the will-to-speak, as when we are "stung by the splendor of a sudden thought" (Browning, "A Death in the Desert"). Will, as a spirit function, governs our aspirations and thereby overcomes incredible barriers. With such an all-inclusive reach, will offers the ultimate prism through which we can view ourselves and communicate with others.

Will and Intentionality

Imagining is intentional through and through.
EDWARD S. CASEY, *Imagining*

The psyche is constantly making intelligible statements. It's
making dreams and symptoms, it's making fantasies and
moods. It's extraordinarily intentional, purposive.
JAMES HILLMAN, *Inter Views*

Intentionality is the human capacity to have aims that funnel into
actions, directing them. We might call it the primary stage of any act of
volition. This part of unconscious Will gathers experiences and shapes
them into perceptions we can integrate into our personalities. In my
view intentionality is the first link in an active and reactive chain leading
to the unity of will and desire.

Intentionality is also best described as the way the soul structures
experience so that it has meaning for us. It follows that meaning is a
basic intention of the mind. Every meaning in turn carries, within it, a
commitment. Every act of consciousness tends toward something, the

human move of turning and focusing, and has inherent within it some impetus toward willful action.

Intent makes it possible for us, as subjects, to understand the objective world. The presupposition is that we could not know anything unless we already in some way participated in it. We are in-formed by the thing understood and, in the same act, our intellect simultaneously gives form to the thing we understand. "Once you touch the object (image) you must go with the intention of the object; not the intention of the subject," is the way Enrique Pardo describes it.[1] This perspective obliterates any pure subject/object dichotomy by saying that objectivity is not possible when involving a desiring/willing subject. The world is a co-creation; an analogy might be that the clay provides the structure to which the sculptor responds. Or the intention of the rain is already in the gathering of the clouds. We live in a participatory universe.

Whatever we are drawn to answers our gaze. In this sense it is the alliance with Eros that allows this avenue of connection to be made. Rollo May's observation is apt:

> We see that eros has much in common with the concept of intentionality...: both presuppose that man pushes toward uniting himself with the object not only of his love but his knowledge. And this very process implies that a man already participates to some extent in the knowledge he seeks and the person he loves.[2]

The theory of intentionality rests on the concept of the human mind as an active, probing participant in what it knows. Edmund Husserl advances this theory, already shown by Kant in the *Refutation of Idealism*, claiming that consciousness never exists in a subjective vacuum but is always a consciousness of something outside itself. So intentionality is an assertive response of the person to the structure of his or her world. Interaction with our world gives us our sense of ourselves, what we call our identity. By my act I reveal myself, not by my thought of myself.

Most definitions of intentionality sound very dry, and circular, like the chicken and the egg. This one of Mihaly Csikszentmihalyi's stresses consciousness as *intentionally ordered information*:

> We may call *intentions* the force that keeps information in consciousness ordered. Intentions arise in consciousness whenever

a person is aware of desiring something or wanting to accomplish something. Intentions are also bits of information, shaped either by biological needs or by internalized social goals. They act as magnetic fields, moving attention toward some objects and away from others, keeping our mind focused on some stimuli in preference to others. We often call the manifestation of intentionality by other names, such as instinct, need, drive, or desire. But these are all explanatory terms, telling us why people behave in certain ways. Intention is a more neutral and descriptive term; it doesn't say *why* a person wants to do a certain thing, but simply states *that* he does.[3]

Consciousness is born of conflict. To say "yes" to one image, idea, or thought is to say "no" to something else. The initial response to any challenge involves an act of volition. There is an either/or choice in every act of perception. To understand acts of volition, we need to explore both conscious and unconscious intentionality. Unconscious intentionality may underlie conscious choices. The structures of meaning we formed in a preconscious period of life set a pattern for sublimation and thus for the blocking of any uncluttered awareness of intentions in later life.

Knowing and willing are inseparable, linked by intentionality. In the enunciation of "I can," we intend or point toward a goal. By implying an action aimed toward the future, a sense of potentiality thus empowers and determines one's self-esteem. Through the capacity of projection we are able to deepen our awareness of the progression of "I can-I will-I am" in our intimate sense of ourselves.

Intentionality implies a latent opening, a projected window of opportunity, a pointing toward the future. There are, naturally, thorns of anxiety interspersed with the buds of potential. Our anxieties may derive from memories of past difficulties, as the past plays itself out in the present, or they may be imaginary fears that seem to threaten the clear path to our goal. Reinterpreting the past can be creative—choosing not to continue to see ourselves as a victim, for example.

Kinetic energy is inherent in any intention. If not dispersed in the actualizing of that intention, it may detach itself into cool disregard or psychopathological acting-out, which are two opposite ways of actualizing intentionality. If we cannot escape into the act, we try to avoid the tension by pretending that we never cared to act anyway. Our vitality is a correlate of the degree of full-hearted commitment we can make to our plans. Tasks done joyfully are scarcely any effort at all.

One's degree of courage is only indirectly related to the measure of one's intentionality. It is not a simple formula of courage equalling commitment. Sometimes what passes for courage is really an attempt to hide fears under a more acceptable disguise. It takes a lifetime of meeting one crisis after another with strength and fortitude to gauge our supply of courage.

How we conceive the future affects the mood of the present. Action is difficult when the future seems precarious. Sardello explains why any action implies a future: "Thought and feeling come from the past; any action is from the future."[4] Feelings of hopelessness, the sense of checkmate before the game begins, result in a willingness to abandon the effort. Energy evaporates when a sense of futility dominates. When energy is sapped, every movement seems arduous and burdensome. Remember the last scene of Samuel Beckett's "Waiting for Godot," which aptly conveys such apathy.

> Vladimir: Well? Shall we go now?
> Estragon: Yes, let's go.
>
> They do not move. (stage direction)

Will is paralyzed by discouragement.

When personal dignity and self-esteem, the ultimate aim of all our desires, are missing, as Robert Solomon points out,[5] or when we have trouble feeling proud of ourselves, even simple acts require more energy than we can summon. In *Images of Hope*, Father William Lynch addresses the problem: "Hope is, in its most general terms, a sense of the *possible*, that what we really need is possible, though difficult, while hopelessness means to be ruled by the sense of the impossible."[6] He calls apathy "negativity, nonwishing, noninvolvement, retreat into the private imagination, absence of feeling, absence of concern."[7] This retreat into a private introspective world—a world dominated by the wish not to act, not to exist, not to have been born, not even to be bothered by thinking about it, is, in short, nihilism.

Self-reflection, so necessary to self-knowledge, turns negative if we become wrapped up in a circular, introspective cycle, forfeiting our concern for others. Like a dog endlessly chasing its own tail, one becomes closed off, compulsively caught in egocentric anxieties, losing connection with wider dimensions of being that might provide a fresh perspective.

Despair, *des-espoir*, means, literally, hopelessness. This moment may be the distillation of a general attitude of discouragement laid over a bed of fear. A sense of fatalism, Father Lynch holds, stems from absolutizing an idea, any idea, even a good one. Such mental rigidity traps us in stereotypical responses. The *Götterdammerung* of recent concern has been a possible nuclear holocaust. In turning the concept of impending doom into an absolute, we begin telling ourselves, "We are all going to die soon," so "What's the use of caring?" Or a similar apocalyptic equation: "Some unhinged dictator like Quaddafi or Hussein will probably blow up the world, so what does it matter what I do?" This nothing-can-be-done syndrome is both limiting and self-defeating. Imagination ceases to pursue solutions, accepting the fatalistic view that none exist. Trapped in this apathetic vise, image-making and even wishing cease to flow. Freeing the imagination to flow again with its accompanying energies of will hinges on a shift in perspective, an image of hope substituted for that of despair.

When personal undertakings seem too formidable, and the outside world overwhelms with menace, one can sink quickly into a deeply passive state—an intractable psychic dungeon, a trauma of isolation from others whose energy and imagination are still functioning. All is despair and blackness, no light, no glimmer of possibility. It is impossible to imagine that anything can be done or is worth doing. Imagination doesn't stretch beyond the present agonizing moment. At this nadir of despair, suicide becomes a resolution. To Wendell Berry, suicide is mute loneliness, rising out of despair, "a wound that cannot be healed because it is encapsulated in loneliness, surrounded by speechlessness."[8]

At such bleak moments, is there any other solution? Only by overcoming the absolute conviction that we have no inner resources to draw upon nor external sources to turn to for help. In actuality, we may be pleading for concern, crying for someone to step in and do something for us. Father Lynch says that "Hope cannot be achieved alone."[9] This explains why no amount of introspection can help when we really feel hopeless. Psychotherapy, when it is effective, involves imagining *with* someone else.

Assessing the schisms in consciousness between hopefulness and futility requires study of the whole spectrum of emotions from wishing, wanting, expecting, to dejection and lassitude. It is not possible to quantify precisely the act of willing, since we bring different amounts of energy to various aspects of will. But energy is subject to tremendous vicissitudes. On the one hand an existential sense of hope for an advantageous future is prone to constant challenge; on the other a desire for material goods is fueled by a constant appeal to cupidity in the media bombardment of billboards, TV, and magazines. Acute awareness of what others have goads us into excessive wanting for ourselves. In an age of immediate gratification, we are torn between avarice and discouragement, between self-indulgence and self-defeatism. Paul Diel calls anguish "desire in its negative form," and goes on to explain that "anguish is a state of convulsion because it consists of two diametrically opposed attitudes: *exalted desire and fearful inhibition.*"[10]

Allan Wheelis in his book, *The Quest for Identity*, believes that an underlying sense of futility pervades our current culture. Especially outside the successful mainstream, extreme cynicism, skepticism, or despair paralyzes the will to respond with fortitude. Choice dissolves into following the path of least resistance, or adopting an irresponsible *carpe diem* attitude of celebrate today, forget tomorrow, or, worse, using drugs to quell the frustrations. In the 1960s, the allure of drugs signified a spiritual quest, whereas today they seem to be a tool of denial, a blotting out of painful possibilities. But drugs will always be with us, because, as Octavio Paz points out, humankind is always searching for "a beyond." Like Odysseus's men in the Homeric epic who had seen too much pain in the Trojan war and were willing to forget the goal of returning home to Ithaca, the search is for a drug to quell thwarted desires. Odysseus had to use force to drag his men away from the Lotus Eaters and restore their will to strive.

The current drug epidemic argues that our society is failing to provide adequate avenues for desire and will to reach fruition. We have too many marginal people who are impoverished in spirit as well as in material goods and have trouble finding an acceptable place in the community or an adequate sense of potential in visioning the future. We could benefit from some invigorating new images of an inclusive society that would provide opportunities for each individual to realize his/her finest qualities. To Lynch, this "lack of hope is behind one particular facet of our national character, its broad tendency toward running, toward activism, toward overmasculinity. We have not faced and handled our hopelessness. We conceal it under its opposites."[11]

Perhaps the pervasive sense of futility was disguised in the upper middle class world of the 1980s "can do" society, but I suspect that the defense against a sense of futility is similar to a defense against depression. We worry that should we happen to pause in our manic rush forward we would be irrevocably overwhelmed by a tidal wave of depression. Thus we cannot slow down. Even the people in the most successful segment of society run as if they fear that anything less than feverish activity implies that they are falling behind. Some discerning person inserted in *Who's Who* her favorite recreation: "resting." This comment seems amusing in the context of a society where doing something at all times is the norm and resting is regarded as an aberration.

The body is the centrum and the language of intentionality. Our bodies speak a language we can learn to understand, but in our time the connection is strained. After three centuries (from the seventeenth to the twentieth) of regarding the body anatomically, we are caught in acute dissociation from the body, which promotes abuse of it. The body becomes an object that is jogged, flogged, stretched, starved, as if it were an alien entity. We have accepted a veneration for the mechanical, thereby living out the myth of the body as machine. Consider the myriad ways we attempt to analyze it, reduce it to numerical equations (pulse rate, body weight, body mass index, cholesterol count, white cell count, heart rhythms, etc.), all further detachment from the perception of the body as the house of the soul.

In "The Wasteland," that seminal poem summing up so many of our contemporary problems, T. S. Eliot writes of the need for vital images to escape a sense of impoverishment of meaning. "The Wasteland" opens with a longing for images of vitality to renew the deadened earth and, by analogy, the inner sense of deadness of soul life. When there seems to be "no exit," to borrow a phrase from Sartre, the crucial question becomes how to free the imagination and the will to be dynamic once more, how to encourage the will to dream.

The Independent
Will of the Complex

The shadow and the opposing will is the
necessary condition for all actualization.
C. G. JUNG, *Psychology and Religion: West and East*

Where the will to power becomes dominant, the resulting
complex has a most unfortunate effect on the personality.
M. ESTHER HARDING, *Psychic Energy*

Many Native Americans believe that people will die if you step on their
shadow. We react in similar fashion—as if our very lives were threatened by anyone seeing through us too clearly. When we become defensive it is certain that some remark, some circumstance has impinged on
an aspect of our shadow side. Jung says that at such moments we have
come into uncomfortable contact with one of the feeling-toned complexes. These deeply ingrained complexes are constantly warring,
interfering with our conscious choices. When we make New Year's res-

olutions not to get angry at our mother-in-law or husband (his cigar ashes in our bedroom?) or not to react to our children's ploys, when we pledge no more desserts, no postprandial drinks, and then see our resolution vanish, we can be sure some complex has activated a psychic chain reaction.

The giveaway, the sine qua non, of a complex (which Jung revealed through association experiments) is that it is repetitious. Not only in our behavioral patterns but also in our speech, whenever we keep returning, like the proverbial broken record, to enunciate our experiences in precisely the same fashion, we have provoked a complex. It's almost as if they cry for our attention by continually repeating themselves. And this endless repetition can get terribly boring. Often one thinks: Wouldn't it be stimulating to work on a new problem? But instead the old ones keep intruding. Unfortunately, they can't be conquered by frontal assault, as anyone knows who has tried. It is only by indirection, by brief bits of insight, that we gain access to them. We can listen, pay heed to them, try to see how they are organized. But we can't succeed by trying to impose our own sense of order on them. As Hillman often maintains, a complex is not repeating itself just to get rid of something. It's a forgotten bit of the psyche calling for respect, and care, pleading for our attention again.

The individual normally denies or rationalizes these emotional eruptions. Then we make them serve as a smoke screen, a psychic obfuscation. Those intimate with us are more apt to penetrate our shadow complexes than we are. Whenever the blood boils, whenever we react with angry defensiveness or with an excess of fear, a complex has been provoked. When the psychic thermometer rises, or someone trips an emotional trigger, a complex has been activated.

All psychic life takes place in our complexes, and if we pay heed, they can be a wellspring of knowledge concerning our individuality. Jung's definition of the shadow focuses on the complex as the basic, active part of personality: "The contents of the personal unconscious are chiefly the feeling-toned complexes, as they are called; they constitute the personal and private side of psychic life."[1]

We are such a bundle of complexes that it is hard to separate the unified profile, or persona, which we like to present to the world, from the fragments. Our complexes overlap. Hillman describes them as that "upon which we depend for our daily personality and from which we draw our energetic compulsion."[2]

What we call the ego, the "I," is really a complex in itself, a center around which all other complexes cluster. Complexes can never be known by the intellect alone, because we must feel their force if we are to begin to unveil them. They are like painful bulges that rise off the surface of consciousness, drawing upon pustules in areas far below. We aren't aware of them until something bumps into them. According to Jung, they consist "not only of *meaning* but also of *value*, and this depends on the intensity of the accompanying feeling tones."[3] We can be totally unconscious of our complexes, or identify with them, or project them on others.

Two that involve the majority of us most intimately are the mother and father complexes with their bewildering variety of contradictory valencies. We spend a good part of our adult life untangling the many parental complexes, but especially those of security (fright of being left alone, along with actual safety), of approval, of adequacy, and of dependency. Linked together are many symbolic associations, so that our parental complexes carry a baggage overload. Often we find ourselves, in spite of our intention to do just the opposite, adhering zealously to the same path as our parents, teaching our children the same old bromides. Or we may consider ourselves very clever in doing the exact opposite, only to become aware that some entirely independent course might represent our own identity more accurately. Without elaborating in endless detail the powerful thrust of these significant complexes, it is important to emphasize the polarities of positive and negative they always carry. With a positive father complex one is apt to idealize the personal father, often at the expense of one's own identity and creativity or to be easily led, or deceived, by a mentor. With a negative father complex, women in particular may feel victimized by men or subject to constant criticism of the internal animus.

The magnitude of the mother complex surpasses the personal mother, the already powerful effects fortified by the underpinning of the archetypal Great Mother. As Hillman explains: "The mother complex is not my mother; it is my complex. It is the way in which my psyche has taken up my mother. Behind is the *Magna mater*."[4] All areas of feeling are dominated by the mother complex, just as spirit matters are dominated by the wise, old Father image. The feelings associated with the mother complex Hillman describes as "our most permanent and intractable feelings" and then observes:

> This complex [mother] is the permanent trap of one's reactions and values from earliest infancy, the box and the walls in every situation whichever way one turns. One faces the mother, as fate, again and anew.... The way we feel about our bodily life, our physical self-regard and confidence, the subjective tone with which we take in or go out into the world, the basic fears and guilts, how we enter into love and behave in closeness and nearness, our psychological temperature of coldness and warmth, how we feel when we are ill, our manners, taste, and style of living, habitual structures of relating, patterns of gesture and tone of voice, all bear the marks of the mother; and for the woman the mother-complex comes particularly into play in her self-identity feelings and her sexual feelings.[5]

From our father complex we mold our moral and spiritual principles. At the extreme, we develop a rigid insistence on law and order, a too strict sense of duty, an unimaginative and conventional approach to thought and behavior, an unyielding stubbornness to any new idea, and a removal from the source of instinctual life. We may move to the polar opposite, as Murray Stein indicates:

> The obsessive anti-authoritarian, the deliberate eccentric, the systematic non-conformist [is] devoured not by identification with collective consciousness, but by a severe allergy against it. This counter-type finds it equally impossible [as its opposite above] to experience life individually. His negative father complex has him in maw.[6]

We spend our lives trying to project our substitute mother or father needs on mates, mentors, and friends. Probably the best way to peer into these complexes is to lessen or withdraw the projections, so easy to talk about, so hard to do. We can ask ourselves, what is it in this person, in this situation that resonates pleasurably for me. Or, contrarily, what draws my hate, loathing, repulsion, anger, or fear.

Complexes are generally, but not always, formed early in life in interaction with experiences. Their "nuclear element" is a center of meaning "beyond the realm of conscious will, unconscious and uncontrollable," according to Jolande Jacobi, around which all subsequent events circle and add dimension. There are a number of associations connected with this nuclear element, "stemming in part from innate personal disposition and in part from individual experiences conditioned by the environment."[7] Like scar tissue thickening around a wound, this inexorable tightness and density explain why complexes are so difficult to raise to conscious awareness when we make the attempt later in life. It is not just one forgotten piece of memory that needs raising to consciousness; it is an entire structure of meaning that has guided our reactions.

Jung maintains that complexes, not dreams, provide the most direct access to unconsciousness. Early on, he called his psychology "complex" rather than "archetypal." This particular point led to his schism with Freud. Jung believes that complexes originate out of archetypal images of the collective unconscious, coupled with repression of a personal storage bin of unwanted, unacceptable bits of experience. Freud thinks they are only related to the personal past.

A complex generally embodies an archetypal image at its core, and carries a number of seeming opposites. It is the contrasting valencies, typical of archetypes, that impart the dynamic energy. Bachelard attests to this: "It is in the sum of gathered contradictions that the strength of the complex is measured."[8] Some, such as the Puer/Senex (related to the father), split into very apparent dichotomies. The flighty, irresponsible puer youth seemingly has little connection to the ponderous, senexed old man who takes everything too seriously. They are, though, but two aspects of the same drive. The manic/depressive complex (related to the mother) can swerve from mild awareness of its swings to a pathological syndrome, exhibiting strongly polarized characteristics. The seesaw swings from moods of hilarity to morbid depression. With some complexes the paradoxical parts remain closer in proximity, with less obviously contrasting opposite states. Yet, as Bachelard elaborates: "A complex is always the hinge of ambivalence. Around a complex joy and sorrow are always ready to exchange their eagerness."[9]

Our complexes are psychic hooks, one end embedded in an archetype, the other in us. A splinter of an archetype becomes elaborated with personal experiential material. The word "archetype" has multiple meanings, all related to the notion of original source. One of Jung's singularly important concepts holds that we come into the world with inherited psychic structures, or archetypes, that determine the way we organize our experiences. What is predetermined is the form that governs the common structuring mechanism; the contents we supply out of our personal experience. We know that archetypes exist as underlying structures for containing human experiences by their common manifestations in art, religion, myths, folk and fairy tales where similarities intersect cultural lines. They uniformly appear as primordial images imbued with energy or numinosity, and these images form the structure and nucleus of meaning of our complexes as well. We might say that the complex is formed by the imposition of the archetype on individual experiences.

In one of his playful moods, Jung sees complexes as cockroaches, whirling around, animistic. This image exudes a sense of autonomy that can be relatively mild or quite intense, with the roaches behaving as a law unto themselves. Until we discharge some of the energy of the complex by raising it and absorbing it into consciousness, it will continue to surprise us with the consistency of its reappearance. According to Jacobi: "They [complexes] cast off the compulsive character of an automatism only when we raise them to consciousness which is among the most important elements of therapy."[10] If complexes are at a great distance from consciousness, they take on a mythological character and become infused with archetypal numinosity that "is totally impervious to the conscious will and puts the subject into a state of seizure, of will-less subservience."[11]

Complexes challenge our faith in the preeminence of the will and of ego control. Our complexes have us; we don't have them, as we usually think.[12] I would add that, as with compulsion in any addiction, it is the beginning of wisdom to acknowledge how powerless will is when confronting the more powerful complex. Jacobi stresses that: "This is the crucial point of which we must gain clarity if we are to counter the prevailing smug faith in the supremacy of the will and of ego-consciousness with the doubt it deserves."[13] Complexes are beyond the control of the conscious will and remind us that something in our psyche can be even stronger than personal will power.

Complexes range a wide gamut, from mildly neurotic to psychopathic. Though the underlying cause may be a trauma, or emotional shock, Jacobi suggests that "as a rule the complex has its ultimate cause in the impossibility of affirming the whole of one's nature."[14] Often we become aware of these phenomena as "indirect expression[s] of unrecognized desires"[15] only through the oblique miseries or symptoms we suffer. Jung always believes that the agonies induced by complexes are not present simply to disturb but to provide a stimulus to understand ourselves better: "Suffering is not an illness; it is the normal counterpole to happiness." Complexes press upon us, insisting that we take heed. When we ignore them, we suffer their pathology: "A complex becomes pathological only when we think we have not got it."[16]

With their nuclear images, complexes resonate with fragmented shards of our lives. Some or even all images can have archetypal vitality. According to Hillman, the archetypal quality emerges through: a) precisely portraying the image; b) sticking to the image while hearing it metaphorically; c) discovering the necessity in the image; d) experiencing the unfathomable analogical richness of the image.[17]

Pat Berry observes that each complex has an image and a volition. In other words a complex carries an image combined with its own drive, *telos*, or direction. This drive is what we confront when we try ever so hard to wish or will away our complexes. The real access to the complex is through the image, which often we can intuit only by following the line of attention provoked by the volition.

Nothing stirs in the psyche without concomitant alteration in the image. We can only feel the volition; we cannot directly reach the demanding imperative of the complex, simply to transform it by making up our minds that it would be desirable. Only through conscious attention to the force of the volition can we begin to proscribe the dimensions of our complexes. Then we try to unearth the contents of the images frozen there. Explaining why images that we live out are so unapproachable, Sardello touches on an unimaginable aspect to the image, which is its dark memory. "What keeps us away from the image is that we feel its darkness."[18] And Hillman, echoing Neil Micklem, says: "There is an intolerable aspect to *every* image as image. Its habitation in the undersense of things is their underworld and `death.'"[19] Or Michael Perlman: "The theme of death is always involved since images are themselves psychic shades, remembering ghosts."[20]

We begin to be aware by being alert to the complex's volition. When we experience the tightening of the muscles, the grip around the throat, whenever necessity limits our freedom of choice, the flag of awareness can go up. Although images of our own psychic processes are always difficult to discern, it may be possible to perceive dimly the image that is trapped in the volition. Only by this pathway may we begin to find ways to alter the complex. By small adjustments in revisualizing the image we may be able to lessen its hold.

Hillman's paper on the goddess of Necessity, Ananke, illuminates how, uncomfortable as it is, necessity propels us toward our *amor fati*. Harkening back to Plato, we may say that there are only two original founding forces (arche) or first principles: *Nous* and *Ananke*. Other appropriate appellations might be Reason and Necessity. Neither can permanently conquer the other, although one may be in temporary ascendance. Life is a continual struggle with one in the dominant position now, the other at another time. Making necessity a founding principle, we reflect on its primordial strength. In compulsions, necessity dominates and image is totally obscured. Hillman elucidates:

> Necessity is experienced when one is compelled and there is no image of what is occurring. It is as if there were a relation—even an inverse proportion—between images and drivenness: the more the image and the altar, the less the blind necessity. The more the compulsion, the less we are able to sacrifice, to connect our personal compulsion with something divine.[21]

This is a profoundly different approach to will and compulsion. Their supernatural hold on us cannot be broken by any simple act of willful determination. No matter how adamant our refusal to yield to our obsessions, we are doomed to failure. Only through spiritual conversion can we alter our fiercest compulsions, our addictions. Yet how encouraging that our destiny lies in our compulsions, for they may lead to spiritual awakening.

As we begin to understand a complex intellectually, we must allow ourselves to be emotionally altered. This means to feel it in our body, to feel how the distress, anxiety, or fear that triggers them reacts on our body. It takes an emotional experience to liberate us and bring about the necessary transformation of energies.

The linkage of emotional necessity with spirit explains why Hillman says that ultimately Aphrodite (goddess of love) and Ananke (necessity) are interchangeable. Each grabs us, disturbs us into awareness, and determines our soul's destiny. Each affiliates with Eros; each works closely with Nemesis (revenge). Citing early philosophy, Hillman points out: "Two of the four powers present at birth are Eros and Ananke, and they are paired. Eros is the kiss, and Ananke, the knot or tie."[22] While it is startling that Eros or Aphrodite are paired with necessity, what is less obvious is that either the acute compulsive complexes that won't let go (Ananke) or the unremitting desire to transform ugliness into beauty (Aphrodite) can lead us unsuspectingly and unremittingly toward spiritual understanding, as we seek release from the implacable pressure of our most willful responses.

Bachelard and Complexes
Embedded in Culture

A complex is essentially a psychic transformer.
GASTON BACHELARD, *Water and Dreams*

Psychic life is based in the complex, and pathologizing
never comes to an end.
JAMES HILLMAN, "On the Necessity of
Abnormal Psychology: Ananke and Athena"

Complexes derive not only from our personal life story but also from our interaction with natural instincts and cultural conditioning. Induced by external factors, they are difficult to discern, having been assimilated through a cultural prism that determines the way we perceive our world. In a sense cultural complexes resemble a matrix onto which we overlay successive new experiences. We are probably less aware of their osmotic absorption in our lives than we are of anger, envy, jealousy, and other personal-feeling complexes that erupt and make their presence inescapable.

Emerging from our responses to the natural world and blending in unexpected ways with societal conventions, complexes become in effect a cultural embossment on our personal history. Jung, in particular, acknowledged the necessity of examining these collective factors: "Our psychology takes account of the cultural as well as the natural man."[1]

Cultural complexes cause us to respect one type of behavior and to abhor another. Without wishing to stereotype, we might think of "inscrutability" as an admired Japanese trait, while "friendliness" or "openness" might be considered more generic to America. For those living in a culture that doesn't parallel natural inclinations, considerable pain may emerge in the adaptive process. In addition to the personal history that psychoanalysis attempts to raise to consciousness, the raising of culturally defining parameters is significant too. We can do this by reflecting on what is constellated collectively in our time. By viewing our cultural heroes and heroines, we create a yardstick for collective characterization. These objects of our fascination can embody deep longings or can be a secret attraction, a voyeuristic urge. Only this can explain the cult worship of a Michael Jackson or Madonna, a John Wayne or Marilyn Monroe. Cultural heroes of more enduring stature—such as Oedipus, Prometheus, Don Quixote, Hamlet, Helen, and Pandora—offer far more profound insights into the ageless dilemmas of human nature.

Bachelard is adept at supplying images that increase our understanding of such cultural complexity. He defines cultural complexes as "unreflective attitudes which control the very operation of reflective thought."[2] On the personal level his definition of complex differs from traditional psychology, because he is unconcerned with repression or sublimation. Using an image from botany, he claims interest only in the plant above the cut where the graft has taken hold, not in the fertilizer. He contends that each of the four seminal elements—earth, air, fire, and water—evoke associations of imagery that are helpful in understanding our responses to an animate world. Poets, philosophers, and medieval alchemists have long held that we sustain a fundamental relationship to the elements. Bachelard amplifies how these links are manifested in individual personalities. He receives credit from Edward Casey for probing the fourfold nature of experience that Jung began but didn't complete:

> It took the genius of Gaston Bachelard to suggest how this gap
> in Jung's theorizing [explicit analysis of active imagination in
> terms of fourfoldness] might be filled. Bachelard, who was also
> a student of alchemy, noticed the striking analogy between the
> four ancient elements and the four medieval humors.[3]

Thus instead of the usual Jungian hermeneutic, I will assume a
Bachelardian stance: I will adopt an imaginative openness to the tangibles of the world. Each encounter with matter, each material alliance
rouses the desire to touch, or to conquer the element, and therefore
evokes responsive imaging. Distinctive complexes develop in association
with the imagination of matter in each traditional group; Bachelard calls
them "the hormones of the imagination." By matching these qualities
with individual personality traits, we obtain an amplified portrait of elemental proclivities, a mirror in which to view our reactions. To over-
simplify a bit, we could say that those who are drawn to water respond
to the always changeable, always profound depths of experience. They
are reflective. Those drawn to air value a sense of freedom and lightness, leading to upward, aspiring thinking. Those who associate with
the earth veer toward stability, endurance, practicality, and determination. Those who respond to fire embody liveliness, emotional intensity,
and the heroic. All of us have moments of strong affiliation with each
element, but we have a dominant inclination that remains constant in
our interaction with matter.

We are indebted to Casey for drawing this scholarly distinction
between material and formal imagination in Bachelard's schema:

> He [Bachelard] advances the thesis that the reader's material
> imagination—which is to be distinguished from the formal
> imagination that operates in understanding mathematics and
> natural science—contains *in nuce* four types of elemental imag-
> ining, but that in fact it will resonate most fully when confront-
> ed with literary images featuring just one or two preferred ele-
> ments. Correspondingly, a poet's imagination will tend to
> express itself in terms of certain elements and not others: Poe's
> imagination is basically aqueous, E.T.A. Hoffman's pyric,
> Shelly's aerial, and Rilke's telluric.[4]

Bachelard regards both water, which is responsive to external forces
that move it, and receptive earth as "feminine" dominants. Air, which ini-

tiates action, and fire, the aggressor, are regarded as "masculine" energies. However, each element combines both active and passive manifestations, both fear and exaltation, as would be expected of archetypal images.

Those complexes whose nuclear image is fire are singularly dramatic in demonstrating how will consolidates and concentrates in order to supply the energy needed for materializing desires. What constitutes the force of a complex, what gives it dynamism, is the sum of the contradictions it amasses in itself. Because fire images embody the most vivid contrasts of any element (a beneficent sun versus hellfire, a raging forest fire versus the gentle warmth of a fireplace), these complexes also incorporate the greatest tension. Their inherent contradictions supply the energy of the complex. It is understandable then why fire complexes tend to be the most obsessive, the most difficult to budge. When a complex holds sway, we are possessed by the archetype. Desire is caught in the vortex and will doesn't have its way.

In *The Psychoanalysis of Fire*, Bachelard's first foray into elemental imagination, he explains how the Novalis Complex raises to awareness the prehistoric but still present sexualized image of igniting fire by rubbing two objects together. This complex revives the physical desire to experience the internal warmth of another but also metaphorically to probe any subject in order to experience its deepest nature. What is aroused is the instinct for possession: "This need to *penetrate*, to go to the *interior* of things, to the *interior* of beings, is one attraction of the intuition of inner heat."[5] It is not difficult to make the imaginal connection of fire with desire when we yearn for possession or burn with jealousy over loss.

The Promethean Complex, so invasive in our time, is the subject of the next chapter. Bachelard describes it as "the problem of clever disobedience," the problem of stealing rightful power from the gods. He also links it to the desire to know more than the parent: "the Oedipus complex of the life of the intellect."[6]

A complex named for Faust might also be envisioned—a genetic derivative of the Promethean and Novalis, but with the goal of penetrating the heart of *all* mystery. Goethe gave us a masterful mythological rendition of the Faustian urge, while recasting a fundamental archetypal complex that had been at the heart of Western tradition, even before Marlowe's *Dr. Faustus*.

The Jupiter Complex is related, because Zeus (Jupiter) and Prometheus are bound eternally in a competitive dyad. Once again, relying on Bachelard, this complex is activated by "insane levels of human pride" and vibrates between the two opposing polarities of pride and humility. It "possesses amazing powers of self-disguise. Very often a Jupiter Complex is concealed beneath an appearance of modesty. Pride and modesty constitute as intricate an ambivalence as love and hate."[7]

Amplifying the image of fire, Bachelard names another scarcely less important complex after Empedocles. In history and legend the pre-Socratic philosopher lived in Sicily from 490-430 B.C. To demonstrate his theories, Empedocles devised a spherical model, applying the geometrical figure to both cosmic and personal realms of being. The sphere is alternately sundered by Strife and then returned to a perfect whole by Love. Hatred and Love, like Being and Non-Being, are forever bound together. Love of life is juxtaposed with hatred of loss of being. The Empedocles Complex centers around the desire to spend one's energies passionately in daring acts that reveal the essence of one's soul, to define one's personal identity at whatever cost. We discover it in the will to defy death, or in our insistence that death make a statement about the significance of living.

Empedocles chose to expire by jumping into the volcano of Mount Etna. Thus the Empedocles Complex arrays life's vitality against the need to die a dramatic, heroic death, preferably at the moment of one's choosing. Bachelard describes this complex as fascination with the danger of fire, comparing it to the moth so attracted by the flame's vitality that its reckless proximity leads to a charred end. The moth is "a tiny Empedocles." By extension, the images of the self-immolation of the moth, Icarus in the sun, Empedocles in the volcano—all are fatal extensions of the verticalizing will that defies limitation and thus is an outgrowth of the Promethean urge. Bachelard describes the fatal moment of choice: "Here, in the instant, [when] human desire gives itself over freely to non-desire, human will itself may be apprehended clearly. Being and nothingness are abstract opposites insofar as contradiction is concerned: I desire and will be able to desire no longer."[8]

Yeats also displays an unmistakable attraction for the imagery of fire, with both his poetry and his plays revealing a full-blown Empedocles

Complex. The brilliant Irish poet often identifies the image with desire. For example, "The Mask" begins with a directive: "Put off that mask of burning gold/With emerald eyes." After questioning if the mask conceals love or deceit, the poem ends with these lines: "What matter, so there is but fire/In you, in me?"[9] We see a similar fire linkage not only in sexual attraction, but in *all* desire. In the last stanza of "Two Songs from a Play," the imagination's fire is exhausted in the act of seeking the heart's desires:

> Everything that man esteems
> Endures a moment or a day.
> Love's pleasure drives his love away,
> The painter's brush consumes his dreams;
> The herald's cry, the soldier's tread
> Exhaust his glory and his might:
> Whatever flames upon the night
> Man's own resinous heart has fed.[10]

Note the concentration of fiery images in the last two lines. Fire is the element of Eros, and where there is fire, there is desire. Impulses, intuitions, inclinations, tendencies, compulsions are all interventions of the *daimon*, the fire in the breast, the blood of desire.

Yeats's immortal "Sailing to Byzantium" is laden with fire imagery that purifies the soul's desire for endless experience. Like cures like. As in the "Fire Sermon" of the Buddha, fire purges the fire of desire:

> O sages standing in God's holy fire
> As in the gold mosaic of a wall,
> Come from a holy fire, perne in a gyre,
> And be the singing-masters of my soul.[11]

The companion poem, "Byzantium," describes the final moment of the long voyage of discovery of the nature of desire. It reverberates with lyrical images of a supernal fire that consumes and yet ever renews, a recurrent theme of Yeats:

> At midnight on the Emperor's pavement flit
> Flames that no faggot feeds, nor steel has lit,
> Nor storm disturbs, flames begotten of flame,
> Where blood-begotten spirits come
> And all complexities of fury leave,
> Dying into a dance,

An agony of trance,
An agony of flame that cannot singe a sleeve.[12]

Flame and fury coalesce in a moment of intense stasis before the tumultuous natural world crowds in again:

Marbles of the dancing floor
Break bitter furies of complexity,
Those images that yet
Fresh images beget,
That dolphin-torn, that gong-tormented sea. [13]

We could identify an infinite number of additional cultural complexes, the yardstick being their hold on the collective imagination through
the centuries. A Hamlet Complex comes into play when will falters and
cannot trust intuition; similarly, a Don Quixote Complex when honor
is worth defending at whatever foolish cost. All figures (literary, historical or religious) that speak to the truth of the soul at a mythological
level provide paradigms for self-exploration. My examples are chiefly
from the Western poetic-mythological sphere, but only because I am
more familiar with its traditions. An analysis of Oriental or African literature would undoubtedly uncover many soul images of those cultures.

What I call the Tristan Complex is related to the Empedocles—the
same willingness to risk everything for the ecstasy of the fire of passions, in this case those doomed to be perpetually unfulfilled. Eleanor
Bertine explains that only a magical potion makes this blinding to
responsibilities possible:

Perhaps the supreme expression of the daemonic, force-of-nature
character of erotic love has been given by Wagner in his *Tristan
and Isolde*. There the irresistible flood of passion sweeps aside all
ordinary human values and the lovers—their individual wills
helpless against it—are inexorably rushed toward death, the only
possible outcome. To justify their complete absorption in this
one-sided drive, regardless of Tristan's personal knightly duty to
King Mark, Wagner introduces the motif of the love potion, pure
magic, which abrogates the power of the conscious will.[14]

The original myth glorified nonmarital love, the thrill coming in part
from the denial of convention and the profanation of sacred vows. Today,
adulterous love has been robbed of that illicit aura, because it has

become so commonplace. Prohibition strengthens the impulse; permission lessens the desire. Yet there are still people titillated by the thought of abandoning all commitments for the sake of guilt-filled interludes. Denis de Rougemont proposes a "mythanalysis" to clarify our current motives, to determine if we are still under the romantic sway of Tristan and Isolde. The Tristan Complex is a desire for unlimited, even unattainable passion, an urge diminished by this permissive environment. As de Rougemont concludes, "The absence of the sacred dims the passions."[15] Yet this complex still resides within us, egging on our impulse to deceive or shock the world, to pursue desire for desire's sake. The affair between Lara and Dr. Zhivago in Boris Pasternak's novel and the one detailed in Vladimir Nabokov's *Lolita* are cited by de Rougemont as twentieth-century embodiments of the Tristan Complex, which still enthralls.

A slight alteration can produce a Don Juan Complex because Tristans are "Don Juans in slow time," according to de Rougement. All the fire is consumed in the chase, with nothing left for consummation. Courtship—the genteel pursuit of male or female—is replaced by conquest. An impersonal quality permeates every affair—another scalp added to the belt. With a Don Juan complex, each successful seduction enlarges the ego but does nothing to enlarge the capacity to love. "No love for Don Juan, only desire; and not for his 'neighbor' but only for objects,"[16] is the way de Rougemont describes it. Pierre-Ambrose F. Choderlos de Laclos's novel *Les Liaisons Dangereuses* captures the devastation of the Don Juan Complex. Often this sterile syndrome masks its true motivation—fear of impotency or of being unable to give oneself fully to another. The refrain, so often heard today, about the difficulty of finding someone to love may actually point in the opposite direction—to an inability to love the other truly.

Bachelard often links cultural complexes with either historical or literary characters. In *Water and Dreams* he names a complex after Ophelia. It embodies a circular, sucking descent in which we feel we are drowning in our woes, like Shakespeare's tragic heroine. In Bachelard's view the image of water provides an easily accessible connection between watery death and disaster: "Her name is the symbol for a great law of the imagination. The imagination of misfortune and death finds in the element of water a particularly powerful and natural material image."[17]

The Swinburne Complex, on the other hand, involves the conquest of water, rather than being seduced by it. In swimming, for instance, water is subdued, a feat that reinforces the will: "More than anyone else, the swimmer can say: the world is my will; the world is my provocation. It is I who stir up the sea."[18]

The Xerxes Complex, as perceived by Bachelard, in the same work, takes its name from the Persian leader who attempted to quell the Athenians at Thermopylae but finally capitulated to them at Salamis. When some of his troops drowned crossing the Hellespont, he ordered 500 lashes inflicted on the water. Similarly a child throws stones at the retreating sea, gaining a sense of power over an element, yet knowing when to flee as a new wave breaks. In both cases it is a complex of will, of wishing to punish someone or something unable to resist (even though the water is blissfully impervious to such ploys). This complex constellates whenever we blame other sources for our mistakes or stupidity. People who work for us, or young, dependent children are often foils for all our Xerxes tendencies. Against ourselves as well, we can invoke this complex through self-flagellation for supposed mistakes.

We can never gauge the depth or breadth of all our complexes, but relating them to classical mythological imagery provides an access tool. We could name a complex for Atlas and recognize it as part of earth imagery. Here we feel that we bear on our shoulders the crushing weight of the world with no Hercules in the wings to assume the burden. Women often feel the Atlas Complex in the imposition of too much lone responsibility in child raising, particularly as a single parent, or when their partner contributes little. Anyone in business feels this onerous burden if unsupported by associates in problem-solving.

Pursuing Bachelard's notion of cultural intrusion, we broaden our awareness of where and how we may be trapped. The Sisyphus Complex derives from the legendary son of Aeolus, ruler of Corinth, who was banned to Tartarus for evil deeds. Doomed in perpetuity to push a boulder up a mountain, only to have it roll down every time he neared the crest, Sisyphus forges an image of endlessly repetitive and unappreciated chores. It can happen with household drudgery, or with any work we are unable to infuse with imagination or purpose other than utility. The only solace for those chained to such apparently futile

tasks (which befall all of us at one time or another) may be this observation by an anonymous sage: "Recognition of the complex as our fate is
the beginning of finding meaning in an otherwise meaningless fatalism."
When we have trouble bringing creativity to any task, the tedium of
repetition can only be redeemed by recognizing it as our love gift to the
world or, at the least, to people we care about.

Sisyphus would be an appropriate image for all obsessive-compulsive
disorders. Translating Sisyphus's pain and sense of futility into a more
positive emotion might lead to better results. In his interpretation of
the myth, Albert Camus emphasizes the joy of striving to overcome a
challenge, whatever the outcome: "If the descent is thus sometimes per-
formed in sorrow, it can also take place in joy.... The struggle toward
the heights is enough to fill a man's heart. One must imagine Sisyphus
happy."[19] (Sorry, I can't.)

A demonic complex could appropriately be named after Tantalus,
son of Zeus and father of Pelops and Niobe. Here the insatiable side of
unrealized desire is unveiled. Accused of stealing ambrosia and nectar
from the gods and goddesses, and, more diabolically, of testing the
Olympians by serving the flesh of his son Pelops to them at a banquet,
Tantalus was exiled to the underworld and there inflicted with a raging
thirst. Fiendishly, the waters receded every time he attempted to drink.
Thus the word "tantalize" relates to that which is always just out of
reach. Not a normal striving for improvement but rather a crazed grasp
for what we think we should possess, a Tantalus Complex implies a
satanic dissatisfaction with our blessings. It is the shadow side of desire.

The element of air suggests a high-flying complex named for Icarus
involving the endless inflation of our own worth. The gods would thus
be tempted to clip our wings, reminding us that we are Earth-bound
creatures. The higher our soaring pomposities carry us, the more
resounding and abject the crash. Those who disdain the mundane or
practical are often imbued with air complexes, with a yearning to
remain detached, free of earthly shackles.

In illustrating the poetic imagery of air, Bachelard recalls the historical Nietzsche who was a poet of high, cold air and who obtained physical
renewal in his early life by striding through vigorous mountain winds.
He fought being Earth-bound. The coupling of Nietzsche with air sug-

gests his abiding love of freedom and his belief that the strength of the will must always be fortified. Can we extrapolate and say that, with a Nietzsche Complex carried to its apogee, we feel the desire to escape human limitations of time and place—we will to be above it all? "It [coldness] corresponds to one of the greatest principles of Nietzschean cosmology: *cold*, the cold of the heights and glaciers and uncontrollable winds.... Thanks to cold, air acquires *offensive qualities*; it takes on 'joyous malice' that awakens the will to power, a will to react coldly, in the ultimate freedom of coldness, with a cold will,"[20] Bachelard adds.

Bachelard utilizes the eccentric French poet, Lautréamont, to illustrate "a complex that is clearer than all the others, a dangerous, terrifying, powerfully unnerving one."[21] In his original but highly unusual work, *Le Maldoror*, Lautréamont associates human will with the animal in us. Amplifying the image of the claw—a "symbol of pure volition"— Bachelard says the instinctual response to an attack is born of fear. This immediate, always-close-to-the-surface instinct for cruelty characterizes the Lautréamont Complex: "How impoverished and cumbersome is the will-to-live of Schopenhauer compared to the will-to-attack of Lautréamont!"[22] Although defensiveness can be cruel when aroused, the Lautréamont Complex is not identical with protective anger. Bachelard claims that defense is round, trying to avoid pain or deflect the blow, but attack is pointed. With a Lautréamont Complex, one enjoys the sadistic act, the swift thrust of the rapier.

To Bachelard, will is the binding force of psychological complexes. He broadens our definition of will, even restoring its honored name as a central aspect of human nature. Psychology tells us that complexes center around an inflexible image. Will, originally responsive to experiences, assembled the images that reverberate in our complexes. Because complexes have generally been formed in a prereflective stage of early life, we are powerless to change them through a simple, conscious decision to do so. We cannot will them away. Nor can will be easily released or the images uncoupled from their tedious, repetitive pattern of occurrence. As Bachelard stresses: "One never does any good against one's will, that is to say, against one's dreams."[23] Our conscious will is overridden by our obsessions and compulsions. We can only change by dreaming better.

The Promethean Will

Ah, but a man's reach must exceed his grasp,
or what's a heaven for?
ROBERT BROWNING, "Andrea del Sarto"

Hope is the pathological belief in the occurrence
of the impossible.
H. L. MENCKEN, *Chrestomathy*

Prometheus, the Titan who stole fire in a reed from the Olympian gods, casts his long shadow over our age. His gift to humanity of the essential tool—fire—and of the craftsmanship that made possible the transformation of the raw into the edible, of clay into the pot, was obviously an enduring boon to mankind. If not for his daring theft, the immortals might never have released this mighty force for the benefit of lowly humankind. So doesn't it seem unjust that Zeus punished him so severely—and for such a protracted period? Chained to a rock, he had his liver eaten by Zeus's eagle each night and then renewed each day. For many years I sympathized with him. But now, because of the excessive impact of Prometheus on our time, I have begun to understand Zeus's point of view: to see the impetuous Titan's act as one of hubristic defiance, a way of expressing his contempt for any heavenly edict. In effect, he was saying, "I'll decide; forget the gods!"

Prometheus's bequest to humanity is the gift of the essential element of transformation, that which can change the coarse substance into a consumable or an artistic end product—in effect, a fabulous gift. In an analogous way it is the spiritual gift of imagination. Among current scholars, Donald Cowan emphasizes that "The Promethean fire is imagination, not simply skills, or reason; and imagination is the power from a divine source whereby matter is permeated with spirit."[1]

In this century we have become the first to fail to acknowledge that imagination is a spirit manifestation, a divine spark. For instance, we never consider it necessary to begin a creative endeavor with an appeal to the Muses to sing through our words. Cowan's concern is that "the theft of so mighty a power, even though man did not himself do the deed, allows the human race to declare its independence from divine order, and through imagination and inventiveness, elevate the human lot."[2]

Then too, Prometheus's gift was tainted, since it carried the curse of a blood feud. It was motivated by his desire for revenge, because Zeus orchestrated the Olympian destruction of his generation of Titans. Prometheus wanted humankind to be able to challenge and even flout the gods and goddesses in return.

Today this forgetfulness of divine guidance is exacting a heavy toll. A continuing shift toward secularism, toward the abandonment of the sacred in our daily lives, is cresting. The lack of connection with the spiritual is accompanied by an elevation of the importance of individual choice. Frances G. Wickes writes about the consequences of choice:

> "Prometheus stole the divine fire, the creative flame; he who consciously accepts his right to individual choice steals an attribute of God. Through this theft he brings upon himself the punishment of consciousness, of responsibility, of self-awareness, and of self-judgment. Yet this theft is also a gift, for the inborn creative spark, which makes the theft possible, is the potential of divinity implanted in man in the act of creation; and the punishment, which is also the gift, is that he must now enter upon a way of transformation, a journey through darkness into light."[3]

Few of us truly grasp the degree to which we have unleashed the Promethean will. As Northrop Frye says, we have raised "the human state to a quasi-divine destiny."[4]

Negative consequences of the gift which was also a theft have emerged. Along with the tremendous power over nature that fire provided came the questionable "blind hopefulness" of which Aeschylus spoke in "Prometheus Bound," plus a general miasma induced by lack of acceptance of limits. Even though granted the divine gift of creative transformation, humans often found themselves unable to foresee boundaries, stipulations, and the perilous repercussions their actions produced. In his book *Christ and Prometheus*, William F. Lynch has a baleful description of modern Titanism:

> The Prometheanism which we have often associated with the image of secularity itself is a rigid, simplistic, unilinear image of movement through the human, based on power and the will and ultimately involving a lack of imagination. It is an image of power, victory, invention, engineering, unilinear progress, and unilinear evolution, the conquest of the world.[5]

In his poem "Prometheus Unbound," Percy Bysshe Shelley accurately foresaw Prometheus's acceptance as the secular god in Western intellectual recesses. Indeed, everyone in our culture today shares some degree of Promethean attributes. In Bachelard's view of this epoch, "all educated persons organize their thinking around one figure of Prometheus or another.... There is a personal Prometheus for everyone."[6] This willful deity is the prototypical American hero, always probing for new realms to conquer, quickly dismissive of past burdens or debts. His special gift is peering into the future, and he finds it teeming with opportunity. He is the future tense governing our projections. When we say, "I will learn," we are projecting our Promethean urge. Prometheus is the will to new knowledge, the spur to experimentation. He is also our power overdrive, our will to exceed limits, our denial of all restraints, our defiance of the gods in the cause of self-aggrandizement, our glorification of what it means to be human. The Prometheus complex reigns today in the secular environs of "exhausted spirituality" (Solzhenitsyn's phrase), ever generating the lamentable belief that the gods are passé.

While recognizing that will is needed to stay the course, we should realize how often it becomes overextended, muscle-bound, in effect Promethean. In earlier times, poets, philosophers, and theologians engaged in fierce debate about the proper use of the will. A consistent thread woven throughout Christian theology—from Abraham, Moses, and Job to Heidegger, Kierkegaard, and Martin Buber—has been fabricated around the conflict. In the seventeenth century, Milton focused on those aspects of choice belonging to mankind and those belonging to divine Will. He contended that paradise is lost when we forget our derivative link with the Heavenly Father and that man's will is devilish when it runs counter to God's. Struggling to recognize God's place in an increasingly secular world, John Donne expressed in his "Holy Sonnet XIV" the difficulty of keeping attuned to God's Will through the fragile faculty of human reason. He used the language of desire to address will that wavers in its devotion: "Batter my heart, three-personned God.... Take me to You, imprison me, for I,/Except You'enthrall me, never shall be free,/Nor ever chaste, except You ravish me."[7]

As the modern world emerged and religious urges weakened, Shakespeare's Iago could be regarded as a predecessor of Machiavelli in describing will as the instrument of choice in human nature and one that could work to bend another's purpose to one's own:

> Our bodies are gardens; to the which, our wills are gardeners: so that if we will plant nettles, or sow lettuce; set hyssop and weed up thyme, supply it with one gender of herbs, or distract it with many, either to have it sterile with idleness, or manicured with industry; why the power and corrigible authority of this lies in our wills. (*Othello* 1.3.320-326)

In the nineteenth century, Schopenhauer and then Nietzsche emphasized the significance of the will, but not in guiding man toward God. Will power became a desirable quality in itself, underpinning leadership and dominance. At the other end of the scale, lack of will along with certain willful aberrations became subjects of poetic interest for the English Romantic movement and the French Symbolists. In Russian literature the novelist Ivan Goncharov (1812-1891) created the bizarre character of Oblomov (in a novel of the same name) that quickly became an archetypal masterpiece. When his romance failed to flower, the young aristocrat Oblomov found he had little will to accomplish anything. Finally his energy for dealing with people and problems evanesced so that he could no longer get out of bed. "Oblomovism" became a recognized word for lassitude or paralysis of the will. "One cannot will desire," as Mary Watkins says.[8]

Acknowledging the difficulty of precise delineations, we can still attempt to weigh will power in its more conscious applications on a quantitative scale from Willfulness to Hopelessness. Any current evaluation must be all-encompassing, for never has humanity been more tormented between feelings of inflation on one hand and powerlessness and despair on the other, both in individual personal problems and as a omniprevalent aspect of collective consciousness. An arbitrary assembly of the quantitative distinctions of will on a scale from overzealous to inadequate might appear thus:

> Willfulness—obstinacy, disregard of other's needs.
> Strong Will—imaging a goal, adhering to a purpose.
> Wanting—determination, accompanied by action.
> Wishing—passively wanting, fantasizing, reverie.
> Dreaming—images, less conscious direction of will.
> Vacillation—wavering will, irresolution.
> Apathy—little will energy, indifference.
> Hopelessness—no will energy, lassitude.
> Despair—no will or imagination of any alternatives.
> Suicide—giving up, cashing in, checking out.

Do we have free will? Or is our destiny predetermined? These questions have preoccupied other centuries more deeply than our own. Always admired in the West for its quality of tenacity, will requires focus and direction. But no longer does religion inspire and shape it. Individual will-to-success is the path to glory. The prayer "Let Thy will be done, on Earth as it is in Heaven" is mostly lip service.

The ultimate expression of admiration of the personal, secular will is detailed in Nietzsche's *Will to Power*. To the question, how does one become stronger, he answers:

> 1) By coming to decisions slowly and by clinging tenaciously to what one has decided.... The sudden and the changeable: the two species of weakness... 2) Beware of the good natured! Association with them makes one languid. 3) All associations are good that make one practice the weapons of defense and

offense that reside in one's instincts. All one's inventiveness
should be bent toward testing one's strength of will.[9]

The tone of defiance is unmistakable. Dominance in life depends on that
strength of will one is able consistently to enforce—tenacity under
stress.

Nietzsche insists that individualism is only a modest stage of the will
to power, not the ultimate goal. He gives three criteria for delineating
desire and will:

> The man of will says I want.
> The man of desire says I wish.
> The man of faith says I know.

Wishing leaves one in a passive state of longing; only willing supplies
the energy of action. In Yeats's words, "Only the greatest obstacle that
can be contemplated without despair rouses the soul to full intensity."[10]

To Nietzsche happiness is not desire's apogee, only power. "One
must be English," he writes, "to be able to believe that man always seeks
his advantage. Our desires want to violate things with a protracted passion—their accumulated strength seeks resistance."[11] This definition
makes will into a counter-will, toughened by opposition to it.

The ultimate glorification of Nietzschean will may be in turning man
into God. In defiant tone, it proclaims: My will instead of Thy will be
done. Thus emerges Nietzschean moral justification for suicide as a personal decision in terms of time and way: "One must convert the stupid
physiological fact into a moral necessity. So to live that one can also will
at the right time to die."[12] It is not surprising that the twentieth century
lives out the Nietzschean assertion. With this total preoccupation with
materialism, God is expiring of inactivity—nothing left to do.

Among contemporary writers Raphael López-Pedraza perceptively
criticizes choosing one's own way of death as "a Titanic, Romantic inflation, coupled with an avoidance of the constant reflection which death
plays alongside life—the value of life that comes from the reflection of
death."[13] Certainly a longer view of the future includes some concept of
what happens after we die. The twentieth century is the first in which
many live without the solace, or hope, of an afterlife. Is it any wonder
that we vigorously repress the idea of death when hope of immortality
has dwindled?

López-Pedraza believes a characteristic of our time is its inability to make images. He identifies psychopathology as modern-day "Titanism," driven by image-less compulsions. I read this as a summons to enlist images in order to allow will to be cosmically creative, certainly not as a direction to be more willful.

In mythology the majority of the Titans ended up in Tartarus or Hell. Prometheus was actually one of the more well-regarded of his generation of Titans, but his name came to symbolize, in my judgment, the inflation of desires, overblown one moment and totally blown away with disappointment the next. When not in the euphoric mode, we may feel the counter sensation of being chained permanently to a rock with no vision of any foreseeable future, our hopes dashed cruelly. This is the core problem of our Promethean era: hope is out of joint—either too expansive or too constrained. As the Greeks knew, hope is hard to fathom and not unambiguous. In Aeschylus's *Prometheus Bound*, the Titan says: "I made men cease to live with death in sight," and instead "blind hopes I caused to dwell in them."[14] Hope is demonic when it takes the form of self-delusion. Hope and its improper use pushes us into Titanism. The word Titan derives from *titanein*, "to overreach oneself," and from *tises*, "punishment."[15] To be driven to excess and to suffer subsequent punishment is the nature of the Titanic (even when a ship?). Karl Kerényi faults this generation that preceded the Olympians, saying "the Titans had overreached themselves in their foolhardiness."[16]

As part of Prometheus's punishment, the goddess Pandora was fashioned by Hephaestus on Zeus's orders to pay back the theft of fire. In *Works and Days*, Hesiod's rather misogynous account, Pandora is called "an evil thing" who gets all the blame for mankind's ills. This story may have had its genesis in a political attempt by the newly emerging pre-Homeric patriarchy to downgrade the terrible power of the earlier earth goddesses. Prometheus warns Epimetheus against accepting any gifts from Zeus. Why is it that Hope, one of Pandora's gifts, remains hidden from mankind? Is Hope an illusion or a blessing?

In other renditions, Pandora is called the goddess "who is bringer of all," acknowledging her positive attributes. Since pan means "all," her name, Pan-dora, can be translated as "all-gifted," Gail Thomas explains.[17] In a masterful interpretation, Thomas sees Pandora as "the bearer of hope, the blind assurance of the continuance of life that goes together with the realization of mortality."[18] Thomas elaborates: "She [Pandora] becomes the image we experience attempting to live in the midst of the real and the ideal. Pandora, the beautiful, the lure of matter, of material forms, of unexpected gifts, moves us. But in our embrace of her we acknowledge mortality…. She sparkles and shines, compels our passions and desires, then fades, creating in us the profound awareness of age, of limited ability, of faded glory."[19] Thus she brings an important sense of the finite. Through her we appreciate all the glories of the earthly existence, its beauty, our memories, our desires, but we also are reminded of our debt to the Gods. And though we may have to face the fact of death, through her we are again bonded to the Gods, a tie that Prometheus attempted to sunder. "Pandora as gift breaks the titanic hybris; man confronts his mortality through reflection of the divine. A new bond—the acceptance of the mortal condition—limits man's freedom of motion,"[20] Thomas adds.

If we think of Hope as being procreative, fertile, and generative of the future, then Hope embodies positive qualities, albeit of an often-dreaded feminine nature. If we think of Hope as an illusion obscuring truth and reality, we might conclude that mankind is abysmally ignorant when hopeful—perhaps even blaming the feminine for this monumental miscalculation.

The *pithos* or box, oftentimes called a jar, which is so intrinsic to the image of Pandora, is ambiguous too. Some see it as kin to the Coptic jar that holds the vital organs after death. Thus Pandora reminds mankind of its mortality (which is probably why she is hated). Polly Young-Eisendrath and Florence Wiedemann provide a provocative study:

> Hope remained in the jar, resulting in some versions of Pandora as a hopeful figure who, like Eve, stands at the juncture between divinity and humanity.
>
> We now remember Pandora largely for having opened this jar, later called a "box." Her curiosity seems wastefully evil to humans who want to be immortal like the gods. Looked at from a theogonic perspective, Pandora's curiosity reconnects her to those powers hidden in the earth, the natural powers of death which relate to her origins as an earth goddess.[21]

In *Aesop's Fables* the poet Babrius tells a different tale with less blame placed upon Pandora and more simply on mankind's curiosity:

> Zeus once collected in a jar
> All of the useful things there are,
> And put it covered up beside
> A man, who by temptation tried
> And keen to know just what it hid,
> With weakened will removed the lid,
> And let the contents out to fly
> To the God's dwellings in the sky,
> But Hope alone was left within,
> Caught by the cover, and kept in
> When he had put it on again.
> So Hope remains behind with men,
> Pledged to give each the useful things
> Which had escaped from us on wings.[22]

Emily Dickinson, in one of her poems (Johnson 254), also speaks of hope as winged: "'Hope' is the thing with feathers—/That perches in the soul—/And sings the tune without the words—/And never stops—at all—"

Dante's message affirms that we must never lose hope if we are to find salvation. The sign at the entrance of the *Inferno* warns: "Abandon all hope ye who enter here." Hopelessness equates with hell; hell is hopelessness. Dante bears witness that we can achieve no upward mobility, or forward motion, or even a change of pace in the soul's journey, without a sense of hope. The initiation of the process and the attainment of the summit of Mount Purgatory are possible only as long as "hope bears a leaf that is green."

Hope linked to the notion of man's perfectibility became so dominant in the nineteenth century that many in the twentieth began to question the viability of continuous growth. Jung often took a negative attitude toward wishing, as though it were the handmaiden of those who lacked the physical strength and courage to press will into action. He believed that women were more susceptible to vain longing than men. This disapproving view contrasts with Martin Buber's more positive definition of wishing as "imaginative mutuality, judgment, passion, a joining of all that is human in a move toward what is not yet but could be." To Buber, wishing is a measure of potential.

Recently Albert Camus has given hope a pessimistic connotation by calling it a negation of life and vitality, a passive wait for the future. Camus believes that mankind shows great courage in simply carrying on, even with the knowledge that ultimately all our effort is hopeless. Is our only choice then to live for the day? With the telescoped view of time we currently espouse, with our lack of interest in historical precedent (history is presently not a popular subject in universities), don't we rob ourselves of any long vista of the future? Paradoxically, by developing the skill to plumb our personal and cultural history, not nostalgically but in pragmatic reflection of how previous experience plays into the present, don't we strengthen our capacity to look forward in hopefulness? Surely by remembering our success in previous situations, we can more easily cope with future moments of despair.

At some primal level will can stir and carry us forward even at our darkest moments. Then we are grateful for its ability to sustain us. Not just perennial optimists, but even the most gloomy find that, if they can ride out the paralyzing, energy-draining periods when depression sucks up all desire, a glimmer of hope and the will to set things right eventually return.

At the opposite end of the scale, when will rides the wave of its strength, Bachelard helps us understand how the imperative Promethean complex takes over. Always Bachelard fuses abstract qualities of personality with images of the elements, thereby grounding psychology in the phenomena of matter. For instance, the human desires of *willing* and *wanting* are joined to hoping and reaching in the image of the vertical flame, an image that Bachelard returns to frequently (although he claims water as his own preferred element): "One who dreams of the verticalizing will, who learns the lesson of the flame, realizes that he must right himself. He rediscovers the will to burn high, to go with all his strength to the summit of fervor."[23] The archetypal conjunction of fire naturally connects with Prometheus in a combination of this prevalent twentieth-century complex that infiltrates all our lives.

The Prometheus Complex has many manifestations. It represents Jung's thrust toward consciousness and Bachelard's spirit entering into the intellectual realm: "An aesthetics of the mind [*du psychisme*], or mental processes which both consolidate and energize the life of the spirit," in the French philosopher's words.[24]

Bachelard focuses attention on how the Prometheus Complex tempts us to ignore restrictions: "The many figures of Prometheus inherited from past myths and cultures have rooted themselves in us, making psychological techniques of *self-transcendence* possible.... But if these imposing figures of Prometheus are to have any psychological effect on us, they must be experienced as attempts—or, better yet, temptations—to transcend our own natures, to experience the human, more than human."[25]

The will-to-intellectuality, one aspect of an upwardly mobile imagination, easily turns into a Prometheus Complex. Describing the complex as "the intellectual mastery of fire," Bachelard recognizes that "there is in man a veritable will to intellectuality." Thus this complex involves "those tendencies which impel us *to know* as much as our fathers, more than our fathers, as much as our teachers, more than our teachers."[26] It is the desire not only to surpass one's father but also to defy the gods, to steal their fire, their creative energy. It could perhaps be considered an Oedipal-Prometheus Complex ensconced at the level of the intellect.

Freud, attracted to the Prometheus myth, made an unusual interpretation of the complex as the sublimation of instinctual life (the id) to the ego and the super ego in bringing mankind to the civilized state. "A culture-hero who is still a god," Prometheus represents "a defeat of instinctual life." Along with libido sublimation, Freud directs attention to the meaning of the punishment meted out to the Titan and the character of his act ("an outrage, a theft, a defrauding of the gods"). He saw the image of the chained Titan, his liver being eaten out each night by Zeus's eagle and then renewed each day as "an apt picture of the behavior of erotic desires, which, though daily satisfied, are daily revived." The liver was the perfect organ for punishment, because "in ancient times the liver was regarded as the seat of all passions and desires; hence a punishment like that of Prometheus was the right one for a criminal driven by instinct, who had committed an offence at the prompting of evil desires."[27] Igor Stravinsky makes this novel observation: "The Greeks must have divined that the liver is a regenerative organ, though medical science has only recently determined the fact, for otherwise Prometheus's punishment would have had no retributive meaning—the birds would have had of him no more than an hors-d'oeuvre."[28]

We know that Goethe was keenly drawn to the image of Prometheus. In his autobiography, *My Life: Poetry and Truth*, he couples himself with the god: "The fable of Prometheus came alive in me." He composed a "Prometheus Ode," a monologue addressed to Zeus, that was much discussed in German literary circles. It ends with Prometheus saying: "I am no God/Yet look on myself as not less worthy." The Ode was planned as part of a play, *Prometheus*, that was never finished. Prometheus proved unconfinable, even for a man of Goethe's genius.

In a Faustian way, with our American passion for infinitude, we reach for immediate perfectibility of mind and body, forgetting the discipline involved in even approaching these ultimate goals. As Father Lynch reminds, hope "is not absolute in its range: part of reality belongs to hopelessness." Humility, for instance, is essential if we start thinking of any lofty ideal; yet, it is conspicuously missing in those self-improvement programs that admit no limit to the ability to acquire new skills. Consider the number of how-to books on best-seller lists. A lifetime habit of learning is commendable, but expecting to master Spanish in a week or two (as some broadcast commercials suggest) is pure chimera. Again Father Lynch: "nothing creates as much hopelessness as an ideal that is not human" in its attainability.[29]

That threadbare maxim, "Where there's a will, there's a way," has a hollow Victorian ring today. The implication that nothing is beyond reach if one is determined enough exalts will over imagination. It rarely occurs to us to question whether certain wishes may in themselves be immoderate. Traditionally Americans have rebelled against the idea of limits; always, until recent years, there was new territory to explore and exploit, an easy substitute for that which we had sullied or depleted. So the virginal vision, with its prospect of endless horizons and ever-greener pastures, tended to eclipse whatever beauty still remained in our immediate surroundings. In his poem "Shadows," Williams Carlos Williams recognizes this: "The instant trivial as it is/is all we have/unless—unless/things the imagination feeds upon,/the scent of the rose/startles us anew" (*Pictures from Brueghel*).

Restless, never satiated, propelled by grandiose dreams, we tend to lose balance in our lives. The superfluous abounds in our overly congested information age. We can travel anywhere in the world, experience any titillation, possess any bauble (until our funds give out). The danger of this Promethean excessiveness is the disillusion that inevitably occurs when reality sets in. The Greeks had experience with such overextension, and they countered it by advocating the value of the golden mean. This is a principle we need to adopt both personally and culturally, recognizing that cupidity constellates deflation, as well as crime.

Stravinsky speaks of the value of limitations imposed upon an artist by the tools of his trade. They define the area in which to operate, restricting and confining it. Instead of curtailing artistic imagination, Stravinsky felt this allowed a free flow of ideas within the parameters of achievability. "Not the fact of possibilities, of course, but choice is the beginning of art," he explained. "The stained-glass artists of Chartres had few colors, and the stained-glass artists of today have hundreds of colors but no Chartres. Organs, too have more stops than ever before, but no Bach."[30]

Poets testify to the efficacy of limits, of boundaries in which individual skill becomes apparent in the ability to compress creativity. The act of choosing a verse form, a ballad or a sonnet, for example, works less as a constraint than as a stimulus to imagination by providing a container for creativity. The poetic form functions like the alchemical vessel. For transformation to occur, for the heat to fuse disparate parts into a unity, a solid container is required. Discussing the process of therapy, Hillman points to the loss of momentum that occurs if the analysand is a leaky vessel, spilling out and disbursing the essence of the experience. Without containment the energy of will and imagination evaporate from any endeavor. Circumscribed and focused, will can be adequate to the task of fulfilling the dreams of imagination, even exceeding them, if there is a form and defined boundary to our wishes.

In a world of vast possibilities or none, of creativeness or destructiveness, of too much or too little, we need ways to free our imaginations from extremes of either grandiosity or stultification. Will can run wild when desire carried by the image is ill-defined. Will requires imagination to be effective; imageless, it turns harsh and imperious.

I do not argue for the renunciation of will. How could I when our very life instinct itself is so embedded in the will? My plea is for greater awareness of the origin of desire, of how it triggers the frequently unconscious, egotistical emotions through which we energize will. Rilke calls it "the first gritty infusion of my will" (*Duino Elegies*). By examining these wellsprings of desire, we can sense their harmful potential and restrain them. If my desire does not contaminate the rights of others or take advantage of them in some fashion, then will can come into proper focus, with imagination as projector for unfolding and foreseeing the effects of will in action. The triad of will, desire, and imagination can thus function as a harmonious entity.

In similar counterbalancing fashion, Promethean will can be offset to some degree by tapping into the Titan's superior aptitude to foresee. In Adlerian psychology this ability is described as the final goal of maturity:

> Foresight is a willed understanding of the effect of one's actions—physical, mental, or emotional—on oneself and one's future and on others and their future. Foresight involves goal setting and the goal. Flexibility, sense and discrimination of values, deferring emotional reactions, sustained efforts, self-control and synchronization are all determined, governed and increased by foresight. Together they can bring about the maintenance and increase of security at which one aims and/or, what matters so much more, the decrease of the fear of insecurity.[31]

By sensibly utilizing this special Promethean ability to foresee, we feel more powerful, less insecure, and therefore able to resist the exaggerated will as power source. By infusing wishes and goals with imagination as well as will, we can evaluate possibilities before they become obsessions. We thus avail ourselves of Prometheus's strengths but curb his flaws.

Fear Interferes

The sense of death is most in apprehension.
SHAKESPEARE, "Measure for Measure"

The heart, for all it's virtues, is a restless and emotional thing,
all too easily swayed by the body.
C. G. JUNG, *Civilization in Transition*

Fear is the most pervasive of all the emotions that combine in the human psyche. It permeates every facet of our being. It feeds despair, promotes apathy, stultifies ambition. How often in our lives does fear translate the positive impulse of "I will" into the negative "I won't" or "I can't"? Far more frequently than most of us imagine.

Ambiguity lurks within each human personality, a clash between differing desires. If we engage in purposeful self-reflection, we may be able to sort out these differences and channel them constructively into a clarity of purpose. However, fear frequently insinuates itself, numbing our conscious wishes. Thus the desire to be kind is countermanded by the fear of leaving oneself defenseless. The will to be generous is thwarted by the fear of depleting one's resources. Where the ego is deficient or insecure, fear can strangle even the best of intentions.

Fear has many faces. It can be an enormous, intimidating monster, terrifying as it suddenly intersects our path, panicking us into fleeing or hiding. In another guise, fear is a tiny termite, unobtrusively boring away year after year at our emotional foundations until they fatally crumble.

The basic primordial fear of humankind is one we are born with: fear of death, or fear of dissolving into nothingness, *Thanatopsis*, the Greeks called it, a contemplation on death beginning in childhood. Deepak Chopra describes it as "the basic insecurity of mortality."[1] As we mature, many ancillary fears build on this primary one, such as fears of failure, of disgrace, of inadequacy, of losing our health, our loved mates, or children. Today fear of AIDS inhibits the free expression of sexual desires in all but the most foolhardy. Fear of the physical domination of a man or worse, of rape, plagues many women, even as they age. Marguerite Duras expresses it succinctly in *The Lover*: "I wasn't raped, but I sensed rape, like all little girls." Fear of the allure of a woman's beauty, of her feminine wiles or her power to disturb often dominates men.

In even the most loving of relationships, partners often have some difficulty adjusting to one another's desire for closeness. It is almost impossible to share a precisely equal requirement for intimacy. Some like constant touching. Some prefer a more remote approach with intense moments of passion reserved for special times. Some like to be always a little beyond reach, and, in fact, may secretly fear close contact and may never be able to cement a lasting partnership. In almost all of us some threshold of fear of intimacy can be encountered if we are pushed too hard, or if we find our partner too possessive. It is as if the physical body, with varying levels of tolerance, demands an inviolable area of surrounding space. More than a fear of intimacy, this may result from the more generic fear of losing control.

Otto Rank pinpoints two specific, primal fears—one of life, one of death. Often overlapping, they are not experienced in single, separated, one-at-a-time fashion. Freud had already defined the Eros/Thanatos conflict—the former life-enhancing, the latter pulling toward death.

The fear that life is without meaning can be an intertwined combination of both fears. The two are fused into a terror of being separated from protection and security, or simply the fear of being alone. Feeling helpless or excessively dependent will attenuate our enthusiasm for living. Even at an older age when the techniques of survival have forced us to subdue at least some aspects of the terror of being left alone, it is difficult to avoid a lingering residue of the abandonment complex. Feeling anxious, feeling inadequate to any task in life, we are prone to retreat into the silent sanctuaries of our own isolation.

Fear of Growing Old

The fear of getting old is not synonymous with the fear of death. Often this fear surfaces in teenagers. With bodily changes signaling oncoming maturity, they begin to feel the fear of adulthood and with it the fear of aging. Fear strikes at various stages on the ladder of life, but particularly as the decades roll on and we become progressively enfeebled. As Yeats versifies in his poem, "After Long Silence": "Bodily decrepitude is wisdom;/Young we loved each other and were ignorant."[2] The dual fear of poverty and declining health accompany us as we pass into traditional midlife and may induce us to be less generous, more complaining. The spectre of aging also prompts some who can afford it to resort to cosmetic surgery whenever a seam or sag appears, in keeping with our worship of perpetual youth and the athletic body. Often, rather than simple joy in healthy living, these fears haunt aerobic classes and stimulate our obsessive eating phobias.

Fear of Death

The fear of death has its paradox: it tempts us either to live more acutely or to collapse in despair. To those afraid the end will come before they have had time to crowd it all in, this fear can press the panic button. In the last decade of this millennium (probably common to the *fin de siècle* of each century), we observe many Americans in a frantic, mad rushing to see and do everything before the grim reaper beckons. "I want to live before I die," could be this century's theme song.

From the source waters of this life and death struggle, tributaries of fear flow in innumerable directions. One estuary nourishes the bigotry that motivates many unstable personalities. As June Callwood points out: "Prejudice is the product of pure fear." She adds, not so surprisingly: "Angry adults...are bigots."[3] Often the fear of inferiority exposes itself on a personal level in antisocial attitudes—a disdain for persons of other races, religions, or lesser or greater (i.e., different) economic status. On an even more profound level, bigotry translates into holocaust, or racial extermination. Fear becomes a standard tool of dictators, first in exploiting mass prejudices and then as an instrument of genocide. It is expressed tangentially when we pin the image of an evil empire onto another nation. In retrospect, how easy it is to see that anti-Soviet fear provoked the witch hunt of the McCarthy era. How easy to vilify others, to regard difference with suspicion! The battle is automatically enjoined, because others inevitably cast us in the same guise, thus cementing a fear-inspired circle of mutual hostility.

Fears can be a response to a perceived danger, or to one hardly understood, ranging from anxiety to panic. The great god Pan holds sway over a number of groundless fears. When we can be more specific about our fears, name them, give them a face, it becomes easier for us than struggling with abstract dread. An analysis of the daily newspaper will reveal that the most overworked headline verb is "to fear." From Seneca to Franklin Roosevelt, a basic verity—that fear generates fear—has been articulated in parallel terms. Seneca said, "Nothing is terrible in things except fear itself." Franklin Roosevelt echoed across the centuries: "We have nothing to fear but fear itself."

Social fears trivial to some can be acutely painful to others. Not to be invited to some function, or if invited not to have suitable attire, or not to find acceptance with our peers—any or all can cause withering anguish. The preferred response to such feelings of social inadequacy may be either to search for some permanent ways to improve self-image or to achieve understanding of how little it really matters what casual acquaintances think if we have a few cherished friends.

As we all know, the pervasive fear of failure, even before failure manifests itself, can cause paralysis of the will and self-fulfilling results. Concentrating on the positive side of our longer-range desires sometimes ameliorates the sense of shame that stems from not living up to our own immediate expectations. Chopra says that the problem lies in one's being "object"-referral rather than "subject"-referral, meaning that one runs into conflicts when tuned more to the expectations of others than to our own innate needs.[4] We also hand over control of our lives if our happiness depends upon what others think of us, upon a job, or upon our worldly successes. We relinquish power to the object of reference. If we know ourselves only through the eyes of others, it follows that fear will always haunt us. According to the Ayurvedic tradition, there are *only* two energies: fear, which is alienation; and love, which is unity. If our primary reference is self-approval, then we can become fear-cleansed and save that energy to expand our individual sense of self.

With all the negatives it inspires, fear surprisingly also can stimulate pleasure. Mild fears are exhilarating. Roller coaster rides, downhill skiing, sky diving, hang gliding, and car racing get the adrenaline going. Communal fear can be exciting: a mob forms over a real or imagined grievance and then risks violence to achieve its goals. Soldiers embarking on foreign wars, the plaudits of the crowd cheering them on, experience a tingling sense of excited apprehension. Napoleon spoke of "the joy in danger" and his love of "the excitement of battle."[5] We are always tempted by experiences that present themselves to us, just as a match tempts us to strike it. Indeed courting danger can be an effective antidote for anxiety. Mountain climbers face disabling injury or death in attempting to scale the Matterhorn or Mount Everest. Danger to them becomes an intoxicating release, a challenge that obscures the prosaic nature of their everyday lives. Whether experiencing thrills vicariously (via action films, or spy or detective stories) or precariously (doing it oneself, i.e., mountain climbing) the individual is making a statement of a need to sense peril and to conquer fear. Studies of what we find humorous (often as a relief of an underriding anxiety) indicate that male humor, as opposed to female humor, frequently reflects the fears that physical strength might fail.

Today the precarious life has become institutionalized. "Survival schools" such as Outward Bound, designed specifically to impart the skills and confidence necessary for endurance under adverse conditions, have a long history in England. They have now found fertile ground in America, where training oneself to be fearless and strong under hostile circumstances has become a way of life.

In Jung's definition of the pathway toward individuation, facing our fears means facing the shadow, that part of us that we try to disown. Still it trails us and others can see it, even if we are blind to it. Robert Bly calls the shadow "The Long Bag We Drag Behind Us," filled with all that personal detritus that we decided to put in the bag to be "nice." Some of our sexuality and most of our shame are hidden in the bag, but also hatred, greed, anger, envy, jealousy and any other emotions unacceptable to our self-identity. In Bly's memorable words:

> We came as infants "trailing clouds of glory," arriving from the farthest reaches of the universe, bringing with us appetites well preserved from our mammal inheritance, spontaneities wonderfully preserved from our 150,000 years of tree life, angers well preserved from our 5,000 years of tribal life—in short, our 360-degree radiance—and we offered this gift to our parents. They didn't want it. They wanted a nice girl or a nice boy.[6]

Facing and absorbing our shadow ("eating" it, in Bly's term) means confronting our fear that we are unlovable, along with our other anxieties. This, in turn, leads to the ultimate fear of being unable to survive, and the fear of death. Hillman explains why facing the shadow, life's most tangled task, is so difficult. It holds us in acute awareness of our limits, nags at our fears of mortality: "Shadow is the very stuff of the soul, the interior darkness that pulls downward out of life and keeps one in relentless connection with the underworld."[7] Often it is a trauma caused by sickness, a brush with death, a divorce, or severe career reversal that initiates the discovery of the shadow. Or the urge to look underneath may come from a deep commitment to contemplation. In any event, it is hard to commence the jolting journey into the netherworld of unconsciousness without a sense of foreboding.

The image of chaos, dark and deep, provokes our terror. This image has powerful physical associations with the maternal womb (the symbol of all beginning) and with the underworld (the symbol of possible end). The primal abyss arouses feelings of being lost between existence and nonexistence. Fear of darkness starts early in most children, and often, even as adults, we can only sleep with a night-light on. In discussing the meaning of language, Theodore Thass-Thienemann compares darkness to "a general ambush for powers that remain unknown and unknowable and strike invisibly. Security means the realm of Apollo, light and visibility, enlightenment and 'foresight'; while darkness is the realm of insecurity, implying fear."[8] The fear of falling into an unknown abyss is aggravated by the word association in "falling" to sleep. Dreams often involve images of falling, as if the dream ego constantly seeks to solve this fundamental fear. Thass-Thienemann explicates the paradoxical fascination and horror of falling : "Where there is an abyss there is also the ambivalent fear and desire 'to fall' and 'to be swallowed' by this primary darkness. Vertigo as a neurotic symptom is the call of the abyss. It represents the self-perception of regression."[9] In a lighter vein, the Japanese believe that Westerners have nightmares of falling because they sleep on elevated beds, rather than close to the earth on a tatami mat.

In our culture we treat death as a rude intruder. We resent it. We postpone consideration of it. In contrast, Native Americans, as well as many Eastern philosophical and religious disciplines, accentuate rituals that confront the fear of death while in life's prime. Such practices require strenuous individual rites that concentrate on withdrawing or muting those pulsing energies—they might be described as longing desire—that are accepted as the prime motivation for living. The Tantric law holds that attachment to the senses and to earthly desire is the source of all man's evil. Years of devotion and diligence are required to discipline oneself to be beyond desire. Within this spiritual rubric, when detachment can be achieved, images of the transformation process in which death continually lives through life can be substituted for the persistent images of desire that hold us captive to the living world. When successful, the believer can face death with awareness of having already crossed the boundary many times; therefore, the final entry is fearless. To most Westerners, and many Easterners, this release of earthly attachments is an exacting discipline. Westerners are simply too conditioned to material blessings to accept easily such a sacrifice. Consequently we face the impending reality of death in less salutary ways and with a less serene mode of living.

Fear of Rejection

In the human life cycle, fear begins at birth (or perhaps even earlier in the womb). Fearful of not getting enough to eat or enough air to breathe, the baby's cry becomes a tocsin of want. For several years the growing child exists in a state of total dependency on others, and fear of severing this dependency is the paramount concern in life. Intense cravings emerge along with a nascent sense of being unfulfilled, the sense of never getting enough. This fear of want matures into a sense of greed, thus creating the paradox that even when the want is fulfilled, it is not enough. A society dependent upon high consumption plays upon fears of want to sustain its survival mode.[10] It becomes a clangorous demand for conspicuous and excessive consumption that can ultimately enslave us, as Thorstein Veblen warned. The sociological question might be: How do we sustain full employment in a society such as ours without being a slave to the fears of want?

The bodily ache of perpetual emptiness, of never being truly filled or satiated, colors emotional needs as well. We compensate fear of rejection by trying overly hard to please. No matter how much love we are given, it is insufficient. No matter how many friends, they aren't enough. These neuroses in turn whet the demand for more possessions, making some of us simply voracious grabbers. Enough for one person becomes deprivation for the next. More money, more cars, more houses, more wives, more girlfriends, never enough! The image of this fear is one of an omnivorous, yawning pit that voraciously sucks up everything within reach. In psychological parlance it translates into a negative Mother Complex projected onto the world of matter. In the background is an image of a personal mother who never gave us enough (how could she?), and this projects onto the material world that supplies us inadequately. On the more positive side of this complex are the great collectors of the world who refine the art of never having enough.

As childhood proceeds we acquire a sense of defiance toward those in authority and envy toward those who seem to have an easier time of it or a greater share of life's cornucopia. It is also at this stage that jealousy first appears, jealousy of the affection parents give to siblings and to each other. As we become aware of rivals for attention, a sense of not getting our share of the beneficence that grownups bestow may intensify. In later life, avowing to be loving and giving and not to repeat our parents' sins, we are dismayed to realize we too have become petty hoarders of feelings or goods. The will to be loving cannot prevail if fear of losing blocks its pathway.

Self-hate adds to the baggage of misery, often taking contrary forms. Beyond the more obvious "selfish" souls who are forever demanding, there are those who seem "selfless" but in reality are overcompensating for an acute feeling of worthlessness. The apparent giving, caring aspect only reinforces the underlying predominant image of unlovableness, the notion that only through excessive effort will one who is intrinsically unworthy receive even a meager return of affection.

As we mature we can develop the ability to supply some of our own needs for nurturance. While motivation is Abraham Maslow's primary thrust, he recognizes this fact in discussing how fear thwarts will and obstructs desire. He explains that we have a love quotient to satisfy and that only after it is fulfilled can we freely move on to anything approximating uncluttered love of others. "D-love" (*deficiency-love*) is like a cup that must be full before we can give anyone else a drink. If we can acquire a good dose of "B-love" (*being-love*), we will have more to give than those fearful souls who always feel deprived. Loving one's neighbor as oneself is much more difficult than it sounds, because loving oneself is a complex affair.

Arguing for the expansion of human qualities through growth motivation, Maslow juxtaposes *striving* (doing, copying, achieving, trying, purposeful activities), which generally preempts all our time and creates anxieties, with *being-becoming* (existing, expressing, growing, self-actualization), which might ameliorate the worries. He believes traditional psychology has been oriented toward the former, while ignoring the latter, more life-enhancing processes. Maslow wants to move toward the self-actualizing potentiality of personality, preferring to concentrate on its capacities rather than its deficiencies. His studies unearthed "a relative absence of fear in self-actualizing people. They were certainly less enculturated...less afraid of what other people would say or demand or laugh at," while "average and neurotic people walled off through fear much that lay within themselves."[11]

Americans tend to worship the concept of growth and progress, often failing to recognize either the discipline or the price tag entailed. To enjoy the unfolding of being-becoming generally takes hard, selfless work in peeling away complexes, repressions, defensiveness, and thus rediscovering the spontaneity that comes from being in tune with our inner nature. In the most creative people, as Maslow points out, "approval and acceptance of their deeper selves made their behavior more spontaneous (less controlled, less inhibited, less planned, less 'willed', and designed)."[12]

This brief review of reactions only skirts the periphery of how such fears inhibit choice, and it does not begin to exhaust these complicated areas of personality. A detailed elaboration is not feasible here where the focus is on the contaminating effect of fear on will and its interference with the realization of desires, of dreams. Suffice it to say, the perpetuation of fears and their demoralizing hold condemns us to both individual and collective mediocrity, unable to free potentialities. Conversely, having the courage to penetrate those fears, to break their restrictive shackles, allows uniqueness and imagination to commence a beneficent flow. According to Starhawk's wisdom: "Change is frightening, but Witches have a saying, 'Where there's fear, there's power.' The culture of estrangement teaches men to deny fear—and women to let fear control them. Yet if we learn to feel our fear without letting it stop us, fear can become an ally, a sign to tell us that something we have encountered can be transformed."[13]

Fear blocks access to Eros. By giving loving attention to our soul's pains, we allow Eros in—Eros who stimulates imagination and thus offers a bypass of fear, a way out of the stuckness, the deep freeze, the immobility, or the escapism. While imagination can indeed be frozen with fear in a single, warped frame, without images of alternatives, it is against the inherent nature of imagination, forever dynamic, to be thus rutted. Bringing imagination to our fears can liberate them. Love may make the world go round allegorically, but in reality love frees the imagination to be expansive. For we only love what we can imagine as part of us.

When we sense that fear is crippling us, it is informative to search our hearts for images of our deepest desires. It may seem an oxymoron to couple the two together, but fear is, in fact, the flip side of desire. Gerald May holds that "in desire, you seek after something you want. In fear, you seek to get away from something you do not want."[13] Generally we recognize the getting away as disagreeable, but forget it is the desiring nature that makes the judgment.

Finally, in paying attention, giving reflection to our fears, to anger, envy, jealousy, and depression, to our wounds, we bring imagination to illumine them. This sounds so simple. Actually it's very hard work, since the ego has an obsidian quality, a rocklike resistance to change. By confronting the woundedness of our egos and allowing Eros, the transformer, into our lives, we can experience a release from those fears that hold us in intractable bondage. Eros announces himself as both a new beginning and death to old patterns of fear. Traversing the pathway through our fears can lead to new strengths. A memorable Yeats poem, "Crazy Jane Talks with the Bishop," suggests why we can take heart: "For nothing can be sole or whole/That has not been rent."[15]

Anger, Depression, and the Excessive Demands of the Ruling Will

Rage—felt, held, not shut out nor denied
nor acted out—leads to compassion.
ROBERT SARDELLO, *Facing the World with Soul*

Anger, as well as those other relatives of fear—envy and jealousy—offer, at worst, acute pain, and at best a dilution of life's joys. While it seems to be an affect, anger in reality is a symptom induced by either fear or frustration. In its acute form it becomes an instrument for survival, spurring the adrenaline flow that gives us the energy and will—you might call it courage—to defend against attack. Interestingly, these primal emotions are with us long before we begin to learn to love.

Fear is often coupled with rage. In infancy this rage is focused on the parent. Our caretakers can never supply our needs quickly enough to overcome the panicky sense that we are going to be left alone, defenseless. Mother-induced rage, directed against the very person on whom one is dependent and through whose help we expect to avoid catastrophe, leads to fear of retaliation, more anxiety, deeper guilt, and more rage, which accompanies the excessive need of dependence in the first place. The infant's period of helpless dependency is an extended one, so the build-up of resentments escalates over time. June Callwood believes that "the new born baby feels fear because helpless, anger at the world that dominates him and hatred of the mother who only intermittently helps."[1] Certainly fear for security is ever present, but hatred comes later, when frustration persists.

Often without awareness, the child may soon learn to turn hate and anger back upon itself (Winnicott's "false self"), not willing to risk excessive rage against the parent on whom it depends. So, a new pattern of guilt develops in the infant: an inability to be truthful, or true to one's feelings, for fear of losing the protective maternal mantle. The primitive, defensive nature of such feeling interferes with, and on occasion overpowers, the feeling of love.

No matter how nurturing our parents, it is almost impossible to escape some early sense of self-denigration. Much remains to be explored as we mature if we don't wish fear or insecurity to dominate our lives. Until anger or fear subside to a manageable level, we can't begin to express love. Only through self-knowledge can we disentangle these disparate emotions. The challenge to do so is particularly acute in intimate relations, when the inevitable love/hate syndrome takes us by surprise. The only antidote is to try to be self-forgiving, in order to sidestep the guilt inspired when hate temporarily eclipses love. Of course, this doesn't mean capitulating to hate's transcendence. Hillman quotes Freud in reminding that hate actually serves the ego's struggle for power: "The ego hates, abhors, and pursues with intent to destroy all objects which are for it a source of painful feelings...the true prototypes of the hate-relation are derived not from the sexual life but from the struggle of the ego for self-preservation and self-maintenance."[2] The ego, when impinged upon, utilizes hate for its survival.

All strong emotion requires understanding of its genesis. What is hate trying to tell us, not about the other person, but about ourselves? What kind of fear is masked in what and whom we hate? Intense reactions, if we question them, can increase self-awareness. Psychologists know we can learn more from negative reactions to enemies (and to friends) than from placid encounters in life. Wisely, Immanuel Kant said: "Man wishes concord, but nature knows better what is good for the species." Anger gets our attention.

While anger is more difficult to disguise than its twins, envy and jealousy—those true green-eyed monsters—the onset in each instance is nonvolitional. We don't choose to be any of the three. Ann Carson explains the etymology of the word "jealousy" and the fear of displacement it embodies. Jealousy, which feels so physical, is a movement of spirit, which may explain why it is so difficult to budge:

> The word "jealousy" comes from the Greek zelos meaning "zeal" or "fervent pursuit." It is a hot and corrosive spiritual motion arising in fear and fed on resentment.... This is an emotion concerned with placement and displacement.[3]

With attention, we don't have to be frozen in these fear complexes forever. Many neurotic symptoms are fueled by a basic need for unfulfilled gratification. Our pathologies are mutilated, misdirected impulses that have somehow become stymied. By following the path of attention, to paraphrase Bly, one notices where the anger or fear leads. Perhaps that is the whole point—to get our attention.

There is little to be gained in blaming ourselves for being angry, since even a strong will cannot control its breakaway surge. Sardello describes it as "pure force, pure vitality":

> Mythically, we might imagine anger as Mars. Mars is not angry at anybody; that is just who he is. And when we feel anger, another person or thing is not the cause of the anger but its occasion. The work, then, is to detach the anger from supposed connections, which always make us live in the past, and to experience that quality as pure force.[4]

Hillman also speaks of the importance that Mars has in an age that experiences much frustration in terms of inability to surmount global problems:

> Mars gives answer to the hopelessness and drifting powerlessness we feel in the face of nuclear weapons by awakening Phobos, his Greek companion or son, *ira*, wrath. Mars is the instigator, the primordial activist. To put the contrast in escha-

tological terms, Mars is the god of beginnings, the sign of the ram. March is his month, and April, *Mars Apertus*, opening making things happen.[5]

In a sense, anger becomes our basic survival kit, a spontaneous response to what we perceive as an attack. We don't have it; it has us. Anger is red. Anger stirs actions, reactions, the blood. Precipitous action is demanded, and this can be exhilarating. The blood feud feels totally justified. Sartre claims that anger is a reaction to the experience of defeat; as such, it is the primitive defensive system of ego survival. Our defensive anger tells us more about the nature of the lacunae in our ego than we often care to face.

Lamentably, anger also gives us a sense of self-importance. Often we employ it to browbeat others into compliance with our desires. We feel endless self-justification when our dander is up. Dante portrays angry penitents under the image of a smokescreen in the fourth circle of the *Purgatorio*. When we start feeling self-righteous, angry illusions serve to blind us from the knowledge that we have (only momentarily perhaps) failed at a living relationship. Such disguises enable us to avoid looking squarely at ourselves as we really are.

Anger is also, paradoxically, part of the power complex. People who feel impotent are forever blaming some person (since Freud, usually their parents), or some circumstance for their difficulties. In this century it has been fashionable to blame a hostile environment or an unappreciative world for undermining or obstructing the pursuit of goals. In fact, the moment we begin accepting responsibility for our lives we begin to feel more powerful. We give away some of our power when we blame a scapegoat. Hitler, in blaming the Allies of World War I and his country's Jewish population for Germany's problems, aroused his countrymen to feel impotent and angry. By intensifying this resentment as a compensation for the feeling of powerlessness, he was able to justify attacking and exterminating his enemies. The death and pain thus visited upon a whole generation stand as an immutable reminder of mankind's inability to plumb the depths of anger and the sense of revenge engendered by feelings of impotence.

Because threats to our self-esteem can feel like physical as well as psychic blows, anger becomes the retaliatory weapon. It can be a useful act of self-assertion, if we have assimilated the anger well enough to curb violent, pathological excesses. If a vital part of our personality is threatened, an outburst of verbal anger is a normal reaction and can be clarifying, even cleansing, so long as it is not accompanied by corrosive, wounding thrusts (such general accusations as: "You're always self-centered" or "You're just as impossible as your mother"). It is far better to avoid a confrontational posture by describing one's own feeling rather than placing blame on the other. Above all, when possible, avoid striking at a loved one with such venom that any chance for interactive consideration of differences is destroyed. In some instances, it can be helpful to ventilate one's ire with a trusted friend prior to confrontation with the primary opponent (often one's mate).

In a loving relationship, two people can discover ways to de-escalate anger. First, try understanding what triggers defensiveness in your partner. Disagreements can be discussed—but only *before* clashing viewpoints are polarized. Beware of storing up hurt feelings and then erupting Vesuvius-like. It is possible to find ways to talk about conflicts sequentially and with restraint. Why toss in the kitchen sink and garbage can when the imperative is an emotional atmosphere both clean and honest? A good sense of absurdity can help at such times, hard as it is to energize when we most need it.

We can choose what to do with anger, but only if we are on familiar terms with our feelings and when the affect is not too intense. In the first book of the *Iliad*, Agamemnon triggers the wrath of Achilles, offending him by taking Achilles's war prize. But the half-god, half-man responds to the goddess Athena's cautioning tug on his yellow hair. He restrains himself from giving full vent to his outrage against Agamemnon's insult. So too can we search for the best ways to work with our anger. What are the internal restraints, the Athena internalized, that can come to us in inflamed moments and contain the full fury of anger?

Each of the Olympian gods and goddesses has a particular way of mirroring anger, and we can learn from them. Anger can be cathartic. Zeus's anger is the thunderbolt that cleanses the air with its directness, and is thus soon over. Hera reflects the anger we feel when faced with multiplicity and complexity rather than the singular concentration we yearn for in any relationship. Ares demonstrates the least acceptable form of anger—aggression without reason, mindless death, and destruction. But as we have seen above, Ares is sometimes the force to get things activated. Dionysian rage can be invigorating, pleasurable even, allowing new outbursts of creativity. Apollonian anger, like his arrow, gets right to the point, clarifies. Aphrodite expresses that anger we feel when we stifle our sense of beauty and accept ersatz shoddiness. Artemis captures the sense of rage when our quiet time is interrupted. As a cherished daughter leaves for college we might sense a slowing of our energy pulse, even a touch of the depressed rage experienced by Demeter when she loses Persephone. Kathleen Raine sums up the invigorating power of anger:

> Ares takes over the warrior when, like the Irish Cuchulain, the battlewarp seizes him, his hair stands on end, his face is distorted with rage and his body filled with the berserk courage the Vikings delighted in, a transport of rage in which the warriors scarcely felt the wounds of battle. To each god his kingdom.[6]

Bachelard celebrates anger because it floods us with pure energy and he offers a novel solution on working with it. Realizing that it cannot be avoided, he extols its invigorating potential as an energizer: "My joyous anger, my ever-victorious, ever-conquering anger."[7] The arduous physicality of the world provides us with singular opportunity to convert the rush of the energy of anger into creative endeavor. Bachelard points out that hardness, a knotty tree to be cut down, a bar of iron to be forged, offer a challenge to man's enterprising will. Such obstacles confronting our volition to conquer also integrate our anger. But, as society has become increasingly more technological, and less physically demanding, the question arises: Will we have to devise other bodily ways to convert anger, since we don't have wood to chop any more? Using the energy to do some onerous job we have put off doing, such as cleaning out the attic or the garage, can help to work off the steam. Anger and fear increase bodily tensions; therefore any physical exertion can smooth the stress. Aerobic exercises often fulfill this function.

We live in a society that has severe problems with pent-up anger. Sardello makes the point that current violence is a rage against the expulsion of beauty from our world.[8] With ugly buildings, dirty streets, and little aesthetic relief, anger exacts an unremitting toll in irrational eruptions. The study of ways to defuse anger is never taught in grade schools, but it should be. The standard curriculum could include methods of handling youthful frustrations and irritations before they ignite. In psychology we know that the less articulate the personality, the greater the likelihood that hostilities will be vented in violence. Few of our children's role models demonstrate acceptable ways to release anger. In films and the media the standard approach is etched in violence—traditionally the gun or the knife, or more recently the laser.

When we fear our reactions because they seem too violent, or fear loss of love if we voice irritations too freely, then we can fall into the trap of thinking that anger will go away if we just bury it. Evasion is never curative. Bachelard distinguishes resentment from anger: "Resentment is a matter that builds up. Anger is an act that can be differentiated."[9] Bernie Siegel contends: "It is unexpressed anger that is harmful. Too many people confuse anger with resentment. Anger can be positive, whereas festering resentment can cause people to become murderous. It is the things that have never been said that harm us most."[10] Recall William Blake's poem, "The Poison Tree," on this point:

> I was angry with my friend
> I told my wrath, my wrath did end.
> I was angry with my foe;
> I told it not, my wrath did grow.

The will, no matter how strong, cannot suppress feelings or emotions. We will still sulk and seethe inwardly. In pretending we don't feel an emotion, we deaden our spontaneous reactions, leading to lack of acuteness and specificity in awareness. Denial never permits avoidance of pain. Beyond that, vetoing feelings will block any ultimate sense of joy, pleasure, or satisfaction. Peace at any price, the desperate search for harmony, can cause us to act evasively, deceitfully, and finally force a displacement of anger and dissociation upon the physical body. Being out of touch with feeling fosters being out of touch with bodily functions as well, dissociating us from our most intimate interrelationships. Schopenhauer is correct in seeing the body as objectification of the will. Will, unfulfilled, becomes an instrument of bodily afflictions, as suppressed feelings inflict a lethal revenge.

Inner feelings are better managed if confronted before these secondary symptoms begin their invidious infiltration. Facing up to problems in the present, with faith that the future will be better, requires telling oneself: "This is my problem and it is up to me to solve it." Refusing responsibility, trying to wiggle out of the painful need to know oneself, can only prolong the nagging, repetitive problems of life. Pain in concentrated doses, though bruising to our egos, can be therapeutic in dissolving stomach knots.

Life, after all, is a series of personal choices and decisions. If we face them responsibly, a considerable sense of freedom can result. Conversely, if we don't recognize the choices, we will always feel like victims. The simple exercise of courage, facing whatever the trauma, can weaken fear's bondage. Will released from fear and engaged in creative problem solving becomes an active force in life, not a reactive one, not a counter-will.

Depression

When anger becomes inverted, depression results. Somewhat akin to an economic cycle, when the inevitable down side catches up, people are surprised and disheartened, since they want and expect the up side in perpetuity. When the pace unexpectedly slows in our personal lives, we try to pretend that we are not depressed by fleeing into more intense activity. In actuality, if we settle into the slowness, the darkness a bit, allow it to be, we may discover that depression may even assist us in realizing our desires. We often become depressed when will feels thwarted, but we may also have a will to depression because we need a rest from a mistaken course. It may be an announcement that we need quiet time for regrouping and redefining our goals.

In depression we reverse the direction of rage and fling it back at ourselves, making an indirect substitution for the original object of our wrath. By inversion we most often flail ourselves, along with those caretakers (from childhood) or circumstances (from later life) that we feel failed to accept some essential part of ourselves. Underneath we are still angry for not receiving a due sense of worth, still fearful that we will not find approval if we are not "perfect." Choices, some made long ago in childhood, constituted an attack on our defenseless persona. Depression is aggression turned around 180 degrees, inducing self-hate, and thereby engendering additional intense feelings of helplessness. Dana Crowley Jack provides important details about the gap between ego ideal and the actual self and the feeling of hopelessness it engenders:

> The greater discrepancy between these two senses of self, the lower the self-esteem. Despite important theoretical differences, theorists agree that depression results from an early environment where the child learned that, in order to be loved, she or he had to repress authentic feelings and present an outwardly conforming, false self, becoming self-alienated and cut off from emotions in the process.[11]

Aaron Beck's *The Diagnosis and Treatment of Depression* phenomenologically describes depression and how best to manage what he calls "a depletion syndrome." The give/get balance is upset. Loss of satisfaction or gratification is the central feature. Beck regards depression as a kind of hibernation brought on by loss of energy. Low self-evaluation envelopes one in a deep sense of hopeless pessimism. Unable to be mirthful or carefree, we become indecisive, vacillating, increasingly dependent, needing help or advice. Our already paltry supply of self-esteem vanishes. In severe cases will is virtually paralyzed.

Depression obliterates any possibility of pleasure in success. Gloom can range in intensity from a bleak, sepia shade, all pervasive, to an intense, black pit of despair and hopelessness in which suicide seems the only refuge. No energy, no joy, only endless nothingness ahead. It is akin to mourning for something dead or lost—in reality, mourning the loss of part of one's self. Death, of course, is the ultimate loss of the self. Depression feels like death without being the actual fear of death. Beck finds that fear of death is *not* a causative factor in bringing on depression. If Otto Rank and Freud are correct, that there are really only two basic fears—of life and of death—then depression would be classified as a fear of life. This seems logical. It is life that feels insurmountable. In a depressed state, whichever way one turns, life offers little source of gratification.

An unrecognized depression is at the core of most addictions, particularly alcoholism, but also of some physical problems such as peptic ulcers. Feeling inadequate, we revert to the earliest stage in infancy, activating the desire to drink more, or eat more, or not to eat at all. The body always triggers memory. A person feeling starved for love may find multiple ways for destroying the body in the grasping need for energy, or unconscious will, to overcome this depressive drain. Actually despair can be harnessed to help in overcoming a problem, one technique utilized by Alcoholics Anonymous. Rollo May explains how:

> Although we usually regard despair as a negative emotion, it can actually bring a person a sense of humility and love for a greater power in the universe. We can see, therefore, that emotions we often regard as negative are sometimes the most effective catalysts in particular types of healing.[12]

The primary cause of depression is anger over the loss of some essence of our particularity. It is the deep, unacceptable hurt of the loss of self-hood, the pain of emptiness in the feeling: "I am nothing." Calling it a narcissistic wound in psychological jargon is not adequate to the experience, so intense is the hurt. Internal tapes assault the weakened self-image, hammering home messages such as these: "You are worthless; no one could really love you." The mate of such a stricken person has a heavy responsibility, because the inside voice nags: "I can't stand to let him (her) know who I really am. There's nothing there. He (she) would hate me if he (she) really knew me. His (her) eyes must reflect love back to me every minute if I am to feel worthwhile at all." Depression is a trough of emptiness with no mitigating vent, no windows of hope.

Depression intrudes when self-esteem is not secure enough to withstand assault from inner voices or when outer circumstances don't match our vision of ourselves. Because this sense of low self-esteem may never have been realistically evaluated, we may expect achievements from ourselves that are unattainable. It actually lessens the self-punishment if we can make a plan and begin to image a way to implement it. This attitude initiates the process of examining our expectations to see if they collate with what we can reasonably expect. We might have exaggerated ideas of what life owes us without a clear picture of what effort or skills are required to achieve our goals. We could have an exaggerated Prometheus Complex.

Depression feels like we have given up something we loved, and we can't stand living with that feeling for long. So we seek substitutes to counter the emptiness. Yet any such defensive mechanism limits our awareness of ourselves. We would do better to accept depression as a part of living, a prompting to come to know ourselves better. Referring to both pagan and Christian theology, Hillman's appendix to David Miller's book elaborates the viewpoint that depression may provide insights into meaning:

> Depression...may be led into meaning on the model of Christ and his suffering and resurrection; it may through Saturn gain the depth of melancholy and inspiration, or through Apollo serve to release the blackbird of prophetic insight. From the perspective of Demeter depression may yield awareness of the Mother-Daughter mystery, or, through Dionysus we may find depression a refuge from the excessive demands of the ruling will.[13]

Perhaps we enter depression seeking to find release from willful demands that have assumed a too-dominant position. We could adopt the attitude that depression can be healthy reestablishment of equilibrium in the psyche. Living with depression can be a shortcut to self-knowledge, for as Pat Berry explains: "When we no longer cling to the light, blackness loses its darkness." When we split the "Demeter realm of concrete, daily life, devoid of the spiritual values, the sense of essence and the dark (and beneath the dark) carried by her underworld daughter, Persephone,"[14] we suffer a breach of soul. It is possible to make our anger and depression an asset to understanding.

In our culture we see multiple manifestations of a manic defense against depression—hyperactivity, running from experience to experience, from sensation to sensation, literally running away from ourselves. Long ago Lucretius said: "Everyone is forever trying to get away from where he is, as though mere *locomotion* could throw off the load" (*The Nature of the Universe*). A manic defense is a denial of harsh reality, but as T. S. Eliot says in "The Four Quartets," "humankind cannot/bear very much reality."

Typically, then, we totter on an emotional seesaw between grandiosity and despair. Marie-Louise Von Franz reasons: "Depressions and melancholy are often a cover for tremendous greed.... When you dig into a black mood you find behind it there is overwhelming greed—for being loved, for being very rich, for having the right partner, for being top dog, etc."[15] Standing in our depression, looking into the dark shadow of it, may provide insights into our desires, their limits, their far-fetchedness. Our depression or our fear-ridden rage may turn into compassion for the human condition. In the *Iliad* the high moment of the heroic mode is the transformation of Achilles's rage and despair at the loss of Patroklos, his dearest friend, into compassion for the suffering of his enemy.

Oddly enough, we can acquire a sense of worth simply through suffering. It is sometimes easier to achieve a false sense of the uniqueness of self or distinctiveness by deprivation rather than gratification. Even in despair we can derive hidden pleasures and covert satisfactions that encourage us not to change our behavior patterns. We can prove our strength by simply enduring. We may even acquire power over misfortune this way. One of the most frequent defenses against humiliation is, surprisingly, self-humiliation.

Depression can reinforce the constricted self in that, if it is mild, it provides a welcome sense of limits. It has a season and then it departs. For some unfortunate sufferers, being boxed in by depression may provide reason in itself for continuing the symptoms. In serious cases, such as borderline disorders, the chief problem is defining one's individual self in what feels like an unstructured existence: both time and space feel unlimited and frighteningly unbounded. The physical body is horrified when threatened by exposure to an unlimited openness. Any existential routine will be rigidly adhered to in an effort to provide the missing boundaries. To create a sense of uniqueness, the ego requires containment to assure separation from others. For people stricken with boundary difficulties, the desire for love often goes unsatisfied, because the lowering of ego perimeters in order to accept another may be too difficult. Thus, sadly, with fears of borderlessness, the erotic god, Eros, the breaker of boundaries, may not be available to those very people who need his liberating energy the most. To be without Eros is to be without the imagination needed to get out of the stifling box.

However, as Hillman emphasizes, love itself hides submerged within our difficulties: "Problems sustain us—maybe that's why they don't go away.... There is a secret love hiding in each problem."[16] Wherever anger surfaces—against self, against others, against the intangibles we covet or despise—the only cure may be to embrace the problem in order to discover what we love. If Eros connects with soul, we can be reminded of the beautiful and the good that reposes within us as well as the muck that obscures it. One of the sayings attributed to Buddha is that hatred does not cease by hatred; hatred ceases by love. The same may be said of anger or depression too.

The Revival of Will:
Bachelard's Novel Approach

The will...is entirely occupied in loving,
though it understands not how to love.
SAINT THERESA, *Life of St. Theresa*

In the course of a whole life, the intervention of
will over character is practically nil.
JOSÉ ORTEGA Y GASSET, *On Love*

As we have seen, no area of philosophical or psychological study has produced more contradictions over the centuries than that embracing the human will. From the absolutist realm of the gods, will moved to the more contentious province of philosophers or theologians. Then, in the twentieth century, it almost disappeared as a subject of scholarly interest, eclipsed by fascination with the ego.

Fortunately, however, will has been rescued from its subordinate status by the imaginative pen of Bachelard. His refreshing and provocative approach suggests that will is more than a control mechanism over errant human behavior, more than a power play to subdue others. He moves will away from concentration on will power, relating it, for the first time, to image, to the dream, to desire. Thus the ways of the will, historically an area of acute disagreement, now find a new venue as natural, instinctive responses to experience. Bachelard, a man of the twentieth century, dramatically casts the theme of volition as a soul song.

To trace his singularly original approach, we need to examine the period when his writing shifted from a concentration on science (with such titles as *The Dialectics of Duration*) to phenomenological studies of earth, air, fire, and water images. This was a major change for the Sorbonne professor holding a chair in the Philosophy of Science. For the first time, he was elevating imagination and will to the level of science. Discussion of the will emerges as early as 1942 in *L'eau et les rêves* (*Water and Dreams*), then continues in *L'air et les songes* (*Air and Dreams*) in 1943. Surprisingly he couples will to dreaming, although the latter is traditionally associated with wish fulfillment, compensation, bodily needs, desires, or image making. His thought progression can be sensed through subtle variances in his choice of book titles. The word "dream" comes into play in both volumes, but in French the word "*songes*" in the second title implies a direction to fantasy or dream, with more participation of will than with the word "*rêves*" or "*reveries*" (in the first treatise on air), which we usually think of as daydreams. Thus will has an increasing role in dreaming, and this relationship comes to full fruition in 1948 in *La terre et les rêveries de la volunté* (*Earth and Reveries of Will*), where will is nominally part of the title. We are intrigued, indeed puzzled, by this putative partnership between reverie and will. A new perspective of phenomenology is unfolding.

To Bachelard no act of will is possible without imagination's participation. In his initial division between what he classifies as material or dynamic imagination (*Water and Dreams*), we sense his starkly different approach. Ever the contrarian, he places imagination and will in the forefront of all action, but he does not presuppose the usual antagonism between them. Rather he opposes imagination to the function of rational thinking, to precepts, but not to will.

Bachelard emphatically stresses that "The two principal psychological functions [are] imagination and volition."[1] Will and imagination together thus form a continuum: "Both considered antithetical in an elementary vision are in essence closely aligned."[2] This landmark concept is roughly analogous to Jung's observation that instinct and image are but different manifestations of the same driving force, one physiological, one psychological. Like the red and ultraviolet ends of the lightwave spectrum, will and imagination are intertwined energies. Will can, in fact, only be projected through imagination. Rather than relegate them to traditional clashing, contradictory roles, Bachelard, in an entirely new perspective, sees them as complementary forces marching pari passu:

> Imagination and Will are two aspects of a single profound force. Anyone who can imagine, can will. To the imagination that informs our will is coupled a will to imagine, a will to live what is imagined.[3]

Bachelard sometimes joins imagination and will together is a single word "imagination-will," as in *Air and Dreams.*

Will prompts us to engage with the world where we discover pleasure by interacting with it. Assigning values to this exchange, we experience the alignment of imagination and will. "When the imagination assigns value to a substance, it also assigns it the will to act," Roch Smith asserts in his comprehensive book on Bachelard.[4] This is the process Bachelard calls "valorization," where feelings govern, rather than intellectual knowledge, in bestowing judgment. When value is conferred, volition is engaged. Will therefore comes into play when we can imagine conquering any situation, thus forming an inseparable primary bonding between feeling, imagination, and will.

By removing will from the traditional disciplinary, rationalistic habitat, Bachelard posits its origination in a provocative and unique pattern. He conceptualizes will as the product of embodiment, as an energetic response to the living world, a reaction to being engaged with it. In an individualistic, ego-oriented culture such as ours, will is usually perceived as the freedom to make a considered choice. By this definition will is generated by and through the ego; in fact, it often equates with the ego. Thus will weighs alternatives and then makes simple or complex rational decisions. But no—not to our French iconoclast who views will as a primordial function. For him, individual will begins to express itself when we first engage in choosing among alternatives, in our earliest precognitive responses. It emerges as the initial summons in the pre-reflective stage of life, and thus will always has an opaque, unconscious profundity.

Our earliest engagements with matter evoke will. In Bachelard's view: "Matter...possesses all the multiplicity of the hostile world, the world to be dominated."[5] Because matter resists us and provokes us, we are compelled to try to penetrate it. Matter not only excites us to action but challenges us as well. Bachelard notes that "if the world is my will, it is also my adversary. The greater the will, the greater the adversary."[6] In other words, taking on the world empowers the will and increases its strength. Each conquest enlarges the arena of possible further conquest. "Matter, confronted by will, energizes our whole being," Edward K. Kaplan explains Bachelard's thesis.[7] If matter compels the emergence of will, then we begin to appreciate why will seems so pervasive in the Western world, oriented as it is primarily to material well-being. This also hints at what can go wrong if will becomes inflated.

Working with each of the four elements, Bachelard explores the coupling of material imagination with dynamic will. Matter demands our engagement, matter evokes images that distinguish and develop our souls. In the process energy is released and joy experienced: "Matter is our energetic mirror; it is a mirror which focuses our powers in illumining them with imaginative joys."[8] These mirroring images call forth will to fulfill their *telos* or imaginary potential, and in this animating evocation "material imagination is transformed into dynamic imagination."[9] Bachelard defines dynamic imagination as the *extroverted* aspect of will's work, but interestingly he implies that will initially assumes an *introverted* form. First, there is an unconscious, passive stage of taking in; only afterwards can there be a taking hold.

By their very existence, material things challenge us to probe them. The world entices us to be engaged with it. Provocation by the material world is the prime experience needed to initiate individual life into meaning. In the first awakening, elements arouse us to an awareness of *their* nature, but also to *our* very existence. Substances summon us. With our attention captivated, we feel impelled to act. We are motivated by the will to power, which, in turn, "awaken[s] in us primitive acts, primary drives, the imperious joy of ordering the world."[10] By extracting images from engagement with matter and then projecting them, the imagination awakens, moves, and seeks to transform the unawakened psyche. Bachelard defines will as the impetus for forming and expressing identity. He thus heralds will's participation in the life process in ways we may never understand, the quintessential cohesive force of a unified mind/body/spirit. Discovery of the ways of the will is a discovery of identity. The will asserts itself in a revelation of what Jung calls the Self, more inclusive, more extensive, more central than even the ego with which we often confuse it.

In rescuing will's reputation, Bachelard provides a broader appreciation than is habitually attributed to it. His definition embraces the alignment of meaning and order in one's life, for will is "an invitation to action, that call for the intervention of man in the world, that channel the chaotic forces of creation."[11] Faced with an incomprehensible confusion of material forces, will begins its job of defining us. These choices serve the impersonal urge of furthering our physiological growth and pushing us along the road of individuation.

We unconsciously make an affiliation with one of the elements. This shapes our psychology and the way we respond to future experiences. Bachelard maintains that pride gives dynamic unity to a being, "a proud victory over an adverse element."[12] The conqueror, feeling victorious, experiences an *élan vital*, a renewal of energy. All resistance awakens the same wish: "In the realm of will, there is no distinction to be made between things and men."[13] Man is an integrated being. He has the same will against all adversaries. The world is our provocation, shaping our value system.

The will to power always carries a kind of naiveté. We imagine we are capable of unlimited possibilities. Imagination is expansive and naturally exaggerates. Through images of power, will discovers a royal road to power: "The will to power needs images; the will to power is thus matched by an imagination of power."[14]

Defensiveness aroused by confrontation is the negative aspect of a material provocation that can be awakened by things as well as persons: "[T]he adversary who does the insulting is not necessarily a man, for things also question us."[15] A surge of energy is as available for defense as for conquest: "Defense reflexes that truly bear the human stamp, that man acquires, conditions, and holds ready, are acts that defend while attacking. They are constantly dynamized by a will-to-attack."[16] In this way will's assumption of a passive defense suddenly turns into a jolting offensive jab.

The common tendency is to think of will as that part of the psyche that impels us to follow through and complete an action. In contrast, Bachelard makes will the initiator of all action and thought. (Didn't Immanuel Kant do the same?) When closure takes place, it is because the will-to-power finds a match with the imagination of power. In the act of initiating, will is seen in its most unadulterated, extroverted form.

Perhaps we are unable to will not to do anything because of the nature of will itself. Will is a volition to or toward, moving always toward a *telos* that is inherent in its inception. When we try to break habits or obsessive behavior, will loses its usual tenacity; it is powerless against a strongly engraved habit, and certainly against a complex. We can say, for example, "I will not eat, or smoke, or get mad," but still we find ourselves resuming the old behavioral modes with nauseating consistency. The preposition *contra*, against, is only activated, in Bachelard's rather grandiose view, when the challenge is to conquer the world.

The word "will" itself gives evidence of its complexity and expansiveness. In English it is pervasive; it can be an adjective, a verb, or a noun (which is its most extensive usage). It means "acceptance" when a present participle—for example, when one is "willing." In Bachelard's style, "will" needs a modifier that, in a subtle way, specifies the kind of will under consideration: i.e., will-to-beauty, will-to-contemplate, and the other multiple ways he employs. He rarely uses the word adjectivally (as in "will power").

As part of the verbal form, will projects to the future. In such sayings as "I will go," the present is ordered toward a becoming, a futurity. In French or Italian one does not say, "I will have"; such a phrase sounds too insistent to be polite. "I would like to have" sounds better. Bachelard might insist that instead of "I will reach my goal," it would be more accurate to say: "I can only reach my goal if I can imagine myself in the act of getting there."

Dreams of the will dominate both daytime and nighttime realms. Bachelard insists that "everyone who labors dreams a cosmic dream."[17] The world presents jobs waiting to be done. The destiny of work is present in our bodies. Bachelard alludes to the clenched fist, which is linked to toil and needs toil, as "the digital will…a will to build."[18] By being endowed with a hand, we can dream of holding the world in it. Every action, even the most simple, is fortifying to the will and establishes our relationship to the universe we live in. Knowledge is in the world. The world affords or supplies knowledge—"affordance" (J. J. Gibson's term). Every labor thus can be an exaltation when will is expressing essential identity. To distill this joy, we can imagine will realizing itself. "Before any act, we need to say to ourselves, in the silence of our own being, what it is we *will* to become; we need to *convince ourselves* of our own becoming and to *exalt* it for ourselves,"[19] Bachelard declares.

Daytime reverie and nighttime dream are both opening curtains for the will-to-imagine: "It is through its dreams that the will for power is most aggressive."[20] Imagination traps will in the possibility of the fulfillment of our dreams. Will seeks employment in whatever imagination suggests, and this is the way the dream of the will unfolds. Dreaming takes different modes. Bachelard has nothing against the nocturnal dream—indeed he has very novel ideas concerning it—but he leaves its full exploration to psychoanalysis and archetypal psychology. He chooses, generally, to explore daydreams (reveries), because they are "less *insistent* than a night-dream"[21] and in them the sense of the "I" is never obliterated. Yet, if we retain power of direction, is it not a contradiction that he calls reverie anima-oriented, rather than animus-dominated (generally his term for any forming, controlling action)? Obviously, his "anima" and "animus," while close to the Jungian derivations, are much more generic and loosely defined than those of the archetypal psychologist. I presume he means that in daydreaming we can become receptive to the psyche's meanderings.

Though he writes enthusiastically about reverie, his words about night dreaming, while less detailed, are also typically original. One might suppose that during sleep will ceases to exert itself, but not to Bachelard. To him sleep is a manifestation of a specific will, the will to return to a psychological center, to shut out the daylight world. The sun's sleep fortifies our sleep, which is governed by the need to be closed-in, away from the light that energizes us to dream of action. In the Stygian dark we cherish aloneness: "Night is my solitude, my will to solitude. Night, too, is representation and will, my nocturnal will."[22] After the sunlit clarity of daytime, will longs for the occult: "the sleeper partakes of a will to occultation, the will of night."[23]

The nighttime horizon, no longer unlimited as is daytime, encircles us. The oval-shaped eye, a body part, gives contour to dream: "The symbols of night are governed by the ovoid."[24] As the horizons of the world blur, we retract our vision of distances, moving toward enclosure, a closing in: "To sleep properly we must obey the will to envelopment, the will of the chrysalis; with the smoothness of a well-coiled spiral we must follow the movement of envelopment right to its center—an essentially curved, circular process eschewing all angles and edges."[25] As we surrender to night, the eyelid droops. The eye itself, thus curtained, has a heavy "will to sleep, a heavy, irrational, Schopenhauerian will."[26]

In exquisite detail, Bachelard explains how "after the relaxation of the eyes comes the relaxation of the hands, for they, too, come to reject objects."[27] The hands, those seekers of work during the day, relax at night. Indeed relaxation of the hand is a requisite if we wish to sleep: "When we bear in mind that the whole specific dynamism of the human being is *digital*, it follows inescapably that oneiric space unfolds as and when our knotted fists unclench themselves."[28]

Dreams of early night differ from those before awakening at dawn. In the deep of night we probe for our psychic center. Withdrawing into primitive space, the "will to reconstitute" enfolds us in basic primordial forms: "With the smoothness of a well-coiled spiral we must follow the movement of envelopment right to its center." We follow "the systole and diastole of nocturnal space about night's center."[29] After reaching it, we retrace the pattern in a reverse cycle of enlarging circular expansion, a kind of "turning and turning in the widening gyre," to borrow from Yeats's poem, "The Second Coming."

As dawn approaches, the will to concentrate, to hold to the center, is replaced by "the will to irradiation." The light summons us to the contemplation of action: "A hand as it waits to wake up is a living cluster of muscles, desires, designs."[30] Bachelard, as usual, binds bodily action together with will, image, and dream, demonstrating that each is part of the same fabric. As sleep retreats:

> Our dreams become augmentative. We dream of a dimension and immediately it grows; dimensions that were coiled up straighten out again. Instead of spirals we have arrows tipped with aggression.[31]

Will can be likened to an instinct for engagement, and at some level we share this inclination with all creatures. Once again Bachelard adopts a novel approach. In communicating with others, he suggests, our most basic link is through the shared understanding of dreams of the will, for "in the roots of the will lie the most powerful of communions."[32]

A function of daytime will that intrigues Bachelard is language usage, for "Nowhere in the whole area of will is there a place where the distance between will and its manifestation is shorter."[33] He relates the pleasure of speaking to breathing, to aspirating, with the thought that, in a speaking being, images of will and desire are exultantly combined:

> The will, if we catch it in the act of speaking, reveals its natural self. This is where we must seek the meaning of poetic ontogenesis, the bridge between those two radical powers, will and imagination. It is with the reference to the will to speak that we can say that will *wills* the image or that imagination *imagines* will.[34]

At times Bachelard's love of word-pictures is so potent that the lyric writer supersedes the philosopher. To him a poem is an evocation of what one translator calls "will toward expression" and another "will to logos" (*volonté de logos*).[35] He proclaims that "The will to see and the will to show constitute the poet's direct action."[36] A poem becomes a dialectic between reader and poet, a dialectic between reason and speech, between expression and reflection. A poem demands a total review of one's essential identity, a calling forth of the "I am" to respond to its queries. An active, appreciative reader becomes united to the poet in recreating the poetic act; together, they celebrate the act of becoming.

Similarly, Richard Wilbur attributes the genesis of the poetic act to a dual causation: "Poetry [is] the impulse to name the world, and the impulse to clarify and embody the self."[37] Bachelard carries this definition beyond a simple naming of things, insisting that imagination wants to exalt the tangibles of the world. More than a re-presentation of the world, poetry is an exaggeration of its beauty: *"Poetry is truly the pancalistic activity of the will.* It expresses the will for beauty."[38] Kaplan appends the unusual assertion that "this will to beautify an object of perception reflects the general tendency of imagination to surpass given reality by valorizing it, by poeticizing it."[39]

Bachelard affectionately lays to rest any notion that valorizing the world, poeticizing it, is a passively submissive act. He assures us that the poetic act is essentially the will-to-power:

> The conqueror and the poet both want to put the brand of their power on the universe. They both take the branding iron in hand; they brand the dominated universe.[40]

Correspondence between nature's will and man-in-nature set up reciprocal resonances. *Pancalism*, an arcane word in English, is invoked repeatedly by Bachelard in speaking of love of beauty. The Gallic word comes from *pan*, meaning everything, from the god's name, and from *kalos*, meaning beautiful. This combination accords beauty its highest value. Never altogether quiescent, in Bachelard's view, "will...creates eyes to contemplate, to feast on beauty.... Does it [the eye] not bear the mark of pancalism? It must be beautiful in order to behold beauty."[41] We have a will to see the world's beauty that matches the world's wish to be seen. This reciprocal desire, when we participate wholly in absorbing nature's beauty, moves us from individual narcissism to a much less onerous cosmic narcissism.

Through this broadened perspective, Bachelard removes some opprobrium from the popular concept that reflection on self-beauty is mere idleness or fawning self-absorption. While it is easy to dismiss him as a romantic idealist, no one was more pragmatic concerning the natural world: "We take some knocks from nature too. Its very beauty is no placid thing."[42]

Nature is both a demiurgic force and a revelation of beauty, but its greatest value is that it "forces us to contemplation."[43] Contemplation, in turn, is not the opposite of the will; it is but another branch of the will. Thus man, in contemplating the world, must confront and conquer it. The process is initiated by dreams of the will-to-power: "Man, if he would taste the enormous fruit that is a universe, must dream that he is master of it."[44] Here we have the unabashed Bachelardian dream of the will.

In one of his impalpable reversals, Bachelard confounds us by saying that even the Earth is in a continuous process of expressing its own will: "The meadow is not a mantle of greenery, it is the earth's primordial will."[45] This viewpoint is reminiscent of the lyrical moment in Faulkner's *The Hamlet* when Mink Snopes, sprawled in the meadow, feels enfolded by its earthiness, or what Bachelard would call the will of the Earth. This impersonal impetus of life's energy is not simply biologically directed. Earth's will involves some mute form of consciousness, which Yeats acknowledges in this quatrain: "Come, heart, where hill is heaped on hill:/For there the mystical brotherhood/Of sun and moon and hollow and wood/And river and stream work out their will" ("Into the Twilight"[46]).

The struggle to resolve ambivalence in our lives is endless. Bachelard teaches us not only that this is fruitless, but indeed that to seek unities is to stultify imagination. He assures us it is perfectly plausible to live with ambivalence and uncertainty. Imagination and will have forever seemed in opposition to one another—but not since Bachelard's breakthrough concept coupled them in the dream's desire to work with matter through engagement with images. To couple will and being-in-the-world provides a healing linkage of living matter to soul and spirit.

In shifting will from its naked power function, the Nietzschean approach, and projecting it into the living world of images and dreams and desire, all interrelated, Bachelard gives powerful impetus to the centuries old effort to link, indeed to bond, those disparate elements that together form the human psyche.

Notes

The Enigma

1   C. G. Jung, *Memories, Dreams, Reflections*, rec. and ed. Aniela Jaffè (New York: Pantheon Books, 1961), 349.
2   Robert Bly, James Hillman, and Michael Meade, eds., *The Rag and Bone Shop of the Heart: Poems for Men* (New York: HarperCollins Publishers, 1992), 418.
3   Raphael López-Pedraza, *Cultural Anxiety* (Einsiedeln, Switzerland: Daimon, 1990), 34.
4   James Hillman, "On the Necessity of Abnormal Psychology," in *Facing the Gods* (Dallas: Spring Publications, 1980), 10.
5   Jung, *Memories, Dreams, Reflections*, 347.
6   C. J. Jung, "The Realm of the Archetype," in *Collected Works of C. G. Jung*, vol. 8, *The Structure and Dynamics of the Psyche*, trans. R. F. C. Hull, Bollingen Series XX (Princeton: Princeton University Press, 1969), para. 415.
7   Robert Sardello, "Soul Tasks of the Coming Age," *Common Boundary* 10, no.6 (1992): 43.

The Summons of Eros

1   *An Intermediate Greek-English Lexicon, founded upon the seventh edition of Liddell and Scott's Greek English Lexicon* (Oxford: The Clarendon Press, 1991), 371.
2   Hesiod, *Theogony*, trans. Richard Lattimore (Ann Arbor: University of Michigan Press, 1968), 130.
3   C. G. Jung, *Memories, Dreams, Reflections*, ed. Aniela Jaffe (New York: Pantheon Books, 1961), 353.

4   Denis de Rougemont, *Love Declared: Essays on the Myths of Love* (New York: Pantheon Books, 1963), 36.

5   Walter F. Otto, *The Homeric Gods —The Spiritual Significance of Greek Religion* (New York: Pantheon Books, 1954), 53.

6   Otto, 161-162.

7   Otto, 161.

8   James Hillman, "On the Necessity of Abnormal Psychology," in *Facing the Gods* (Irving, Tex.: Spring Publications, 1980), 32. f.7.

9   M. Esther Harding, *Psychic Energy, Its Source and Its Transformation*, Bollingen Series X (New York: Pantheon, 1963), 226.

10   Harding, 224-225.

11   *The Upanishads vol. 1, The Sacred Books of the East,* trans. F. Max Muller (Delhi: Motilal Banarsidass, 1965), 142.

12   *Encyclopedia Britannica*, vol. 4 (1957), 326.

13   Jung, *Collected Works of C. G. Jung*, vol. 11, *Psychology and Religion: West and East*, trans. R. F. C. Hull, Bollingen Series XX (Princeton: Princeton University Press, 1969), para. 770.

14   St. Augustine, *Confessions* (Cambridge: Harvard University Press, 1977), 8.5.

15   Louise Cowan, "Introduction, Epic as *Cosmopoesis*," *The Epic Cosmos*, ed. Larry Allums, gen. ed. Louise Cowan (Dallas: Dallas Institute Publications, 1992), 24.

16   Monica Sjöö and Barbara Mor, *The Great Cosmic Mother: Rediscovering the Religion of the Earth* (New York: Harper & Row, 1987), 298.

17   Dante, *The Divine Comedy-(Paradise)*, trans. Dorothy L. Sayers and Barbara Reynolds (Baltimore: Penguin Books, 1969), 347.

18   Friedrich Nietzsche, *The Will to Power*, trans. Walter Kaufmann and R. J. Hollingdale (New York: Random House, 1967), 366.

19   Nietzsche, 550.

20   Jung, *Collected Works*, vol. 10, *Civilization in Transition*, trans. R. F. C. Hull, Bollingen Series XX (Princeton: Princeton University Press, 1970), para. 658.

21   Martin Heidegger, *Nietzsche: The Will to Power as Art*, vol. 1 (New York: Harper & Row, 1979), 60.

22   James Hillman, *Re-visioning Psychology* (New York: Harper & Row, 1975), 68.

23   Adolf Guggenbühl-Craig, "The Archetype of Invalid and Limits of Healing," *Spring 1979* (Irving, Tex.: Spring Publications, 1979), 40-41.

Eros, Psyche, and the Wings of Desire

1   Quoted by Marie-Louise Von Franz, *Projection and Re-collection in Jungian Psychology* (London: Open Court, 1980), 133-134.

2   Robert Sardello, "Psyche and Eros," Lecture, University of Dallas, Irving, Tex., Sept. 17, 1979.

3   Noel Cobb, "The Fires of Eros," *Sphinx 3, A Journal for Archetypal Psychology and the Arts* (London: Claughton Press, 1990), 103.

4   Plotinus, *Enneads III*, trans. A. H. Armstrong (Cambridge: Harvard University Press, 1967), 203.

5   Plato, *Collected Dialogues*, ed. Edith Hamilton and Huntington Cairns (New York: Pantheon Books, 1962), 559, para. 207.

6   José Ortega y Gasset, *On Love* (New York: Meridan Books, 1971), 82.

7   Lyn Cowan, *Masochism, A Jungian View* (Dallas: Spring Publications, 1982), 59.

8   Anders Nygren, *Agape and Eros*, trans. Philip S. Watson (New York: Harper & Row, 1969), 175.

9   Karl Kerényi, *Hermes, Guide of Souls*, trans. Murray Stein (Dallas: Spring Publications, 1976), 55-56.

10 James Hillman, "Blue Fire, Part I" (Dallas: Spring Audio, 1991).

11 Ann Carson, *Eros, The Bittersweet* (Princeton: Princeton University Press, 1986), 10.

12 Carson, 70.

13 Raphael López-Pedraza, *Cultural Anxiety* (Einsiedeln, Switzerland: Daimon, 1990), 58.

14 Donald E. Kalsched, "The Limits of Desire and the Desire for Limits," in *The Fires of Desire—Erotic Energies and the Spiritual Quest*, ed. Frederica R. Halligan and John J. Shea (New York: Crossroad, 1992), 80-81.

15 Apuleius, *The Golden Ass*, trans. Jack Lindsay (Bloomington: Indiana University Press, 1960), 122.

16 Carson, 157.

17 Thomas Moore, *Care of the Soul—A Guide for Cultivating Depth and Sacredness in Everyday Life* (New York: HarperCollins, 1992), 91.

18 Kalsched, 91.

19 Kalsched, 82.

20 Rainer Maria Rilke, *Letters to a Young Poet*, trans. Stephen Mitchell (New York: Random House, 1984), 69-70.

21 C. G. Jung, *Collected Works of C. G. Jung*, vol. 7, *Two Essays on Analytical Psychology*, trans. R. F. C. Hull, Bollingen Series XX (Princeton: Princeton University Press, 1975), para. 33.

22 Sigmund Freud, *Beyond the Pleasure Principle*, trans. James Strachey (New York: Liveright Publishing Corp., 1961), 55.

23 Rollo May, *Love and Will* (New York: Dell Publishing Co., 1969), 78.

24 May, 79.

25 Kerényi, 58.

26 James Hillman, *The Myth of Analysis* (Evanston: Northwestern University Press, 1972), 62.

27 Denis de Rougemont, *Love in the Western World*, trans. Montgomery Belgion (New York: Pantheon Books Inc., 1983), 41.

28 Rougemont, 310.

29 Jalal 'Uddin Rumi, "Odes From the *Divan Shams-I-Tabriz*," trans. Coleman Barks and John Mayne, 1990, quoted in *Sphinx 3*, (London: Claughton Press, 1990), 20.

30 Cobb, 104.

31 The incident described happened several years ago. Now, thanks to Robert Sardello and Tom Moore, we are more comfortable with using the word "soul."

32 Sardello, 12.

Sulphur and the Fury of Desire

1   C. G. Jung, *Collected Works of C. G. Jung*, vol. 13, *Alchemical Studies*, trans. R. F. C. Hull, Bollingen Series XX (Princeton: Princeton University Press, 1967), para. 237.

2   C. G. Jung, *Memories, Dreams, and Reflections*, trans. Richard and Clara Winston (New York: Random House, 1961), 205.

3   Titus Burckhardt, *Alchemy—Science of the Cosmos, Science of the Soul*, trans. William Stoddart (Baltimore: Penguin Books, 1971), 200.

4   Jung, vol. 13, para. 127.

5   W. B. Yeats, *Mythologies* (New York: The Macmillan Company, 1972), 284.

6   W.B. Yeats, "Byzantium," *The Poems of W.B. Yeats*, ed. Richard J. Finneran (New York: Macmillan Publishing Co., 1982), 248.

7   Yeats, *Mythologies*, 267.

8   C. G. Jung, *Collected Works of C. G. Jung*, vol. 14, *Mysterium Coniunctionis*, trans. R. F. C. Hull, Bollingen Series XX (Princeton: Princeton University Press, 1963), para. 467.

9   Jung, vol. 14, para. 151.

10 Jung, vol. 14, para. 153.

11 Jung, vol. 13, para. 210.

12 Herbert Silberer, *Hidden Symbolism of Alchemy and the Occult Arts* (New York: Dover Publications, 1971), 409.

13 James Hillman, "The Thought of the Heart," *Eranos Lectures 2* (Ascona, Switzerland: Eranos, 1981), 8.

14 Mylius, quoted in Jung, vol. 14, para. 135.

15 Robert Grinnell, *Alchemy in a Modern Woman: A Study in the Contrasexual Archetype* (Zurich: Spring Publications, 1973), 25. In this statement "appetition" is a perfect word choice meaning: "the direction of desire toward an object or purpose." O.E.D.

16 C. G. Jung *The Visions Seminars*, Book One, from the complete notes of Mary Foote (Zurich, Switzerland: Spring Publications, 1976), 181.

17 Hillman, 43.

18 Paul Kugler, "The Alchemical Theater," *Sphinx 2* (London: London Convivium for Archetypal Studies, 1989), 183.

19 Burckhardt, 189.

20 Burckhardt, 190.

21 Grinnell, 24.

22 Jung, vol. 13, para. 234.

23 C. G. Jung, *Collected Works of C. G. Jung*, vol. 16, *The Practice of Psychotherapy*, trans. R. F. C. Hull, Bollingen Series XX (Princeton: Princeton University Press, 1967), para. 508-509.

24 Walter Burkert, *Greek Religion* (Cambridge: Harvard University Press, 1985), 220.

Aphrodite and the Ensouled World

1   Walter F. Otto, *The Homeric Gods—The Spiritual Significance of Greek Religion* (New York: Pantheon Books, 1954), 161.

2 C. G. Jung, *Collected Works of C. G. Jung*, vol. 13, *Alchemical Studies*, trans. R. F. C. Hull, Bollingen Series XX (Princeton: Princeton University Press, 1967), para. 229.
3 James Hillman, "On Senex Consciousness," *Spring: An Annual of Archetypal Psychology and Jungian Thought* (New York: Spring Publications, 1970), 161.
4 Paul Friedrich, *The Meaning of Aphrodite* (Chicago: University of Chicago Press, 1978), 79.
5 Jean Shinboda Bolen, *Goddess in Everywoman* (New York: Harper & Row, 1984), 233.
6 Ginette Paris, *Pagan Meditations* (Dallas: Spring Publications, 1986), 13.
7 Homer, *The Iliad*, trans. Robert Fagles (New York: Penguin Books, 1991), 376.
8 Kenneth Clark, *The Nude* (New York: Pantheon, 1956), 63.
9 J. J. Bachofen, *Myth, Religion, and Mother Right*, Bollingen Series LXXXIV (Princeton: Princeton University Press, 1967), 205.
10 Otto, 161.
11 M. Esther Harding, *Woman's Mysteries: Ancient and Modern* (New York: G.P. Putnam's Sons, 1971), 124.
12 Ginette Paris, Wainwright House Lecture, Rye, New York, March 1990.
13 John Sanford and George Lough, *What Men are Like* (New York: Paulist Press, 1988), 227, referring to Lyn Cowan, *Masochism—A Jungian View* (Dallas: Spring Publications, 1982), 110.
14 Nancy Qualls-Corbett, *The Sacred Prostitute—Eternal Aspect of the Feminine* (Toronto: Inner City Books, 1988), 68.
15 Homer, *The Homeric Hymns*, trans. Charles Boer (Irving, Tex.: Spring Publications, 1979), 71.
16 *Sappho: Lyrics in the Original Greek with Translations by Willis Barnstone* (Garden City, N.Y.: Anchor Books, Doubleday & Co., 1965), 61
17 Friedrich, 127.
18 Gaston Bachelard, *Fragments of a Poetics of Fire*, trans. Kenneth Haltman (Dallas: Dallas Institute Press, 1990), xviii.
19 Karl Kerényi, *Goddesses of Sun and Moon* (Dallas: Spring Publications, 1979), 59.
20 Christine Downing, *The Goddess: Mythological Images of the Feminine* (New York: Crossroad Publishing Co., 1981), 202.
21 Paris, *Pagan Meditations*, 14.
22 Friedrich, 187.
23 Ronald Schenk, *The Soul of Beauty* (London and Toronto: Associated University Presses, 1992), 37.
24 Henry Corbin, "The Jasmine of the Fedeli D'Amore," *Sphinx 3*, (London: Claughton Press, 1990), 217.
25 Qualls-Corbett, 66.
26 James Hillman, "The Thought of the Heart," *Eranos Lecture 2* (Dallas: Spring Publications, 1981), 37.
27 Erich Fromm, *The Art of Loving* (New York: Harper & Row, 1956), 30, 31.
28 Bachelard, xiii.

29 Hillman, "The Thought of the Heart," 37.

30 Paris, *Pagan Meditations*, 32.

Agape and Eros

1 Philip S. Watson, "Introduction," *Agape and Eros*, by Andres Nygren, trans. Philip S. Watson (New York: Harper & Row, 1969), xx.

2 Watson, xvi-xvii.

3 Andres Nygren, *Agape and Eros*, trans. Philip S. Watson (New York: Harper & Row, 1969), 177.

4 Otto Rank, *Beyond Psychology* (New York: Dover Publications, 1941), 176.

5 Rank, 97.

6 Ross Rizely, "Psychobiological Bases of Romantic Love," in Kenneth Pope et al., *On Love and Loving* (San Francisco: Jossey-Bass Publications, 1980), 104.

7 L. H. Farber, *Lying, Despair, Jealousy, Envy, Sex, Suicide, Drugs and the Good Life* (New York: Harper & Row, 1976), 165.

8 Jesse D. Geller and Richard A. Howenstine, "Adulthood: Men," in Kenneth Pope et al., 84.

9 Geller and Howenstine, 84.

10 Rollo May, *Love and Will* (New York: Dell Publishing Co., 1973), 29.

11 Geller and Howenstine, 72.

12 Ann Carson, *Eros the Bittersweet* (Princeton: Princeton University Press, 1988), 39.

13 James Hillman, *Re-Visioning Psychology* (New York: Harper & Row, 1975), 43.

14 Thomas Moore, *Care of the Soul—A Guide for Cultivating Depth and Sacredness in Everyday Life* (New York: HarperCollins, 1992), 36.

15 Polly Young-Eisendrath and Florence Wiedemann, *Female Authority* (New York and London: The Guilford Press, 1987). This book gives a detailed discussion of the stages required by a woman to free herself from bewitching archetypes in order to achieve a solid base for her identity.

16 Robert Sardello, *Facing the World with Soul* (Hudson, N. Y.: Lindisfarne Press, 1992). This book and much of Sardello's work is devoted to the redemption of the material world through love.

17 C. G. Jung, *Collected Works of C.G. Jung*, vol. 9.1, *The Archetypes and the Collective Unconscious,* trans. R. F. C. Hull, Bollingen Series XX (Princeton: Princeton University Press, 1969), para. 167.

18 M. Esther Harding, *Psychic Energy: Its Source and Its Transformation*, Bollingen Series X (New York: Bollingen Foundation, 1963), 218.

19 Adolf Guggenbühl-Craig, "The Archetype of Invalid and Limits of Healing," *Spring 1979* (Irving, Tex.: Spring Publications, 1979), 40.

20 Viktor E. Frankl, *The Will to Meaning* (New York: World Publishing Co., 1969), 96.

21 M. Scott Peck, *The Road Less Traveled* (New York: Simon & Schuster, 1978), 80-83.

22 Peck, 83.

23 James Hillman, "Blue Fire," Tape 2 (Dallas: Spring Audio, 1991).

24 James Hillman, "The Thought of the Heart," *Eranos Lectures 2* (Dallas: Spring Publications, 1981), 5.

25 Hillman, 18-19.
26 Kathleen Raine, "Poetry and Prophecy," *Lindisfarne Letter* (West Stockbridge, Mass.: Lindisfarne Press, 1979), 70.
27 Gerard Manley Hopkins, *The Poems of Gerard Manley Hopkins* (London: Oxford University Press, 1967), 69.

Image and Will

1 C. G. Jung, *Collected Works of C.G. Jung,* vol. 13, *Alchemical Studies,* trans. R. F. C. Hull, Bollingen Series XX (Princeton: Princeton University Press, 1967), para. 75.
2 James Hillman, "An Essay on Pan," in *Pan and the Nightmare* (Zurich: Spring Publications, 1972), xxiv.
3 Gaston Bachelard, *The Poetics of Space,* trans. Maria Jolas (Boston: Beacon Press, 1969), xi.
4 Gaston Bachelard, *On Poetic Imagination and Reverie,* trans. Colette Gaudin (Dallas: Spring Publications, 1987), 6.
5 Gaston Bachelard, *Air and Dreams,* trans. Edith R. Farrell and C. Frederick Farrell (Dallas: The Dallas Institute Publications, 1988), 253.
6 Liliana Zancu, "Transcendental Dynamics: A Bachelardian Romantic Perspective Including the English Translation of *Earth and Reveries of Volition: An Essay on the Imagination of Forces* by Gaston Bachelard" (Ph.D. diss., Kent State University, 1975), 137.
7 Zancu, 106.
8 Edward S. Casey, *Imagining, A Phenomenological Study* (Bloomington, Ind.: Indiana University Press, 1976), 41.
9 Hillman, "An Inquiry into Image," *Spring 1977* (Dallas: Spring Publications, 1977), 81.
10 Eligio Stephen Gallegos, *Animals of the Four Windows—Integrating Thinking, Sensing, Feeling and Imagery* (Santa Fe: Moon Bear Press, 1992), 77.
11 Quoted in Harold Jantz, *The Mothers in Faust—The Myth Time and Creativity* (Baltimore: Johns Hopkins Press, 1969), 82-83.
12 Jolande Jacobi, *The Psychology of C. G. Jung* (New Haven, Conn.: Yale University Press, 1973), 16, f.1.
13 Robert Sardello, in private conversation.
14 Hillman, *Inter Views* (New York: Harper & Row, 1983), 181.
15 Hillman, "Image-Sense," *Spring 1979* (Irving, Tex.: Spring Publications, 1979), 141.
16 SyberVision is a visual aid technique on video tape that replicates stroke patterns in games such as tennis or golf. Viewing one stroke over and over again fuses the image in memory. The body seems able to adapt to at least some of this image conditioning. After a month of viewing these repeated images of strokes by world class players, a friend of mine played noticeably better tennis.
17 William James, *Principles of Psychology,* Vol. 1, (New York: Dover Publications, 1950; originally published by Henry Holt, 1890), 524.

18 Richard Wilbur, *Responses* (New York: Harcourt Brace Jovanovich, 1976), 118.

19 Mark Kramer, "About Men," in *The New York Times Magazine* (December 16, 1984), 128.

20 Marion Woodman, "Dreams," vol. 2, *Language of the Soul*, audio tape (Boulder, Colorado: Sounds True Recordings).

21 Casey, 173.

22 Bachelard, *Poetics of Space*, 36.

23 Robert Sardello, "Foundations of Spiritual Psychology," lecture, The Dallas Institute for Humanities and Culture, Sep. 19, 1991.

24 C. G. Jung, *Collected Works of C. G. Jung*, vol. 8, *The Structure and Dynamics of the Psyche*, trans. R. F. C. Hull, Bollingen Series XX (Princeton: Princeton University Press, 1972), para 402.

25 Hillman, *The Dream and the Underworld* (New York: Harper & Row, 1979), 201.

26 Raphael López-Pedraza, *Hermes and His Children* (Dallas: Spring Publications, 1977), 7.

27 Martin Rossman, "Illness as an Opportunity for Healing," in *Healers on Healing*, ed. Richard Carlson and Benjamin Shield (Los Angeles: Jeremy P. Tarcher, 1989), 80.

28 Jeanne Achterberg, *Imagery In Healing: Shamanism and Modern Medicine* (Boston: Shambhala Publications, 1985), 17.

29 Achterberg, 5.

30 Ann Carson, *Eros, the Bittersweet* (Princeton: Princeton University Press, 1986), 77, 63.

31 Carson, 77, 169.

Reappearance of Will

1 C. G. Jung, *The Collected Works of C. G. Jung*, vol. 6, *Psychological Types*, trans. R. F. C. Hull, Bollingen Series XX (Princeton: Princeton University Press, 1971), para. 844.

2 Donald Cowan, *Unbinding Prometheus—Education for the Coming Age* (Dallas: Dallas Institute, 1988), 122.

3 Otto Rank, *Will Therapy and Truth and Reality,* trans. Jessie Taft (New York: Alfred A. Knopf, 1947).

4 E. James Lieberman, *Acts of Will—The Life and Work of Otto Rank* (New York: Free Press, 1985), 357.

5 Rank, 32.

6 Rank, 217.

7 Francis Aveling, *Personality and Will* (New York: D. Appleton Press; Cambridge: Cambridge University Press, 1931), 93.

8 Silvano Arieti, *The Will to Be Human* (New York: Quadrangle Books, 1972), 2.

9 Rollo May, *Love and Will* (New York: Delta, 1973), 204.

10 R. May, 207.

11 R. May, 218.

12 R. May, 193.

13 Roberto Assagioli, *The Act of Will* (New York: Penguin Books, 1973), 10.

14 Assagioli, 15.

15 Viktor E. Frankl, *The Will to Meaning* (New York: World Publishing Co., 1969), 170.
16 Viktor E. Frankl, *The Doctor and the Soul: From Psychotherapy to Logotherapy,* trans. Richard and Clara Winston (New York, N. Y.: Bantam, 1965).
17 Gerald May, *Will and Spirit* (San Francisco: Harper & Row, 1987), 50.
18 G. May, 117.
19 G. May, 59-62.
20 W. B. Yeats, "Vacillation," *The Poems of W. B. Yeats*, ed. Richard J. Finneran (New York: Macmillan Publishing Co., 1983), 251.
21 Gaston Bachelard, *Water and Dreams*, trans. Edith Farrell (Dallas: The Pegasus Foundation, 1983), 27.
22 Gaston Bachelard, *The Right to Dream*, trans. J. A. Underwood (Dallas: The Dallas Institute Publications, 1988), 57.
23 Gaston Bachelard, *Lautréamont*, trans. Robert S. Dupree (Dallas: The Pegasus Foundation, 1986), 19.

Will and Intentionality

1   Quoted by Paul Kugler in "The Alchemical Theater," *Sphinx 2* (London: London Convivium for Archetypal Studies, 1989), 181.
2   Rollo May, *Love and Will* (New York: Dell Publishing Co., 1979), 79.
3   Mihaly Csikszentmihalyi, *Flow: The Psychology of Optimal Experience* (New York: Harper & Row, 1990), 27.
4   Robert Sardello, "Foundations of Spiritual Psychology," lecture, The Dallas Institute for Humanities and Culture (Dallas, Tex., Oct. 19, 1991).
5   Robert C. Solomon, *Love: Emotion, Myth and Metaphor* (Garden City, N. Y.: Doubleday, 1981). See last chapter, where love and self-esteem are the subjects.
6   William Lynch, *Images of Hope* (Baltimore: Helicon Press, Inc., 1965), 32.
7   Lynch, 51.
8   Wendell Berry, *The Unsettling of America: Culture and Agriculture* (New York: Avon Books, 1977), 104.
9   Lynch, 9.
10 Paul Diel, *Symbolism in Greek Mythology—Human Desire and Its Transformations,* trans. Vincent Stuart, Micheline Stuart, and Rebecca Folkman (Boulder, Colo., and London: Shambhala, 1980), 9.
11 Lynch, 33.

The Independent Will of the Complex

1   C. G. Jung, *Collected Works of C. G. Jung,* vol. 9.1, *The Archetypes and the Collective Unconscious*, trans. R. F. C. Hull, Bollingen Series XX (Princeton: Princeton University Press, 1975), para. 4.
2   James Hillman, "Going Bugs," *Spring 1988* (Dallas: Spring Publications, 1988), 61.
3   C. G. Jung, "The Self" in *Collected Works*, vol. 9.2, *Aion*, trans. R. F. C. Hull, Bollingen Series XX (Princeton: Princeton University Press, 1959), para. 52.
4   James Hillman, "Feeling and the Mother Function" in *Jung's Typology* (New York: Spring Publications, 1971), 114.

5   Hillman, 113-114.

6   Murray Stein, "The Devouring Father" in *Fathers and Mothers* (Zurich: Spring Publications, 1973), 68.

7   Jolande Jacobi, *Complex/Archetype/Symbol* in *The Psychology of C. G. Jung*, Bollingen Series LVII (Princeton: Princeton University Press, 1959), 8-9.

8   Gaston Bachelard, *Lautréamont*, trans. Robert S. Dupree (Dallas: The Pegasus Foundation, 1986), 70.

9   Gaston Bachelard, *Water and Dreams*, trans. Edith Farrell (Dallas: The Pegasus Foundation, 1983), 167.

10   Jacobi, 11.

11   Jacobi, 11.

12   C. G.. Jung, "A Review of the Complex Theory" in *Collected Works of C. G. Jung*, vol. 8, *The Structure and Dynamics of the Psyche*, trans. R. F. C. Hull, Bollingen Series XX (Princeton: Princeton University Press, 1969), para. 200.

13   Jacobi, 9.

14   Jolande Jacobi, *The Psychology of C.G. Jung* (New Haven: Yale University Press), 38.

15   C. G. Jung, "New Paths in Psychology" in *Collected Works*, vol. 7, *Two Essays on Analytical Psychology*, trans. R. F. C. Hull, Bollingen Series XX (Princeton: Princeton University Press, 1975), para. 438.

16   C. G. Jung, "Psychotherapy and A Philosophy of Life" in *Collected Works*, vol. 16, *The Practice of Psychotherapy*, trans. R. F. C. Hull, Bollingen Series XX (Princeton: Princeton University Press, 1970), para. 179.

17   James Hillman, "An Inquiry into Image" in *Spring 1977* (Dallas: Spring Publications, 1977), 82.

18   Robert Sardello, Lecture, University of Dallas, Feb. 27, 1973.

19   James Hillman, "Image Sense" in *Spring 1979* (Irving, Tex.: Spring Publications, 1979), 141.

20   Michael Perlman, "Images Remember" in *Spring 50* (Dallas: Spring Publications, 1990), 58.

21   James Hillman, *Facing the Gods* (Dallas: Spring Publications, 1980), 9.

22   Hillman, 7.

Bachelard and Complexes Embedded in Culture

1   Jolande Jacobi, *The Psychology of C. G. Jung* (New Haven, Conn.: Yale University Press, 1968), 1.

2   Gaston Bachelard, *On Poetic Imagination and Reverie,* trans. Colette Gaudin (Dallas: Spring Publications, 1987), 17.

3   Edward S. Casey, *Spirit and Soul, Essays in Philosophical Psychology* (Dallas: Spring Publications, 1991), 9.

4   Casey, 9.

5   Gaston Bachelard, *Psychoanalysis of Fire*, trans. Alan C. M. Ross (Boston: Beacon Press, 1964), 40.

6   Bachelard, 12.

7   Gaston Bachelard, *The Right to Dream*, trans. J. A. Underwood (Dallas: The Dallas Institute Publications, 1988), 58-59.

8   Gaston Bachelard, *Fragments of a Poetics of Fire*, trans. Kenneth Haltman (Dallas: The Dallas Institute Publications, 1990), 109.

9   W.B. Yeats, "The Mask," *The Poems of W.B. Yeats*, ed. Richard J. Finneran (New York: Macmillan Publishing Co., 1983), 95.

10   Yeats, 213-214.

11   Yeats, 193.

12   Yeats, 248.

13   Yeats, 249.

14   Eleanor Bertine, M.D., *Close Relationships* (Toronto: Inner City Books, 1992), 92.

15   Denis de Rougemont, *Love Declared: Essays on the Myths of Love* (New York: Pantheon, 1963), 51.

16   Rougemont, 160.

17   Gaston Bachelard, *Water and Dreams*, trans. Edith Farrell (Dallas: The Dallas Institute of Humanities and Culture, 1983), 89.

18   Bachelard, 168.

19   Albert Camus, *The Myth of Sisyphus and other Essays,* trans. Justin O'Brien (New York: Vintage, 1955), 90-91.

20   Gaston Bachelard, *Air and Dreams,* trans. Edith R. Farrell and C. Frederick Farrell (Dallas: The Dallas Institute Publications, 1988), 138-139.

21   Gaston Bachelard, *Lautréamont,* trans. Scott Dupree (Dallas: The Pegasus Foundation, 1986), 32.

22   Bachelard, 17.

23   Liliana Zancu, "Transcendental Dynamics: A Bachelardian Romantic Perspective Including the English Translation of *Earth and Reveries of Volition: An Essay on the Imagination of Forces* by Gaston Bachelard" (Ph.D. dissertation, Kent State University, 1975), 185.

The Promethean Will

1   Donald Cowan, *Unbinding Prometheus—Education for the Coming Age* (Dallas: Dallas Institute Publications, 1988), 168.

2   Cowan, 22.

3   Frances G. Wickes, *The Inner World of Choice* (Englewood Cliffs, N. J.: Prentice-Hall, Inc., 1976), 8-9.

4   Northrop Frye, "Preface" in Gaston Bachelard, *Psychoanalysis of Fire* (Boston: Beacon Press, 1964), viii.

5   William Lynch, *Christ and Prometheus: A New Image of the Secular* (Notre Dame: The University of Notre Dame, 1970), 56.

6   Gaston Bachelard, *Fragments of a Poetics of Fire*, trans. Kenneth Haltman (Dallas: The Dallas Institute Publications, 1990), 66.

7   John Donne, *John Donne's Poetry*, ed. A. L. Clements (New York: W. W. Norton & Co., 1966), 86.

8   Mary Watkins, "Hearts Desire" in *Habits of Being,* audio tape (Darien, Conn.:

Wainwright House, July, 1990).

9   Friedrich Nietzsche, *The Will to Power*, trans. Walter Kaufmann and R. J. Hollingdale (New York: Random House, 1967), 485-486.

10   W. B. Yeats, *Autobiographies* (London: The Macmillan Press Ltd., 1973), 119-120.

11   Nietzsche, 491.

12   Nietzsche, 484.

13   Raphael López-Pedraza, "Moon Madness," in *Cultural Anxiety*, (Einsiedeln, Switzerland: Daimon, 1990), 21.

14   Aeschylus, *Prometheus Bound*, trans. Edith Hamilton (New York: W. W. Norton, 1965), 106.

15   Gail Griffin Thomas, "Pandora" (Ph.D. dissertation, University of Dallas, 1983), 38.

16   Karl Kerényi, *The Gods of the Greeks* (London: Thames & Hudson, 1974), 207.

17   Thomas, 57.

18   Thomas, 41.

19   Thomas, 89.

20   Thomas, 46.

21   Polly Young-Eisendrath and Florence Wiedemann, *Female Authority* (New York and London: The Guilford Press, 1987), 91.

22   Babrius, *Aesop's Fables,* trans. Denison B. Hull (Chicago: University of Chicago Press, 1970), Fable 58.

23   Gaston Bachelard, *The Flame of a Candle*, trans. Joni Caldwell (Dallas: The Dallas Institute Publications, 1988), 40.

24   Bachelard, *Fragments,* 69.

25   Bachelard, *Fragments*, 73-74.

26   Bachelard, *Psychoanalysis*, 12.

27   Sigmund Freud, *The Standard Edition of the Complete Psychological Works of Sigmund Freud*, vol. 22, trans. James Strachey (Toronto: Hogarth Press, 1964), 187-193.

28   Igor Stravinsky and Robert Craft, *Dialogues and A Diary*, (Garden City: Doubleday & Co., 1963), 12.

29   William Lynch, *Images of Hope* (Baltimore: Helicon Press, 1965), 55.

30   Stravinsky and Craft, 26-27.

31   Erwin O. Krausz, "Neurotic Versus Normal Reaction Categories," in *Alfred Adler—His Influence on Psychology Today*, ed. Harold H. Mosak (Park Ridge, N. J.: Noyes Press, 1973), 57.

Fear Interferes

1   Deepak Chopra, lecture, Wainwright House, October 26-27, 1990.

2   W.B. Yeats, "After Long Silence," *The Poems of W.B. Yeats*, ed. Richard J. Finneran (New York: Macmillan Publishing Co., 1983), 265.

3   June Callwood, *Love, Hate, Fear, Anger and the Other Lively Emotions* (New York: Doubleday & Co., 1964), 34, 65.

4   Chopra, lecture.

5   Will and Ariel Durant, *The Age of Napoleon* (New York: Simon & Schuster, 1975), 249.

6   Robert Bly, *A Little Book on the Human Shadow*, ed. William Booth (San Francisco: HarperCollins Publishers, 1988), 24.

7   James Hillman, *The Dream and the Underworld* (New York: Harper & Row, 1979), 56.

8   Theodore Thass-Thienemann, *The Interpretation of Language*, vol. 2 (New York: Jason Aronson, 1973), 288.

9   Thass-Thienemann, 148.

10 Will McKhinney, "Education for the Third Quarter of Life," *Journal of Continuing Higher Education* (Spring 1990): 19.

11 Abraham Maslow, *Motivation and Personality* (New York: Harper & Row, 1987), 162.

12 Maslow, 162.

13 Starhawk, *Dreaming the Dark: Magic, Sex and Politics* (Boston: Beacon Press, 1982), 47.

14 Gerald May, *Will and Spirit* (New York: Harper & Row, 1982), 335.

15 Yeats, 260.

Anger, Depression, and the Excessive Demands of the Will

1   June Callwood, *Love, Hate, Fear, Anger and the Other Lively Emotions* (New York: Doubleday & Co., 1964), 62.

2   James Hillman, *The Dream and The Underworld* (New York: Harper & Row, 1979), 58.

3   Ann Carson, *Eros, The Bittersweet* (Princeton: Princeton University Press, 1986), 14.

4   Robert Sardello, *Facing the World with Soul* (Hudson, N.Y.: Lindisfarne Press, 1992), 10.

5   James Hillman, *A Blue Fire*, ed. Thomas Moore (New York: Harper & Row, Publishers, 1989), 184.

6   Kathleen Raine, "What is Man?" in *Poetry and Prophecy* (West Stockbridge, Mass.: Lindisfarne Letter, 1979), 33.

7   Gaston Bachelard, *Water and Dreams,* trans. Edith Farrell (Dallas: The Pegasus Foundation, 1983), 160.

8   Sardello, 137-152.

9   Gaston Bachelard, *Air and Dreams*, trans. Edith R. and C. Frederick Farrell (Dallas: Dallas Institute Publications, 1988), 133.

10 Bernie Siegel, "Love, The Healer" in *Healers on Healing*, ed. Richard Carlson and Benjamin Shield (Los Angeles: Jeremy P. Tarcher, 1989), 8-9.

11 Dana Crowley Jack, *Silencing the Self—Women and Depression* (Cambridge: Harvard University Press, 1991), 93.

12 Rollo May, "The Empathetic Relationship: A Foundation of Healing," in *Healers on Healing*, 109.

13 James Hillman, "Psychology: Monotheistic or Polytheistic," appendix to David L. Miller, *The New Polytheism* (Dallas: Spring Publications, 1981), 114-115.

14 Patricia Berry, *Echo's Subtle Body—Contributions to an Archetypal Psychology* (Dallas: Spring Publications, 1982), 15.

15 Marie-Louise Von Franz, *The Psychological Meaning of Redemption Motifs in Fairy Tales* (Toronto: Inner City Books, 1980), 38.

16   James Hillman, *Inter Views* (New York: Harper & Row, 1983), 187.

The Revival of Will: Bachelard's Novel Approach

1   Liliana Zancu, "Transcendental Dynamics: A Bachelardian Romantic
    Perspective Including the English Translation of *Earth and Reveries of Volition:
    An Essay on the Imagination* of Forces by Gaston Bachelard" (Ph.D. diss., Kent
    State University, 1975), 137.
2   Zancu, 89.
3   Gaston Bachelard, *Air and Dreams*, trans. Edith R. and C. Frederick Farrell
    (Dallas: The Dallas Institute Publications, 1988), 111-112.
4   Roch Smith, *Gaston Bachelard* (Boston: Twayne Publishers, 1982), 89.
5   Gaston Bachelard, *The Right to Dream*, trans. J. A. Underwood (Dallas: The
    Dallas Institute Publications, 1988), 51.
6   Gaston Bachelard, *Water and Dreams*, trans. Edith Farrell (Dallas: The Pegasus
    Foundation, 1983), 159.
7   Edward K. Kaplan, "Gaston Bachelard's Philosophy of Imagination: An Introduction,"
    Philosophy and Phenomenological Research: A Quarterly Journal, 33 (1972): 13.
8   Kaplan, 12.
9   Bachelard, *Water*, 143.
10 Bachelard, *Right*, 59.
11 Bachelard, *Right*, 58.
12 Bachelard, *Water*, 160.
13 Bachelard, *Water*, 183.
14 Bachelard, *Right*, 59.
15 Bachelard, *Water*, 160.
16 Bachelard, *Water*, 160.
17 Bachelard, *Right*, 60.
18 Bachelard, *Right*, 71.
19 Bachelard, *Air*, 245.
20 Bachelard, *Water*, 179.
21 Gaston Bachelard, *The Poetics of Space*, trans. Maria Jolas (Boston: Beacon
    Press, 1969), 36.
22 Bachelard, *Right*, 184.
23 Bachelard, *Right*, 154.
24 Bachelard, *Right*, 155.
25 Bachelard, *Right*, 154.
26 Bachelard, *Right*, 154.
27 Bachelard, *Right*, 155.
28 Bachelard, *Right*, 155.
29 Bachelard, *Right*, 153-154.
30 Bachelard, *Right*, 156.
31 Bachelard, *Right*, 155.
32 Bachelard, *Right*, 55.
33 Bachelard, *Air*, 243.

34 Bachelard, *Air*, 243.
35 Worthington Campbell Jr., "Gaston Bachelard and the Transformation of Consciousness: Some Implications for Criticism and Interpretation" (Ph.D. diss., Syracuse University, 1973), 153, quotation from *L'air et les songes*, 278 (French, see Dallas Institute Publication, *Air and Dreams*).
36 Bachelard, *Right*, 133.
37 Richard Wilbur, *Responses* (New York and London: Harcourt Brace Jovanovich, 1976), 102.
38 Bachelard, *Air*, 49.
39 Kaplan, 8.
40 Bachelard, *Water*, 183.
41 Bachelard, *Water*, 28.
42 Bachelard, *Right*, 56.
43 Bachelard, *Water*, 30.
44 Bachelard, *Right*, 56.
45 Bachelard, *Right*, 63.

Index